"My dear sister and fellow teacher of the Word of God has poured out her soul in the writing of *God's Portrait of a Righteous Woman*. Marie has spared nothing in executing her 'charge' from the Lord. If you have studied or taught the Word of God, you will appreciate the labor of love that has gone into *God's Portrait of a Righteous Woman: How to Live Out the Life God Has Purposed for Women*."

—**Kay Arthur, Best-Selling Author, Renowned Bible Teacher, Co-Founder & Brand Ambassador Precept**

"Seldom do you meet someone like Marie Strain who has literally spent her entire life studying and teaching the scriptures. For decades she has immersed herself into the study of God's Word and then invested what she has learned into the lives of those God has placed under her teaching. Marie's life is evidence of her lifelong study of God's Word, along with the lives of those she has taught and discipled.

God's Portrait of a Righteous Woman is a storehouse of biblical wisdom and practical applications. Women who follow Christ will be encouraged and challenged by reading this book. The scriptures have much to say about discipleship, relationships, marriage, children, and church. Marie Strain has drawn from her years of teaching and discipling to offer great biblical insights that will draw you closer to Christ and into more of His likeness. Knowing that fact makes this book a worthwhile investment of your time."

—**Dr. Charles A. Fowler, President of Carson Newman University, Former Pastor of Germantown Baptist Church**

GOD'S PORTRAIT *of a* "RIGHTEOUS WOMAN"

HOW TO LIVE OUT THE LIFE GOD HAS PURPOSED FOR WOMEN

MARIE STRAIN

Published by Innovo Publishing, LLC
www.innovopublishing.com
1-888-546-2111

Publishing Books, eBooks, Audiobooks, Music, Screenplays, & Courses for the Christian
& wholesome markets since 2008.

GOD'S PORTRAIT OF A "RIGHTEOUS WOMAN"
How to Live Out the Life God Has Purposed for Women

Copyright © 2023 by Innovo Publishing LLC
All rights reserved.

No part of this publication may be reproduced, stored in a retrieval system, or transmitted in any form or by any means electronic, mechanical, photocopying, recording, or otherwise, without the prior written permission of the Publisher.

Emphasis placed within scripture quotations has been added by the version's translators to add clarity. Underlined words/phrases within these quotations are the author's emphasis.

Unless otherwise noted, all scripture is taken from the New American Standard Bible®, Copyright © 1960, 1971, 1977, 1995, 2020 by The Lockman Foundation. All rights reserved.

Scripture marked "CSB" is taken from The Christian Standard Bible. Copyright © 2017 by Holman Bible Publishers. Used by permission. Christian Standard Bible®, and CSB® are federally registered trademarks of Holman Bible Publishers, all rights reserved.

Scripture marked "ESV" was taken from The Holy Bible, English Standard Version. ESV® Text Edition: 2016. Copyright © 2001 by Crossway Bibles, a publishing ministry of Good News Publishers.

Library of Congress Control Number: 2023933549
ISBN: 978-1-61314-796-2

Cover Design & Interior Layout: Innovo Publishing, LLC

Printed in the United States of America
U.S. Printing History
First Edition: 2023

Has God called you to create a Christ-centered or wholesome book, eBook, audiobook, music album, screenplay, or online course? Visit Innovo's educational center (cpportal.com) to learn how to accomplish your calling with excellence.

To Jehovah God of the Bible, and His Son, my Lord and Savior, Jesus Christ, the Nazarene:

My God and Savior, Who has always been faithful to accomplish in me and through me all that He has called, purposed, and equipped me to do . . . be all glory, honor, praise, and thanksgiving.

To Lee Strain, my beloved, faithful, and devoted husband of sixty-two-plus years:

You have spent sixty-plus years loving me as Christ loves His church, His bride. You have always supported and encouraged me in all that the Lord has called me to do. However, this time you worked countless hours editing every word of every page which has been invaluable to this manuscript. I am so very blessed to have you work with me on this project. Thank you, with much love!

ACKNOWLEDGMENTS

I owe so much gratitude to my husband, Lee Strain, for the countless hours he has spent personally in editing. He did so much by asking me questions that helped me put the words in a clearer composition, as well as helped to clarify some important doctrinal points. He also sacrificed many hours of his personal life to my sitting in front of a computer for many months. Thank you, sweetheart, for your seemingly tireless and dedicated contributions to me as I have worked on this project.

I want to thank Dr. Charles A. Fowler, who is presently serving the Lord through the office of president of Carson-Newman University, located in Jefferson City, Tennessee. Before going to Carson-Newman, he served for nine years as the senior pastor of Germantown Baptist Church, of which I am a member. He not only served the Lord faithfully as my pastor, but we were also co-laborers in the gospel. He knew early of our Lord's calling me to put into print what He promised to download into my mind. He has been my greatest cheerleader through this process—i.e., other than my husband, Lee. His input into this book has been invaluable, having edited several books himself in other projects. Thank you, Charles, for not only serving us well as our pastor but also becoming and continuing to be a very special person in my life.

I want to give a hearty and heartfelt thank you to Dave Keesling for his contribution to the editing of the book as well. Dave currently serves the Lord as the Philanthro Corp founder and its executive vice president and is a dear friend of over forty years. He has written a devotional book titled *Life in Real Time: A Daily Devotional*. He spent many hours going through this book twice, which turned out to be of tremendous help in providing "better wording" than I had chosen, ideas I had not thought of, and some phrases that were best to be omitted. Thank you, Dave, for your invaluable advice in helping to make this book the best it could be.

I also want to thank Mrs. Sarah Maddox, a new friend that had no idea just what she was getting into when our Lord brought her into my life as a genuine gift of grace. Sarah is the author of *You*

ACKNOWLEDGMENTS

Can Learn to Be Content and has co-authored several books herself, including *A Mother's Garden of Prayer* and *A Woman's Garden of Prayer*. Along with her God-given skills and spiritual giftedness, she is also an English teacher. She too has spent countless hours giving me tremendous help in making the manuscript read better and easier. Thank you, Sarah, not only for your invaluable work on the book but most of all for your precious friendship and encouragement through these months. Your input was truly significant. I am so very grateful.

It is imperative that I mention both the names of Kay Arthur, co-founder of Precept Ministries, International, and now serves as Brand Ambassador Precept, and Betsy Bird, who worked at Precept Ministries for many years as the international director of training. I would not be the person I am today without their influence and mentoring me through both the studying of God's Word and training me to teach others in how to study God's Word for themselves, enabling them to know our God more intimately. The Bible study workbooks, along with accompanying lectures Precept Ministries has written and produced, have been the vehicle God has provided me to use for over forty years to sanctify me and disciple others through His Word. I thank them both earnestly and publicly for their investment into my life. I will be eternally grateful for our Lord bringing them and the materials they have produced by God's leading and power into my life and ministry. To Him be the glory!

CONTENTS

Preface..13

Chapter 1: First Things First: 17
Chapter 2: Before You Say, "I Do"......................................37
Chapter 3: God's Primary Role for a Wife 57
Chapter 4: God's Primary Responsibilities for a Wife.........73
Chapter 5: God's Instructions for Becoming a "Righteous Wife"....93
Chapter 6: Some Miscellaneous Relevant Biblical Insights...........111
Chapter 7: What "Works" When It Isn't Working 133
Chapter 8: What "Works" When It Isn't Working 147
Chapter 9: Victorious, Christ-Honoring Living..........................165
Chapter 10: A Snapshot of God's Declared Future 189
Chapter 11: Now What? 217

About Precept & Kay Arthur..230
More from Innovo Publishing..231

PREFACE

As you read this book, whether in part or in whole, I want you to know that I have done this project in obedience to what I sincerely believe the Lord has called me to do. I take no credit whatsoever for any blessings anyone may receive, nor will I have any regrets for what may be rejected. I have, as best as I was able, simply expressed what the Lord God has revealed to me as He has spoken explicitly or implicitly in His Word, the Bible. When I have given an opinion, I will try to make that clear. But my deepest desire is to collect from God's holy, inerrant, all-powerful Word and to make these truths known to young women and/or matured adults who desire to hear, believe, and trust God for His power and divine guidance to live righteously and obediently. This book has been written for any and all women who are seeking and striving to learn from God's Word how He has purposed all women to "walk in a manner worthy of our Lord Jesus Christ" (i.e., those who are seeking to live righteous, godly lives in Christ Jesus). Or perhaps you may have been led to this book and are just curious.

With much passion I am led to speak to you about what God says and instructs regarding living the life of a righteous woman. My earnest desire in writing this book is to bring hope, enlightenment, and encouragement to all who are led to read it. This manuscript is filled with many passages of God's Word printed in the text. When you encounter several passages that are repeated and repeated, understand that it is not that I have forgotten that I had already specifically addressed them. It will either be because they are needful and/or helpful to be repeated and/or I want to address that passage through a different subject's lens.

The title and the goal of all that is written in this book is not only to know what a portrait of a righteous woman looks like before God but also to know what the word *righteous* means as used in the New Testament. Many have described righteousness as "God's right ways." I certainly agree with that description. The Greek word used in God's Word that is translated "righteous" is *dikaios,* and *Dr. Zodhiates' The Complete Word Study New Testament* contains many pages to define this Greek word in the form of nouns, verbs, and adjectives. I want to give you just one definition of the adjective *dikaios*: "Those who are called righteous are those who have conditioned their lives by the standard which is not theirs, but God's. A righteous person is one justified by faith and showing forth his faith by works." And, of course, by the power of the Holy Spirit continuing that transformation.

For many years I have been given the privilege to teach God's Word to adults. My Lord God has consistently led me to teach His Word through staying close to the passage of scripture that I am teaching and also to use biblical cross references to help support and increase understanding and application. As I write these words of exhortation and instruction here, my goal is that as one reads, each will be able to hear from the Lord as to what He says, what He means by what He says, and how He intends for each one to apply these truths you learn to your personal life. That is, to be "transformed more and more into the image of the Lord Jesus Christ," according to Romans 12:2 (and several other passages). "And do not be conformed to this world, but be transformed by the renewing of your mind, so that you may prove what the will of God is, that which is good and acceptable and perfect."

Another thing you will notice is that I am susceptible to "chasing rabbits." You will experience that while I am teaching on one subject, I am reminded of another biblical principle that I believe will help you come to a better understanding of the subject I am dealing with. By the time you finish reading this book, most of you will have been exposed to many, if not most, of my own "systematic theology." Oh well, that's just me. I love and am spiritually blessed to share the truths in God's Word, which includes "knowing the truth that will set us free," according to John 8:32. (*Wow*, I can't even resist chasing a rabbit when I am trying to explain "the rabbits" I chase.) My former pastor, Dr. Charles A. Fowler, now serving as the president of Carson-Newman University, regularly put it this way: "It's the truth that you know (and I add, "and believe") that sets you free."

Point of clarity because we all know that words matter. When you read the words *believer, Christ-follower, Christian, God's children,* and/or *saved*, please know that each of these words have one specific meaning, and I want to make clear that meaning. You will notice that I use these words interchangeably throughout this book, and they are referring specifically to those persons who have been convicted by the Holy Spirit that they are "sinners in need of a Savior." Consequently, they have confessed their sins, repented of their sins (made a conscious, deliberate decision to turn from their sins to God), and surrendered their lives in *faith* to the Person and work of the Lord Jesus Christ, the Son of God. This person's faith is anchored in the facts that Jesus Christ took on human flesh and lived a perfect life (never having committed a single sin), that He was crucified for the very purpose of becoming a substitutionary sacrifice/payment for the forgiveness for every sin committed by every person for all times, and that He was raised bodily from the dead/grave on the third day. There are many more life-changing truths to believe about Jesus' Person and work, but the above facts are the ones that must be believed/trusted in order for God's redemptive work of salvation to have taken place in each individual person.

There will be times when I give you illustrations, some of which are mine personally and some are those of whom I am personally aware. These illustrations will be used primarily to bring a clearer understanding of and obedience to what God has written in His Word about certain circumstances. I believe wholeheartedly that illustrations can be beneficial. However, it is never the illustration of a personal experience that authenticates the scripture. It is the scriptures themselves that make the illustration useful and relevant to our better understanding, because God has given the truth of the matter through His Word. Also, I am well aware that a person does not have to have personally lived through any certain situation to be able to support and encourage someone else through God's Word. God's Word has the inherent power to comfort, bring peace, and grant divine power and guidance to walk victoriously through any and all difficult situations—not a person's "having walked in their shoes," so to speak.

You will come to several places where I say, *I advise you*, or, *My best advice is*. When you come to such places, I want you to know that I am simply asking you to take what I advise to the Lord and seek His opinion as to whether this is good counsel for you or not. I will not have known your background nor your circumstances, but as you know, the Lord does, and He promises to lead us by His Spirit into all truth.

Honestly, I am not a "book writer." I am hoping and praying that you will read the following pages by picturing yourself as a class member in one of my Bible studies. I have written the same way I teach. I have been called and gifted by God as a proclaimer of His Word—that is, to make disciples through the clear teaching of the scriptures. None of us is able to follow this calling, and most assuredly including myself, to understand, teach, and apply God's Word with perfection. But in saying that, my major goal for this project is that those who read these words will be encouraged, inspired, and edified to the point of trust and obedience to following God's plans and purposes for your lives. And in doing so, that you may enjoy the great blessings and rewards through righteously living out the life God has planned and purposed for you. And also that you will bring Him great pleasure and glory as you minister in His name and for the advancement of His kingdom. My prayer is that these pages do not become too long and too detailed but will, by their content, increase each of your abilities to love, to worship, and to serve the one and only true Jehovah God of the Bible, and His Son Christ Jesus, about whom this book has been written.

Let me speak clearly and earnestly to you as I close this portion. I am so well aware that there are biblical subjects that I deal with in this book that are deeply embedded counter-cultural issues. Some subjects I deal with in this book may be very difficult for you to read through because your wounds are so deep, which have been created by past sins committed against you *or* sins you may have committed against someone else. If that is the case for you personally, please simply read the passages in God's Word and let God Himself bring truth, healing, and returned joy to your soul.

Other subjects I deal with may be those which you disagree with my interpretations. As I'll state later, I have not written this book to disparage anyone's beliefs or to try to persuade you to believe as I do. My honest intent before the God I serve is to encourage those who read this book to personally examine the scriptures carefully in context and allow the Lord God Himself to give you revelation of His truth, all for the purpose of getting to know your God more intimately and with ever-increasing understanding—all for the glory of His great name and that your transformation into His Son's image will be substantially increased. Our God is the only One who can do that.

I pray that the Lord my God will speak to you clearly and bless you richly in and through each of these following chapters. To Him be all glory, honor, praise, and thanksgiving.

—Marie Strain

P.S. If you have not looked carefully at the picture of the dove on the book cover, please look again and note that the dove is in a "landing" position. My prayer is that you will experience what this image represents: "The Holy Spirit is positioned to land in your heart with the life-changing truths of God's Word." Please, welcome Him in!

CHAPTER 1

First Things First:

RIGHTEOUS BEHAVIOR IS MANIFESTED THROUGH KNOWING AND OBEYING GOD'S WORD

As the title of this book and this first chapter clearly state, the desire of my heart is to share with all that there is a good and sovereign God Who is the Creator of all things. He is alive and forever ruling over all His Creation. This same living God loves all of His creation but especially those whom He created in His own image—the human race. The most incredible truth of all is that this one and only true and living God wants to reveal Himself—His love—to us. And His revelation is primarily accomplished through His living and active Word, the Bible. Look at Hebrews 4:12:

> For the word of God is living and active and sharper than any two-edged sword, and piercing as far as the division of soul and spirit, of both joints and marrow, and able to judge the thoughts and intentions of the heart.

GOD'S PORTRAIT OF A "RIGHTEOUS WOMAN"

Now, let's hear from God through His Word as He explains His love for us. There are a couple of insights I have learned as I have sought to better understand just what God's love is and how I am to love like God loves. I know that God's kind of love is not based on emotion. God's love is a deliberately demonstrated action through which He meets the needs of the object upon whom His love is manifested.

There are several passages in the book of 1 John that I want to share with you. To help establish its context, I want you to know that this short book of only four chapters contains the word *love* some forty-six times. Read the following passages slowly and carefully because our God wants you to hear His heart. I want us to begin by observing Romans 5:8.

> But God <u>demonstrates</u> His own love toward us, in that while we were yet sinners, Christ died for us. (Romans 5:8)

> See how great a love the Father <u>has bestowed</u> on us, that we would be called children of God. (1 John 3:1a)

> [16]We know love by this, that <u>He laid down His life</u> for us; and we ought to lay down our lives for the brethren. [17]But whoever has the world's goods, and sees his brother in need and closes his heart against him, how does the love of God abide in him? [18]Little children, let us not love with word or with tongue, but in deed and truth. (1 John 3:16-18)

> [7]Beloved, let us love one another, for love is <u>from God</u>; and everyone who loves is born of God and knows God. [8]The one who does not love does not know God, for God is love. [9]By this the love of God was manifested in us, that God has sent His only begotten Son into the world so that we might live through Him. [10]In this is love, not that we loved God, but that He loved us and <u>sent His Son</u> *to be* the propitiation for our sins. . . . [18]There is no fear in love; but perfect love casts out fear, because fear involves punishment, and the one who fears is not perfected in love. [19]We love, because He first loved us. (1 John 4:7-10, 18-19)

1: FIRST THINGS FIRST

> We have come to know and have believed the love which God has for us. God is love, and the one who abides in love abides in God, and God abides in him. (1 John 4:16)

> [A]nd hope does not disappoint, because the love of God has been poured out within our hearts through the Holy Spirit who was given to us. (Romans 5:5)

God wants us to know Him and to live in relationship with Him through our obedience according to His written revelation. I am of the opinion that God's prophetic words through His prophet Amos are being fulfilled even today.

> "Behold, days are coming," declares the Lord GOD, "When I will send a famine on the land, not a famine for bread or a thirst for water, but rather for hearing the words of the LORD." (Amos 8:11)

How I pray that through this book those who are hungry will be fed on God's "bread of life" and be satisfied. That those who are thirsty will receive His "living water" and have their thirst quenched. All through God's Word, He states His desire to bring righteousness to the land but foremost to bring His righteousness through revival within our churches. Now, let's listen to God speak through His Word for better understanding and discover His purposed application on a variety of subjects that have relevant messages and instructions regarding God's portrait of a righteous woman.

This chapter has primarily been written to bring to light or to reinforce what God says about marriage and the family (including relevant truths regarding children) before, during, and after the wedding vows are taken. I am convinced that whatever God speaks about any subject is to be believed, trusted, and obeyed. Marriage and the family became God's foundational institution for all civilization on the sixth day of Creation. We must know as believers in Jesus Christ that marriage is God's physical picture of Christ's relationship to the church, His bride. We'll deal more in-depth with that subject later.

Teaching high school girls in Sunday school (yes, I'm old enough to call small groups that meet together in church on Sunday mornings "Sunday school") was where I first began to heed God's call to "make disciples." This was in the late 1970s and early

1980s. I discovered early that probably the hardest biblical truths for teenagers to believe, trust, and obey are found in 1 Corinthians 15:33: "Do not be deceived: 'Bad company corrupts good morals.'" Please understand, I am not just speaking of the youth who are not regularly within the influential realm of a Christian community, but of those who have been regularly in the company and influence of Christian teachers and many other Christian leaders.

There are two major discernable reasons for this prevalent deception, in my opinion. First, I'm afraid that too many parents today have relinquished to the churches much of the responsibility of teaching their children biblical truths. However, the teachings of the Bible clearly state that the responsibility and accountability rests on their fathers and mothers, according to Ephesians 6:4b: "[B]ut bring them up in the discipline and instruction of the Lord." Second is the constant messaging/brainwashing that our children receive from social media and in many, if not most, of our school systems today. In this time and culture in which they are now living, our children are deluged with evil and destructive information. Their ability to discern what is good and what is evil is greatly hindered, compromised, and sometimes even destroyed by all that is bombarding and stimulating their minds. I have heard it said, and I concur, "It is easier to believe a lie that you have heard a thousand times, than the truth that you have heard only once."

There is a warning for all of us believers in the Lord Jesus Christ, young and old alike, that is quite sobering. Look with me at Hebrews 5:11-14:

> [11]Concerning him [Melchizedek] we have much to say, and *it is* <u>hard to explain, since you have become dull of hearing</u>. [12]For though by this time, you ought to be teachers, you have need again for someone to teach you the elementary principles of the oracles of God, and you have come to need milk and not solid food. [13]For everyone who partakes *only* of milk is not accustomed to the word of righteousness, for he is an infant. [14]But solid food is for the mature, who <u>because of practice have their senses trained to discern good and evil</u>.

1: FIRST THINGS FIRST

Hebrews warns us that there is a possibility for believers to become dull of hearing—that is, hearing as to understand what God is saying. I contend that "becoming dull of hearing" can actually occur unintentionally by two major things: (1) by not regularly feeding on what God has spoken in His Word and/or (2) by refusing to obey the truth of God's Word that you have seen yourself or have been taught by others.

"Use it or lose it" seems to fit perfectly with these warnings in Hebrews 5:11-14. However, Hebrews 5:14 is perhaps one of the most sober warnings Christians are given in scripture. We know clearly that "milk" is good, nourishing, and necessary for infants. Milk is a predigested product by a source not their own and usually fed to an infant by someone else. We also know that an infant physically grows up to the place when receiving milk alone is not sufficient for healthy growth but can hinder and potentially stop physical growth.

"Solid food," the mysteries of the Word of God (those not easy to see and understand), causes spiritual growth. Physical solid food is necessary for the continued growth and health of our physical bodies and is most always personally fed to oneself. The spiritual "solid food" is that which trains us to "discern good and evil," among many other things. However, there is a condition stated: *one must "practice" and obey* what he/she has learned are the "principles of the oracles of God." It is no wonder so many of those who regularly attend Bible-believing and Bible-preaching churches are not able to discern good and evil. I'm afraid that all too many today hear but do not obey what God clearly states in His Word.

The reason I have started with this admonition in Hebrews 5 is because everything in this book will only be beneficial to those who listen closely to what God says clearly in His Word and believe what He says to be true to the point of obedience. After that, we trust Him to accomplish in our lives what He has revealed and promised.

The truth is that teenagers are not alone in their disbelief that "bad company corrupts good morals." First Corinthians 5:2 tells us, "You have become arrogant and have not mourned instead." Look with me at 1 Corinthians 5:1-3, 13:

> ¹It is actually reported that there is immorality among you, and immorality of such a kind as does not exist even among the Gentiles, that someone has his father's wife. ²You have

become arrogant and have not mourned instead, so that the one who had done this deed would be removed from your midst. ³For I, on my part, though absent in body but present in spirit, have already judged him who has so committed this, as though I were present. . . . ¹³But those who are outside, God judges. Remove the wicked man from among yourselves.

This passage gives us God's clear declaration of how He describes those who find themselves thinking they know better than God does in how to deal with a church member who is living in habitual sin. God calls it *arrogance*; perhaps *pride* in one's own ability to navigate life, even though God instructs us otherwise, might be descriptive as well. Do you ever wonder why there is not greater attention paid to and action taken by churches regarding those who are knowingly living immoral and ungodly lives?

There is another commandment in the New Testament that either too few are aware of, or they dismiss its importance. God has commanded believers not to get into any contractual agreement with an unbeliever, according to 2 Corinthians 6:14-15 which states, "Do not be bound together with unbelievers; for what partnership have righteousness and lawlessness, or what fellowship has light with darkness? Or what harmony has Christ with Belial, or what has a believer in common with an unbeliever?"

Even though this passage in 2 Corinthians addresses several issues, marriage and the family (children) are one of my primary focuses here in this opening chapter. Indeed, marriage is a legal contract (being bound together before God). All Christian women should know and believe what God says about marriage *before* they ever get to the place of considering marriage. I am convinced that if our daughters (and of course sons) grow up being taught by their parents the principles and confines of marriage, there would be considerably fewer marriages in conflict today headed down a path toward divorce.

At the time of my salvation, I did not know most of the biblical mandates for those who have been saved. I was ignorant regarding most of the instructions and promises that are recorded in God's Word for those He has purchased for Himself by His own blood. Honestly, there were many things I didn't know (and many I still don't know!) when I was a "dating" teenager. But there is one thing that I have learned since those early, biblically ignorant years. It is that when I got saved, the Lord God Himself wrote the "laws of Christ" (not the Law of Moses) on my new heart of flesh that He gave me when I got saved. So even though I didn't know many biblical truths during the early years of my salvation, they were written on my new heart of flesh by God Himself. The Holy Spirit guided me by what He had written on my heart. When I eventually came to where those things were written in God's Word, my heart rejoiced. Even when one is very young in their walk with Jesus and their heart is to follow Him, He is always faithful to lead and direct their paths. It still happens to me even some sixty-five-plus years after my salvation. Thank You, Lord!

It is essential, in my opinion, that every mother of a daughter (and of a son too) teach this warning by reading and explaining God's Word clearly and often, that they are not to be in a close relationship with an unbeliever. We examined 2 Corinthians 6:14-15 earlier. Most of us are well aware that we cannot *make* anyone do what we know is best if they don't want to, even one of our children. Many children of godly parents have "towed the line, mostly" while still under their parents' roof, so to speak. But when they leave the supervision available in their home, all too many disregard the biblical teachings and moral standards they have been taught. However, I believe that if a biblical truth is taught often and clearly enough by using the Bible itself, there is a better chance that it will be remembered, believed, and obeyed, even in those children who are not yet born again/redeemed by the blood of Jesus.

One thing I know for sure is that my words have no power to change anyone's mind or to make a permanent life change in another. However, God's Word contains inherent power, that when it is believed, it is powerful enough to transform both their hearts and lives, according to Hebrews 4:2: "For indeed we have had good news preached to us, just as they also; but the word they heard did not profit them, because it was not united by faith in those who heard." I'm sure you noticed that this verse gives the principle in the negative. We can just as accurately state this truth in a positive form by saying that "when a person joins their faith to believe what they saw and/or heard in God's Word, their belief releases God's power through which a change of their hearts and lives occur."

Even though it has been several decades since my husband and I have had our own children under our authority, we have been privileged to have grandchildren to love and hopefully influence in the things of God's Word. We have tried to tell them of God's love and exemplify our Lord's saving love, grace, and protection over those who will trust Him and obey His instructions. I am also very grateful to have known the promise of 1 Corinthians 7:14 for the unsaved children in a home where there is at least one Christian parent. We will deal with this verse in depth in a later chapter regarding a different subject, but for now, be blessed and encouraged by the truth revealed in 1 Corinthians 7:14. It should be an incredible blessing and comfort for all Christian parents to realize that their not-yet-saved children who are still under their parental authority are set apart to God:

> For the unbelieving husband is sanctified through his wife, and the unbelieving wife is sanctified through her believing husband; for otherwise your children are unclean, but now they are holy. (1 Corinthians 7:14)

The Christian Standard Bible (CSB) translates this passage this way:

> For the unbelieving husband is made holy by the wife, and the unbelieving wife is made holy by the husband. Otherwise, your children would be unclean, but as it is they are holy.

The Greek verb *hagiazo* is translated in the Christian Standard Bible as "holy" and as "sanctified" in the New American Standard Bible. This Greek word is defined as "set apart, sanctified, consecrated to God as morally pure and blameless."[1] Please know this *does not* mean nor imply that any unbelieving husband, wife, or child is actually saved because of the presence of a believing husband or wife or mother or father. It means that because a child (or children) is under the umbrella of the authority of a believing parent, that child is "set apart to God" and becomes a recipient of God's grace, mercy,

---

1 *The Complete Word Study Dictionary: New Testament* (Chattanooga, TN: AMG Publishers, June 1992).

and protection—that is, the blessings that are those of the saved spouse or parent.

Let me repeat, this passage of scripture does not mean nor imply that any child is ever saved by having a believing parent. It just means that they receive the blessings of God by way of their saved parent(s). Salvation always comes as a result of a personal decision to surrender their hearts and lives to the Person and work of the Lord Jesus Christ. However, never underestimate the spiritual power and influence of a Christian home or a believing parent. And of course, that brings great responsibility to us all to raise up our children in the "discipline and instruction of the Lord," according to Ephesians 6:4b.

Now back to the central subject of this first chapter, "first things first." There is a major cultural truth I want to address. It seems probable, in all too many cases, that our pre-teen and teenage children receive their major influence from their friends and the schools they attend, not their parent(s). As a result, the influences of the pre-teen and the teenagers of this time and culture are all too often in direct conflict with the morals and standards of behavior stated in God's Word.

As most of you already know and would agree, peer pressure in our culture and time is so strong that it is not unusual for teenagers, younger or older, to choose to engage in the activities of the unsaved world-culture that often are in direct disobedience to their parents. That fact in itself must cause parents today to diligently maintain a closer oversight of their children's friends. It is imperative that parents inform their children that they may choose their own friends, but they (the parents) will always retain "veto" power. One of the main reasons is because, when their dating age comes, it is most often that they choose from among their present friends. As I have already mentioned, God says that "bad company corrupts good morals."

Our children's choices of friends are of great importance, but the people they date are of vastly greater importance. Another thing that has become clearly apparent is that our dating system, as we know it today, is one of the most dangerous activities our children engage in. Dating, per se, is an activity mostly made up of deception. Both parties, in most all instances, try very hard to put forth an image that is not an accurate reflection of their true moral character, beliefs, and/or habitual behavior.

GOD'S PORTRAIT OF A "RIGHTEOUS WOMAN"

In our day and time, it is often true for young married couples to find out later that they did not marry the same person they dated. In the late 1950s, during the time I was dating in my teenage years, that was not altogether true, because the moral standard of acceptable behavior, for the most part, came from biblical truth. As you are probably well aware, the world in which our children and grandchildren live today is mostly governed by immoral, ungodly, and often evil standards.

Most likely your child(ren) has been taught from early childhood and may now believe that an abortion is a woman's choice—it is their personal right/prerogative to do so. However, God says abortion is the murder of a helpless, unborn baby. I have heard it said recently, and I agree, that abortion is an act of worship to a false god.

Many, if not most young people in today's culture believe that sex before marriage is simply a social activity you do. God says sex outside of marriage is sexual immorality, which He judges according to Hebrews 13:4: "Marriage *is to be held* in honor among all, and the *marriage* bed *is to be* undefiled; for fornicators and adulterers God will judge." To my horror, I am told that in today's culture, even on a first date, many young men expect to experience some measure of sexual activity. And in far too many cases, the females as well.

Many teenagers today, including Christian teens, believe that the homosexual lifestyle is a good and acceptable choice—that God created them to intimately love those of the same sex and it is to be accepted, embraced, and even encouraged. God says that all homosexual activity is an abomination to Him. According to Romans 1:26-27, sex with a person of the same sex is an unnatural and indecent act. Romans 1:26-27 states,

> ²⁶For this reason God gave them over to degrading passions; for their women exchanged the natural function for that which is unnatural, ²⁷and in the same way also the men abandoned the natural function of the woman and burned in their desire toward one another, men with men committing indecent acts and receiving in their own persons the due penalty of their error.

Many teenagers and even younger kids today use social media to tear apart and demean another person's character. Many of them think that this behavior is an acceptable thing to do. God commands that we do not make false witness or defame another person, according to Matthew 19:18b: "You shall not bear false witness." Whether the information is accurate or not, it seems to make no difference to many today. Social media seems to encourage or embolden negative interaction with no face-to-face accountability. And as we know, some adult professing Christians do this on a regular basis without shame or repentance. God's writes in Psalm 19:14, "Let the words of my mouth and the meditation of my heart be acceptable in Your sight, O Lord, my rock and my Redeemer."

I have painted a pretty bleak picture of today's teenagers, so let me change course here. Many of us are well aware and personally acquainted with teenagers who are some of the godliest people among us. I have the joy of knowing some of our youth who are dedicated followers of Jesus Christ. They are committed to and are diligently trying their best to live in a Christ-honoring way. They are able to live this way—not perfectly as none of us is, but to live a life that can be characterized by a habitual lifestyle that is morally pure and pleasing to our Lord God. We should be so very supportive and encouraging to those who have dedicated their lives to the living and the teaching of God's Word to our youth. And if you are among them, I thank you and pray our Lord will continue to bless and empower your ministry and increase your favor among them all.

So "first things first" implies that we are to know, live, and teach the principles of God's Word diligently. As Christian women, wives, and mothers, we are to live up to our responsibility to oversee and be intimately involved in the spiritual education and growth of our children. This includes knowing the lifestyles of our children's friends and especially anyone they might date.

This is certainly not an easy time to raise children, but God promises to provide everything we need for life and for godliness through the "true knowledge" of God and His Son, Jesus Christ, as conveyed in 2 Peter 1:2-4.

> [2]Grace and peace be multiplied to you in the <u>knowledge</u> of God and of Jesus our Lord; [3]seeing that His divine power has granted to us everything pertaining to life and godliness, through the <u>true knowledge</u> of Him who called us by His own glory and excellence. [4]For by these He has

granted to us His precious and magnificent promises, so that by them you may become partakers of *the* divine nature, having escaped the corruption that is in the world by lust.

I want us not to miss all that this 2 Peter passage promises. The single Greek word *epignosis* in this passage has been translated both "knowledge" and "true knowledge," which is defined as "a knowledge that expresses a more thorough participation in the acquiring of knowledge on the part of the learner; often referr[ing] to knowledge which very powerfully influences, etc."[2]

First, we see in this 2 Peter passage that God's grace (His provision of what we need but do not deserve) and peace are *multiplied* to us through the conduit of the "true knowledge" of God our Father and Jesus Christ our Lord. I am confident that you want God's grace to be multiplied to you. God's Word is the only sure source of God's true knowledge through which God multiples His grace. One gets to know Him intimately by continually/regularly reading, studying, meditating on, and then obeying His Word. Do you want God's peace multiplied to you? I'm sure you do. Get to know Him intimately by continually and regularly reading, studying, meditating on, and then obeying His Word. Do you want to become partakers of His divine nature and escape the corruption that is in the world by lust? I'm also sure that you do. God grants them all to each one of us through our getting to know Him intimately by continually and regularly reading, studying, meditating on and obeying His Word.

To summarize a major point: Most often, dating is the entry passage to finding one's future spouse. You want your children to know that God's Word clearly commands that each believer must not marry an unbeliever. Therefore, I am pleading with you, parents, that you do the best you know how to safeguard your children from ever even dating a person whose habitual lifestyle does not exhibit a true surrender to the Lordship of Jesus Christ. Is that an easy task? ABSOLUTELY NOT! Hopefully, this will be just the safeguard to eventually, hopefully, ensuring that your child(ren) will only marry a person who is a genuine follower of Christ Jesus. I do so encourage you to strive diligently to be a follower of Christ Jesus in a way that is similar to that of Eunice and Lois, Timothy's mother

---

2   *The Complete Word Study Dictionary: New Testament*

and grandmother. Their lifestyles regarding raising children are characterized in 2 Timothy 3:14-15. Oh, that many of our mothers would be and will be described as such.

> [14]You, however, continue in the things you have learned and become convinced of, knowing from whom you have learned *them*, [15]and that from childhood[3] you have known the sacred writings which are able to give you the wisdom that leads to salvation through faith which is in Christ Jesus. (2 Timothy 3:14-15)[4]

If you are one of many who are presently married to an unbelieving husband, be encouraged, we will deal with that circumstance later.

This seems like a good place to share with you a biblical principle upon which this entire book stands. I want to explain why I am using God's Word so frequently to authenticate the statements I make. Many Christians know the passage that tells us that God has written the law on the new hearts He has given us at salvation. I am convictional about my belief that Jeremiah 31:33 is prophesying about the "law of Christ" because all believers are *not* under the Law of Moses. The biblical confirmation follows. As is my habit and style of teaching, I want to support my conclusions by using the following cross references that add to our understanding of the fact that we have the "laws of Christ" written on our hearts in hopes that their meaning and intent will be more easily understood. First, let's deal with the prophesies given to us in the Old Testament regarding a "new covenant" that God would make with Israel.

> "But this is the covenant which I will make with the house of Israel after those days," declares the Lord, "I will put My law within them and <u>on their heart I will write it</u>; and I will be their God, and they shall be My people." (Jeremiah 31:33)

---

3   This Greek word *brephos* that is translated "childhood" is defined in *The Complete Word Study Dictionary: New Testament* as "an infant still in the womb, a newborn child or older infant and implies from the cradle." It goes on to say that this Greek word comes from a root that means to feed, nourish or to bring nourishment.

4   Paul is addressing Timothy in these verses.

This passage and the following Ezekiel passage are God's specific revelation to the Jews, that at some time in the future Jehovah God will make a new covenant with the house of Israel. God gives them some of the key elements to this new covenant. However, we will see just a little later from the book of Galatians that this new covenant God was to make would not only be for the Jews but also for the Gentiles.

It will help us to know that the Law of Moses included the instructions for and the mandate to build the Tabernacle. It told them how they were to worship, live, and have their sins covered/atoned for each year. This "covenant" was given to the Jews so God could dwell among them, and they could live in health and prosperity in the Promised Land. This covenant of the law was never intended to bring salvation to the Jews but to have them experience the value and rewards of God's presence, provision, and protection through their obedience to His laws and precepts. God gave the Jews particular insights into what this "new" covenant would provide. As we just read, Jeremiah 31:33 tells them/us that His law would be written internally on their hearts, not externally on tablets of stone.

Another aspect of this new covenant is that God would be the God of those who would be participants in this new covenant that He would make. And those who would enter into this covenant would become God's people. It is so very important that we are able to authenticate through scripture that God has made it clear that Jeremiah's and Ezekiel's prophesies which were made to Israel would also include the Gentiles. We can authenticate this, and I will show you where in just a few minutes. Look with me first at an additional prophesy God gave Israel about this new covenant, which is recorded in Ezekiel 36:26-27:

> [26]"Moreover, I will give you a new heart and put a new spirit within you; and I will remove the heart of stone from your flesh and give you a heart of flesh. [27]<u>I will put My Spirit within you and cause you to walk in My statutes</u> and you will be careful to observe My ordinances."

In these two verses of Ezekiel, we learn that all humans who have not yet been saved by faith have within them a "heart of stone." This non-visible heart of stone is pretty self-explanatory. So we learn from Ezekiel 36:26 that everyone who enters into this new covenant gets a "heart transplant." Jesus doesn't come into our old hearts of stone. He removes the heart of stone and replaces it with a new heart of flesh, upon which He writes His new covenant laws and comes to personally dwell within each believer's new heart.

In the Ezekiel 36 prophecy they were told that the new covenant also promises that God would put the Holy Spirit, His Spirit, within each believer. Most of you who are reading this book probably know about the Person and the work of the Holy Spirit. But in this promised new covenant, the Holy Spirit's home, His permanent dwelling place, would be inside them. God gives through this Ezekiel prophecy an extraordinary revelation regarding the work of His Spirit. His Spirit would cause them to walk in His statues. The Holy Spirit would empower them to carefully observe and obey God's ordinances. Under the Law of Moses, there was no power given to the Jews to obey God's commands. But the new covenant would include the power to obey; that power would be manifested in them by the Holy Spirit Himself.

Galatians 3:8-14 and Hebrews 11:24-26 explain details about the Law that many have not heard or come to understand. Observe these carefully to understand that Christ redeemed us from the curse of the Old Testament Law of Moses, which was death. That Law has never had the power to save nor to make anyone righteous or justified. The Law of Moses carries with it strict rules and consequences. Observe closely with me the following verses in Galatians 3 and Hebrews 11.

> [8]The Scripture, foreseeing that God would justify the Gentiles by faith, preached the gospel beforehand to Abraham, *saying*, "All the nations will be blessed in you." [9]So then those who are of faith are blessed with Abraham, the believer [i.e., believer in a coming Messiah]. [10]For as many as are of the works of the Law are under a curse; for it is written, "Cursed is everyone who does not abide by all things written in the book of the law, to perform them." [11]Now that no one is justified by the Law before God is evident; for, "The righteous man shall live by faith." [12]However, the Law is not of faith; on the contrary, "He who practices them shall live by them." [13]Christ redeemed

> us from the curse of the Law, having become a curse for us—for it is written, "Cursed is everyone who hangs on a tree"— ¹⁴in order that in Christ Jesus the blessing of Abraham might come to the Gentiles, so that we would receive the promise of the Spirit through faith. (Galatians 3:8-14)

> ²⁴By faith Moses, when he had grown up, refused to be called the son of Pharaoh's daughter, ²⁵choosing rather to endure ill-treatment with the people of God than to enjoy the passing pleasures of sin, ²⁶considering <u>the reproach of Christ</u> greater riches than the treasures of Egypt; for he was looking to the reward. (Hebrews 11:24-26)

Don't you just love how scripture interprets scripture? Galatians and Hebrews explain that both Abraham and Moses' faith was in God's promise of a Messiah. God credited the ledger of their sin debt as "paid in full" based on their trust/faith in a future deliverer, the Christ—the Messiah, which God preached to Abraham. Abraham and Moses believed/trusted that someday God would send the promised Messiah.

Did you know that Abraham was taught and believed the gospel of Jesus Christ? In truth, man has always been saved by faith in the gospel of Jesus, the Christ—a faith/belief/trust that God would someday send the promised Messiah who would deliver them from the slavery of sin. Of course, they believed in what God would do in the future. Today we believe in what God has already done in the past—that God did indeed send the Messiah, and He came in the person of His Son, Jesus Christ, the Nazarene, in order that we could be rescued from the penalty of our sins, which is death, and receive the promise of eternal life.

This prophesied promise in both Ezekiel and Jeremiah was referring to the new covenant of grace which would be mediated by Jesus Christ by His blood, according to Hebrews 9:14-15.

> ¹⁴How much more will the blood of Christ, who through the eternal Spirit offered Himself without blemish to God, cleanse your conscience from dead works to serve the living God? ¹⁵For this reason, He is the mediator of a new covenant, so that, since a death has taken place for

the redemption of the transgressions that were *committed* under the first covenant, those who have been called may receive the promise of the eternal inheritance.

The "first covenant" mentioned in Hebrews 9:15 is referring to the covenant of the Law of Moses. I'm sure you noted that this new covenant "cleanses our conscience from dead works to serve the living God." I vividly remember years ago while leading a Precept Bible study course, one of our members began to sob. She told the class how grateful she was that God had cleansed her conscience from her past sinful behavior prior to salvation, and that now she is able to have a conscience that didn't shame, demean, and condemn her, because Jesus had paid her sin debt. Those past sins no longer held her hostage. She was freed through Christ from the sin debt she had owed and was now experiencing the "joy of her salvation," which included a cleansed conscience.

The following scripture passages state clearly that believers are not "under the Law" (the Law of Moses, that is). Honestly, the previous passages of both Ezekiel and Jeremiah confused me for many years after I had studied the book of Romans and learned that true Christians are not under the Old Testament law. I had been taught that we no longer were responsible to keep the ceremonial laws, but the other laws were to be obeyed. I was confused that God would write the Old Testament laws on the hearts of New Testament believers when the Old Testament laws were no longer applicable to us.

The Lord Himself had clearly shown me in the New Testament book of Romans that I had no obligation to keep the Old Testament laws through these three passages below, along with several others:

> But if you are led by the Spirit, you are not under the Law. (Galatians 5:18)

> [14]For sin shall not be master over you, for you are not under law but under grace. [15]What then? Shall we sin because we are not under law but under grace? May it never be! (Romans 6:14-15)

> [8]After saying above, "Sacrifices and offerings and whole burnt offerings and *sacrifices* for sin You have not desired, nor have You taken pleasure *in them*" (which are offered

according to the Law), ⁹then He said, "Behold, I have come to do Your will." He takes away the first [the covenant of the Law of Moses] in order to establish the second [the covenant of grace—the laws of Christ Jesus]. (Hebrews 10:8-9)

The confusion continued because I couldn't reconcile that the Old Testament law was written on my heart when I was no longer under the Old Testament laws. Hebrews had even told me that God had "taken it away." This went on for years. Then in God's perfect timing, He led me to the following passages of 1 Corinthians 9, Galatians 6, and Romans 8, which clearly state that believers, even though we are not under the Law of Moses, are *not without law*. We now are under the "law of Christ." Look first at 1 Corinthians 9:20-21:

> ²⁰To the Jews I became as a Jew, so that I might win Jews; to those who are under the Law, as under the Law though not being myself under the Law, so that I might win those who are under the Law; ²¹to those who are without law, as without law, though not being without the law of God but under the law of Christ, so that I might win those who are without law.

> Bear one another's burdens, and thereby fulfill the law of Christ. (Galatians 6:2)

> For the law of the Spirit of life in Christ Jesus has set you free from the law of sin and of death [i.e., the Law of Moses]. (Romans 8:2)

The "law of sin and of death" is referring to the Old Testament laws which no one could keep except Jesus Christ, the Son of God, which He accomplished to set us free from the law of sin and death. Notice in Hebrews 8:13 that a "new covenant" (the one Jesus Christ inaugurated) has made the first (the Old Testament laws) obsolete.

> When He said, "A new *covenant*," He has made the first obsolete. But whatever is becoming obsolete and growing old is ready to disappear. (Hebrews 8:13)

It will be helpful for me to bring to your attention that in Galatians 2:15-16 below, the Greek word *dikaioo* has been translated into the English word *justified* is the same Greek word that is also translated "made righteous" or "declared righteous" in other passages of God's Word. In other words, these English words are commonly used interchangeably in the New Testament in the translation of the same Greek word.

> [15]We *are* Jews by nature and not sinners from among the Gentiles; [16]nevertheless knowing that a man is <u>not justified by the works of the Law</u> but through faith in Christ Jesus, even we have believed in Christ Jesus, so that we may be <u>justified by faith</u> in Christ and <u>not by the works of the Law</u>; since by the works of the Law no flesh will be justified. (Galatians 2:15-16)

For some of you this is totally new insight. If this is your experience, I highly recommend that you revisit these passages and meditate on their significance. For others, you had the same questions I had pondered for years, and now you are so grateful to have this confusion settled by God's Word. You now have found peace regarding where the Law of Moses fits into our sovereign God's predetermined plans. If this is the case, I rejoice with you!

CHAPTER 2

Before You Say, "I Do"

In my four decades of teaching and ministry, I have learned a very important principle of "living life" in this world. Jesus Himself warns all believers in John 16:33, "These things I have spoken to you, so that in Me you may have peace. In the world you have tribulation, but take courage; <u>I have overcome the world</u>."

We know from 1 John 2:16 that there are three mentioned temptations from the world that every follower of Christ Jesus should be aware of and carefully and diligently fight against. Look with me as the Lord names them for us in this passage:

> For all that is in the world, the lust of the flesh and the lust of the eyes and the boastful pride of life, is not from the Father, but is from the world. (1 John 2:16)

God promises that when a Christian is led by the Holy Spirit, they will not fulfill the desires of the flesh, according to Galatians 5:16-17:

> [16]But I say, <u>walk by the Spirit, and you will not carry out the desire of the flesh</u>. [17]For the flesh sets its desire against

the Spirit, and the Spirit against the flesh; for these are in opposition to one another, so that you may not do the things that you please.

God's Word tells us that when we walk by faith, we are not allowing our circumstances to control our focus and behavior, according to 2 Corinthians 5:7 which says, "For we walk by faith, not by sight."

When someone makes any decision, they should always make it based on sufficient and accurate information. The first and most important decision anyone will ever make is to recognize and admit that they are a sinner in need of a Savior, confess that fact, repent of their sins, and then surrender their lives to the Person and work of Jesus Christ as Lord, the Son of God.

The second most important decision any person will ever make is whom they should marry. Much incorrect and insufficient information most often characterizes this decision. I am convinced that most Christians aren't fully aware of and/or don't understand what God reveals clearly in His Word regarding this institution which He created on the sixth day of Creation—*marriage*. As I have mentioned previously, almost always in today's time and culture of dating, one does not marry the person that has been presented to them through time spent, energy expended, and emotions experienced prior to the actual marriage.

I believe it is important for me to "chase" a so-called rabbit here. The reason will become evident a little later in this chapter. There are many Christians who do not believe that God created the heavens and the earth in a period of literally *six, twenty-four-hour days*. Please hear my heart as I try to explain one of the most important doctrinal issues that the church of Jesus Christ faces today. It's the subject of *Creation vs. Evolution*. If my words seem to be harsh and unloving, please know from the onset they are not meant to be. In fact, it would be a lack of love for me to skip over this subject. I am truly convinced about the origin of the universe, and I want to clearly share with you what information I am convinced the Bible clearly records about it.

This chapter is going to be long and tedious for some. Biblical creation is rarely taught literally because of the massive invasion of anti-biblical deception that has swept through our churches today. I heard a Christian leader say several years ago that he had in the past purposely chosen not to voice his deep conviction in the fact that God did indeed create the heavens and the earth in six, twenty-four-hour days. He mentioned that at that time, it simply didn't seem to be worth the conflict it would cause. However, later when he studied to preach the book of Genesis, he became convinced that not only was it worth it to be engaged in a discussion about Creation versus evolution, it was critically necessary to address it biblically. He believes, as I do, that one's belief in God's Creation that was accomplished just the way He revealed in Genesis 1–2 is the foundational basis upon which a person will believe, trust, and obey the rest of scripture.

Be aware as you continue this chapter and beyond, that the belief in the inerrancy and applicability of God's Word will be used as the basis for all that I say. The rewards for knowing what He reveals in scripture and trusting Him fully enough to obey is incalculable. Believing God's Word to be true, relevant, applicable, and trustworthy for living a life that is filled with God's peace, guidance, and protection (among many other things) is foundational to understanding the principles for becoming an accurate *Portrait of a Righteous Woman*. My deepest desire is that you will discover and receive from studying and believing that what God says is true for your life as well as the "lifeguard" for your protection and righteousness.

Over the past few decades of my life and ministry, the churches to which my husband and I have belonged could be characterized as ones in which God's Word has clearly taught that the Bible is without error, and that God Himself has protected its purity, accuracy, and reliability throughout the past millennia. However, in these churches, as is true of many churches which are a part of the denomination to which I belong, the vast majority of these members continue to believe in evolution. Most would say, *theistic evolution*—that is to say, God did create the heavens and the earth, but He did it through the means of natural evolution which occurred through millions or billions of years.

There is a scripture that tells us the reason why most do not believe in God's literal creation of the heavens and the earth in such instantaneous productions by His simply "speaking" creation into existence. One of the reasons is found in Hebrews 11:3: "<u>By faith</u> we understand that the worlds were prepared by the word of God, so that what is seen was not made out of things which are visible."

First, it should be obvious from this Hebrew verse that it takes "faith in God and His Word" to believe that the universe and all it contains were created by the Word of God. I am convinced that it takes even more faith to believe that all creation started through one cell (from where this cell came from isn't addressed) which grew and mutated into what is now visible. Obviously, there is no firsthand information. There are variations of opinions as to how evolution occurred, but they all declare unequivocally that it took millions and perhaps even billions of years to be accomplished.

Someone who will not believe that God Himself created everything by the "word of His mouth" (Psalm 33:6) has only the alternative to believe in some "kind" of evolution. I am convinced that *if* that is true of anyone, they have not yet developed a spiritual mindset to take all of God's truth literally when reading Genesis 1–3 or many other passages in scripture that disagree with what the world claims to be true. God's Word clearly contradicts any type of evolution.

Let's reason this issue together. *If* there was no one day and time where "through one man, Adam, sin entered the world," then one has to reject Romans 5:12 where we are told, "Therefore, just as through one man sin entered into the world, and death through sin, and so death spread to all men, because all sinned," and 1 Corinthians 15:21-22, "For since by a man *came* death, by a man also *came* the resurrection of the dead. For as in Adam all die, so also in Christ all will be made alive." Evolution requires that you accept that death entered the world before humans evolved—death of vegetation, death of animals, etc. These two passages clearly state the reverse.

Another unavoidable contradiction is that *if* the first person on earth was not Adam, whom God says He created in the sixth day of Creation, then there is "no single sin committed by one single person" as Romans 5 and 1 Corinthians 15 state. *Therefore*, there is no need nor purpose for Christ Jesus' substitutionary death on the cross as payment for all sin, for all people for all times. But Romans 5 and 1 Corinthians 15 *are true*—God said it, and that settles it.

These two New Testament passages need a closer examination because the accurate interpretation of both requires a belief that God created the heavens and the earth just the way He revealed in Genesis 1–3. Both Romans 5 and 1 Corinthians 15 clearly reveal that death entered the earth through the sin of one man. We are told who this one man was—Adam of Genesis 1–5.

The New Testament contains an abundance of statements that require one to embrace a literal six, twenty-four-hour days Creation and reject any form of evolution, including what some describe as theistic evolution. I did warn you about my inserting "rabbit trails" to help me make clear the foundations upon which I have compiled my systematic theology and doctrinal beliefs.

- *Day 1* is described in Genesis 1:3-5, "evening and morning. . . . *day one.*"
- *Day 2* is described in Genesis 1:6-8, "evening and morning. . . . *a second day.*"
- *Day 3* is described in Genesis 1:9-13, "evening and morning. . . . *a third day.*"
- *Day 4* is described in Genesis 1:14-19, "evening and morning. . . . *a fourth day.*"
- *Day 5* is described in Genesis 1:20-23, "evening and morning. . . . *a fifth day.*"
- *Day 6* is described in Genesis 1:24-31, "evening and morning. . . . *the sixth day.*"

Most of you are probably aware that there were no paragraphs or chapter divisions (and in most instances, no punctuation) in the original writings. Chapter 2 of Genesis is one of many "unfortunate" man-made chapter divisions. It is not uncommon that man-made chapter divisions actually can be context destructive. Look with me at what is revealed to us that happened on the seventh twenty-four-hour period of time, which I believe is a continuation of God's Creation narrative in Genesis 1:

> ¹Thus the heavens and the earth were completed, and all their hosts. ²By <u>the seventh day</u> God completed His work which He had done, and <u>He rested on the seventh day from all His work which He had done</u>. ³Then God blessed <u>the seventh day</u> and sanctified it, because in it He rested from all His work which God had created and made. (Genesis 2:1-3)

GOD'S PORTRAIT OF A "RIGHTEOUS WOMAN"

The Hebrew word translated "day" in Genesis 1:1–2:1-3 is "*yom*," which is defined as a distinct measure of time. The context will normally reveal whether that particular period of time is a day, a year, or another stated period of time. Indeed, this context will reveal exactly what period of time is to be understood here. The text of Genesis 1 requires one to agree that each period of time follows the completion of the preceding period of time. In other words, what God did in "time period two" had to have followed what God declared He completely accomplished in "time period one."

The following is an undeniable truth. Note in Genesis 1:9-13 God created vegetation "bearing fruit" during the "*third* period of time."

> ⁹Then God said, "Let the waters below the heavens be gathered into one place, and let the dry land appear"; and it was so. ¹⁰God called the dry land earth, and the gathering of the waters He called seas; and God saw that it was good. ¹¹Then God said, "Let the earth <u>sprout vegetation, plants yielding seed</u>, and <u>fruit trees on the earth bearing fruit</u> after their kind with seed in them"; and it was so. ¹²The <u>earth brought forth vegetation, plants yielding seed after their kind, and trees bearing fruit</u> with seed in them, after their kind; and God saw that it was good. ¹³There was evening and there was morning, <u>a third day</u>. (Genesis 1:9-13)

Observe Genesis 1:14-19 which records the creations of the "*fourth* period of time," which must follow the "*third* period of time," during which God declares that He created the sun and the moon among several other things:

> ¹⁴Then God said, "Let there be lights in the expanse of the heavens to separate the day from the night, and let them be for signs and for seasons and for days and years; ¹⁵and let them be for lights in the expanse of the heavens <u>to give light on the earth</u>"; and it was so. ¹⁶God made <u>the two great lights</u>, the greater light to govern the day, and the lesser light to govern the night; *He made* the stars also. ¹⁷God placed them in the expanse of the heavens <u>to give light on the earth</u>, ¹⁸and to govern the day and the night, and to separate the light from the darkness; and God saw that it

was good. ¹⁹There was evening and there was morning, <u>a fourth day</u>. (Genesis 1:14-19)

The two great lights are irrefutably "the sun" and "the moon" which "give light on the earth." No one can refute that sunlight is required for vegetation to live and grow. So one must conclude that given the time period of these two chapters, "*yom*" has to be interpreted as a twenty-four-hour period of time—that is, a literal day. It's simply impossible to reconcile that there were multiple kinds of vegetation for thousands or millions of years without the sun having been created to enable them to live and grow.

As you will note in the passage below, the institution of marriage was established on *Day Six* of God's creative activities and is found described in Genesis 1:24-31. Carefully examine this passage by first reading what God tells us occurred, and then allow me to share with you the main points I have observed as to how this passage can help us better understand marriage.

> ²⁴Then God said, "Let the earth bring forth living creatures after their kind: cattle and creeping things and beasts of the earth after their kind"; and it was so. ²⁵God made the beasts of the earth after their kind, and the cattle after their kind, and everything that creeps on the ground after its kind; and God saw that it was good. ²⁶Then God said, "Let Us make man in Our image, according to Our likeness; and let them rule over the fish of the sea and over the birds of the sky and over the cattle and over all the earth, and over every creeping thing that creeps on the earth." ²⁷<u>God created man in His own image, in the image of God He created him; male and female He created them</u>. ²⁸God blessed them; and God said to them, "<u>Be fruitful and multiply, and fill the earth</u>, and subdue it; and rule over the fish of the sea and over the birds of the sky and over every living thing that moves on the earth." ²⁹Then God said, "Behold, I have given you every plant yielding seed that is on the surface of all the earth, and every tree which has fruit yielding seed; it shall be food for you; ³⁰and to every beast of the earth and to every bird of the sky and to everything that moves on the earth which has life, *I have*

> *given* every green plant for food"; and it was so. ³¹God saw all that He had made, and behold, it was very good. And there was evening and there was morning, the sixth day. (Genesis 1:24-31)

Is it as interesting to you as it is to me that God created the animals that primarily lived on the earth (dry land) on the Sixth Day before God created man in His own image? (This Hebrew noun, *elohiym* that is translated "God" is in the plural form, and its plurality means more than two.) So the first thing distinctive about humans is that they alone are created in the image of the Triune God of the Bible—our Father God; Jesus, God's Son; and the Holy Spirit. I do hope you noticed that human beings were created *last*.

The second important distinction here is that God created one male and one female. Both Hebrew words *zakar* (which is a verb meaning "to be a male") and the noun *neqebah* (translated "female"), are singular nouns meaning "only one."[5] I think it will be helpful to mention here that God created only *one* race—namely the human race. Yes, there are obviously different cultures, different ethnicities, different characteristics, including skin color. *But there is only one race,* and all humans belong to a single race that was, is, and will continue to be created in God's image. PERIOD! Not only are all of us descendants of Adam and Eve, but also all of us are descendants of Noah and Mrs. Noah through either Ham, Shem, or Japheth. Only one race; all human beings are equally created and equally loved by God. The only two distinctives among the human race are that some have been saved by God's grace through faith in Jesus Christ, and others have refused salvation by God's grace through faith in Jesus Christ. In other words, the only distinctive among humans is that there are "those who are saved—children of God" and "those that are lost—children of the devil." Perhaps John 8:42-45 may be very enlightening to some:

> ⁴²Jesus said to them, "If God were your Father, you would love Me, for I proceeded forth and have come from God, for I have not even come on My own initiative, but He sent Me. ⁴³Why do you not understand what I am saying? *It is* because you cannot hear My word. ⁴⁴ "You are of your

---

5 *The Complete Word Study Dictionary: Old Testament*

2: BEFORE YOU SAY, "I DO"

father the devil and you want to do the desires of your father. He was a murderer from the beginning, and does not stand in the truth because there is no truth in him. Whenever he speaks a lie, he speaks from his own *nature,* for he is a liar and the father of lies. ⁴⁵But because I speak the truth, you do not believe Me."

There are several things we should note in Genesis 1:28: "God blessed them; and God said to them, 'Be fruitful and multiply, and fill the earth, and subdue it; and rule over the fish of the sea and over the birds of the sky and over every living thing that moves on the earth.'" After the creation of the first male and the first female, "God blessed them" *(plural pronoun)* both. God told them both to be fruitful and multiply and fill the earth. This sounds elementary, but God's intended and created purpose for them both was to procreate to establish the family unit. As you well know it takes both one male sperm and one female egg to do that. So, as humans were created on Day Six of God's creation process, so also was the union of marriage—on the very same day!

Also, God told both the male and the female to subdue the earth and rule over every living thing that moves on the earth. It is important to note that God gave both Adam and Eve the command to rule over His creation. We will also deal with this later, but it's important for us to be aware that when the male and the female were created in God's image, that included the woman also having been given the DNA capability to "rule." This became a real problem for Eve after she and Adam sinned, because she was told that her husband would now rule over her (Genesis 3:16). Many married women (myself included) have struggled with this "ruling thing" since sin entered the human DNA on the day when both Adam and Eve chose not to obey God and ate the forbidden fruit of the tree of the knowledge of good and evil. This act of sin caused the necessity for this first married couple (and all which would follow) to have an earthly ruler. Before sin entered humans, God Himself was the sole ruler. God Himself chose after sin entered His perfect creation that the earthly ruler in marriage be the male, the husband. Again, we'll discuss this further later.

Genesis 2:4-23 is not describing another Creation event. God simply chose to give Moses (whom God used to write the first five books of the Bible) the details He wanted to make known to us regarding His creation of both male and female in His own image. In Genesis 2, we learn that Adam, the male, was created first, and God said it was not good for man to be alone. Therefore, God "fashioned" the female to be the exact human counterpart that would not only complement/complete what the male needed to be "good" in God's eyes but also to be able to accomplish what God would command them to do: create the family unit, which included bearing children (as commanded in Genesis 1:28).

Here we are faced with some of the translation challenges given to us. The Hebrew and the Greek languages are the languages in which the Old Testament and the New Testament are primarily written. There is a rule of interpretation that is extremely important here— *context rules all interpretation.* This is certainly true of the Hebrew word *issah*. *Issah* is a word that can be translated several different ways, governed by its context: "wife," "woman," "female," "widow," an "adulteress" or even a "female animal" (Genesis 7:2).[6]

Obviously we are getting in deep waters here, so to speak, but there are some subjects in God's Word that require an understanding of other passages and the original languages in order to accurately understand what God is saying and what He means and then be able to apply it to one's life accurately. The Hebrew word *issah* is translated into the English word *wife* by most all conservative scholars in Genesis 2:24-25 because the context requires it.

> [24]For this reason a man shall leave his father and his mother, and be joined to his wife; and they shall become one flesh. [25]And the man and his wife were both naked and were not ashamed. (Genesis 2:24-25)

Before we leave this original pair created by God to be the beginning of God's establishment of marriage, we need to note that this union was to be distinctively separate, unique, and exclusive, by God Himself bringing His creation of the female Eve to the male Adam. God gave Moses the commentary which is in Genesis 2:24-25, which defines the parameter and the exclusivity of this union of one man and one woman.

---

6   *The Complete Word Study Dictionary: Old Testament*

2: BEFORE YOU SAY, "I DO"

Again, most conservative Christian theologians believe that God inspired Moses to write the first five books (the Pentateuch) of the Bible, according to Exodus 24:4: "Moses wrote down all the words of the Lord. Then he arose early in the morning, and built an altar at the foot of the mountain with twelve pillars for the twelve tribes of Israel."

One more truth to understand about Genesis 1 and 2 is that when God created this single male and this single female, He not only brought them together and formed the first marriage union, but He also laid the foundation of the "family unit" to be the centerpiece for all human civilization on earth (Genesis 1:28) when God told them to "be fruitful and multiply and fill the earth." In Genesis 4 the words *brother* (v. 8ff) and *son* (v. 17) were used which are family-oriented nouns.

There is one more issue that we need to consider. That is, the "seventh day" in Genesis 2:1-3:

> ¹Thus the heavens and the earth were completed, and all their hosts. ²By the seventh day God completed His work which He had done, and He rested on the seventh day from all His work which He had done. ³Then God blessed the seventh day and sanctified it, because in it He rested from all His work which God had created and made.

Most of you will recall that God placed the "Sabbath" in the Ten Commandments, which is recorded in Exodus 20:8-11. Look with me how this commandment reads, knowing that the Hebrew word *yom* is also translated "day" in this passage, as it is in Genesis 1.

> ⁸Remember the sabbath day, to keep it holy. ⁹Six days you shall labor and do all your work, ¹⁰but the seventh day is a sabbath of the Lord your God; *in it* you shall not do any work, you or your son or your daughter, your male or your female servant or your cattle or your sojourner who stays with you. ¹¹For in six days the Lord made the heavens and the earth, the sea and all that is in them, and rested on the seventh day; therefore the Lord blessed the sabbath day and made it holy. (Exodus 20:8-11)

God commanded the Jews *not* to do any work on the Sabbath day. They could labor six days, but on the seventh day they were to rest because God had rested on the seventh day and had blessed it and made it holy. It is impossible for us to even consider that God was speaking in Exodus 20 that man was to work during six periods of millions and possibly billions of years. And then they were to rest for one period of millions and possibly billions of years. One has to conclude that the "day" of Creation mentioned in Exodus 20 is the same length of time because of Genesis 2:1-3 mentioned previously. The day in Genesis 1 has to literally be made up of a twenty-four-hour period of time, or one must reject the fourth commandment and reduce the number to the "nine commandments." And I am sure that is too ridiculous a thought to even consider. This is only one example of very many passages in God's Word that require a belief in a literal six, twenty-four-hour days Creation timeframe.

One day as I was meditating on some of the facts about God's creation, God all of a sudden connected the dots of the Genesis Creation account to a Matthew passage. God's Word records in Genesis the exact ages lived of all the males from Adam to Abraham. The New Testament book of Matthew records that there were forty-two generations from Abraham to the Messiah. God spoke to my heart and said, *I have revealed the age of My universe in My Word.* God Himself has told us in His Word the age of His universe! I have no idea why it took me so long to connect these dots to arrive at the God-given age of His creation. This revelation didn't change my belief. It confirmed it biblically, and I hope it will confirm yours as well. The following is what God says in His Word is the age of His created universe. Let me add that I am aware that there are those who say that God doesn't literally mean what He tells us in Genesis regarding the ages of each male from Adam to Abraham—that there were many more who were excluded from what is listed. However, the text tells us the person's name and age and includes his son's name and age and then his son's son and his name and age. There is a chart below that I am using with the permission of Precept Ministries, International, that is of great value, and I personally use it often to reference deferent things.

The only remaining challenge is to somehow determine to some degree of accuracy the number of years that make up "one generation," according the God. All I have to go on is an obscure passage found in Genesis 15:13, 16a. Below is my process:

¹³*God* said to Abram, "Know for certain that your descendants will be strangers in a land that is not theirs, where they will be enslaved and oppressed <u>four hundred years</u>. . . . ¹⁶Then in the <u>fourth generation</u> they will return here.

BIBLICAL AGE OF THE UNIVERSE

2,183 years—Number of years from the birth of Adam to the death of Abraham (Genesis 5:3–25:7). Below is a chart created by Precept Ministries, Int., that states each man's name from Adam to Abraham, the length of each man's life, and the name of each man's first son.

4,200 years—42 generations total from Abraham to the Messiah, Christ (*Matthew 1:17)

*42 times 100 = 4,200 (if one defines a "generation" as one hundred years (Genesis 15:13, 16a), which may or may not be totally accurate, but it cannot be more than 969 years, which is the longest length of time a man ever lived (Methuselah's age, Genesis 5:27). By using 969 years as a generation, the age of the universe would then be **40,698 years** from Abraham to Christ, which I totally discount.

* "So all the generations from Abraham to David are fourteen generations; from David to the deportation to Babylon, fourteen generations; and from the deportation to Babylon to the Messiah, fourteen generations" (Matthew 1:17) = 42 generations total from Abraham to the Messiah, Christ.

2,020 years—The approximate years from Christ until today

8,403 years—The approximate biblical age of the universe

So, according to God's Word, the universe is approximately 8,403 years old. At the oldest, according to scripture, the universe could be 40,698 years when using 969 years as 1 "generation" (Methuselah's age), which I don't believe is possible. Neither of these interpretations get us *anywhere close* to the supposed age of one million years, much less many tens of millions or billions of years, as is commonly believed by many to be true today.

GOD'S PORTRAIT OF A "RIGHTEOUS WOMAN"

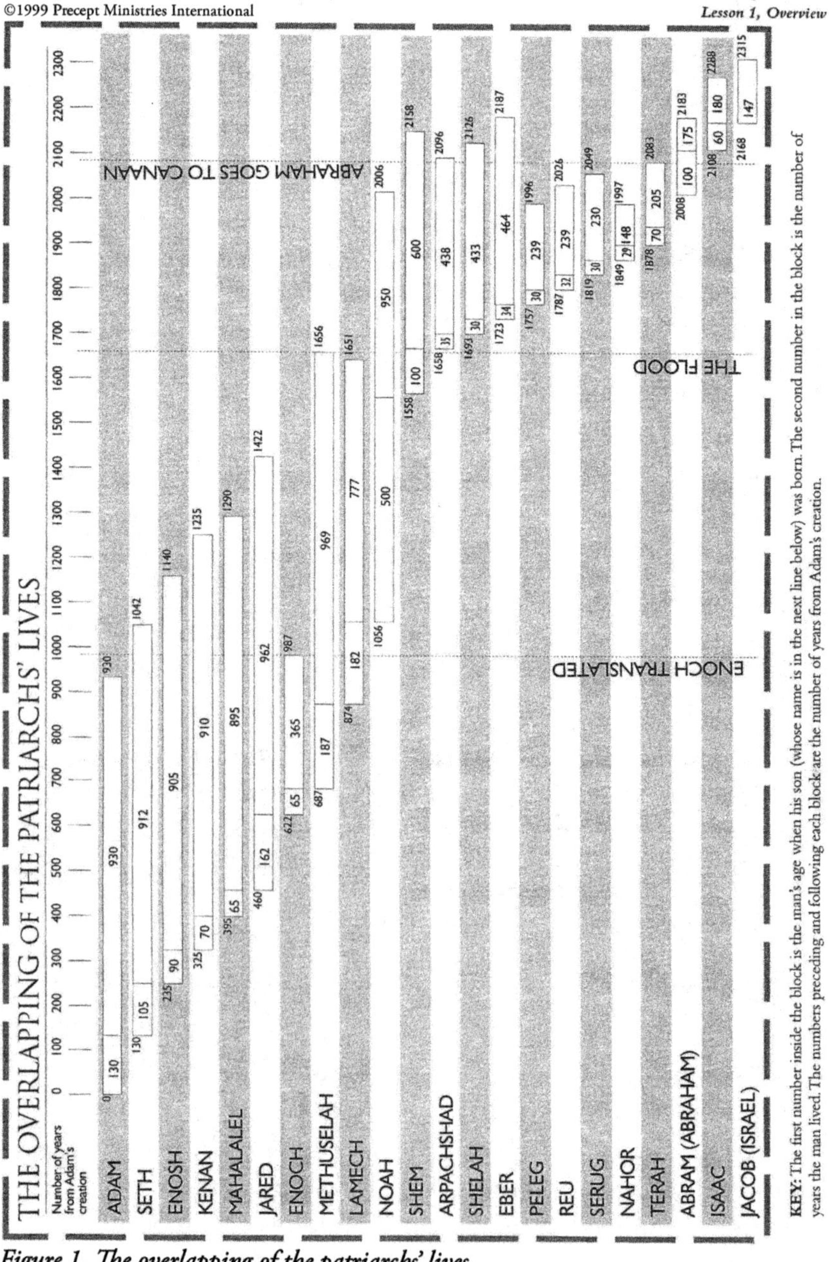

Figure 1. The overlapping of the patriarchs' lives

Now that we have about settled (I hope) the approximate age of the universe according to God Himself, let's turn our attention back to our primary subject, marriage. There is another aspect of the marriage union that is necessary for us all to understand. It is found in Malachi 2:14: "Yet you say, 'For what reason?' Because the Lord has been a witness between you and the wife of your youth, against whom you have dealt treacherously, though she is your companion and your wife <u>by covenant</u>."

The making of covenant vows is a well-established practice early in God's Word. The word *covenant* first appears in Genesis 6:18: "But I will establish My covenant with you; and you shall enter the ark— you and your sons and your wife, and your sons' wives with you." We just saw in Malachi 2:14 that marriage is a covenant agreement most often made before witnesses. Most reliable Hebrew dictionaries define a covenant as a solemn, binding agreement made consciously, intentionally, and voluntarily between two or more persons. Most covenants contain rules, conditions, and/or a timeframe that applies to all the covenant participants. There are covenants God has made with man that are recorded in scripture that are unconditional. In other words, on one side the participants of the covenant are not required to do anything. For example, God's covenant promise to Noah was to never again destroy the earth with a flood, and nothing was required of Noah. However, as we all well know, the marriage covenant does require the male and the female to agree to live by the vows they make *not only* to their new spouse but ultimately it is to God Himself.

Perhaps this is the very best place for us to start—to examine some specific passages from God's Word that give us greater understanding about this most important topic: marriage. Before we go any further, it is necessary that since our God is the creator and sovereign ruler over all that was, is, and/or will be created, He has the sole sovereign right and authority to set the rules.

Before I go any further, I want to make it clear that I am fully and compassionately aware of the fact that what I will be commenting on next may be of great offence to many females today. As I previously mentioned, this was a huge issue for me as well until I came to understand God's ways always work incalculably better than our manmade alternatives. All I am asking is that you take these passages in God's Word, read them carefully and in context, and ask the Lord to give you His revelation of how they are to be applied to your own belief system.

GOD'S PORTRAIT OF A "RIGHTEOUS WOMAN"

God explicitly states the "rules" that govern the marriage union (after sin entered) that we first see in Genesis 3:16: "To the woman He said, 'I will greatly multiply your pain in childbirth, in pain you will bring forth children; yet your desire will be for your husband, and <u>he will rule over you</u>." We will deal with this passage more thoroughly in a future chapter, but for now, the following will suffice. God determined after sin entered the world that the headship in a marriage is given to the husband. This fact should be seriously considered before a woman says, "I do." It is found in 1 Corinthians 11:3: "But I want you to understand that Christ is the head of every man, and the man is the head of a woman, and God is the head of Christ." This is also found in Ephesians 5:22-24, which we will also examine later. But before any woman plans to marry, she should ask herself before God, *Am I willing to voluntarily be subject to—that is, to place myself under the authority of—the leadership of this man for as long as we both shall live?*

Consider with me that many women often evaluate a potential husband by the wrong criteria. I have been told ladies are to note how a man treats his mother. Well, that might give some information about his character and behavior, but I believe and propose that the only true way to know the genuine character of any person is to evaluate them spiritually—not by what they say but most importantly by observing the habits of their lives. Does this potential husband unashamedly speak of the Lord Jesus and his love for and gratitude to Him? Does he openly and habitually worship and serve the Lord Jesus through a local church fellowship? Jesus Himself told us twice that "you will know them by their fruit" (Matthew 7:16, 20).

This subject of "fruit inspection" is worthy of close and careful study, but I'll not succumb to the temptation to do a topical study here. There are two major passages that I want to bring to our attention in this matter of one diligently examining the habitual lifestyle of a potential lifelong partner in marriage. The first is the "fruit of righteousness" found in Philippians 1:11, Hebrews 12:11, and Ephesians 5:9. So the question that begs to be answered is, *Does this potential husband habitually live in a way that exhibits living God's right ways* (which is the way I often define "righteousness")? No one is perfect, but according to 1 John 3:7, every believer, who "practices righteousness is righteous." It will be very helpful in this endeavor to examine 1 John 3:4-10:

⁴Everyone who practices sin also practices lawlessness; and sin is lawlessness. ⁵You know that He appeared in order to take away sins; and in Him there is no sin. ⁶No one who abides in Him sins; no one who sins has seen Him or knows Him. ⁷Little children, make sure no one deceives you; the one who practices righteousness is righteous, just as He is righteous; ⁸the one who practices sin is of the devil; for the devil has sinned from the beginning. The Son of God appeared for this purpose, to destroy the works of the devil. ⁹No one who is born of God practices sin, because His seed abides in him; and he cannot sin, because he is born of God. ¹⁰ By this the children of God and the children of the devil are obvious: anyone who does not practice righteousness is not of God, nor the one who does not love his brother.

Carefully examine verse 10. This message from God's Word clearly states that the "children of God and the children of the devil are obvious" by whether they "practice sin" or whether they "practice righteousness." This Greek word *phaneros* that is translated "obvious" here means "apparent publicly, externally visible." The NASB is known for trying to translate the verb tenses as accurately as the English language permits. Most of these descriptive verbs in 1 John 3:4-10 are in the present tense, which describes a person's continual, habitual lifestyle. That is to say, if a person had access to examine the way a person lives habitually, that person could in most cases accurately evaluate the true character of that other person and the true spiritual condition of his heart.

The second "fruit," the one most familiar to believers, is the fruit of the Spirit, found in Galatians 5:22-23. The question you need to find the answer to is, *Can this man's true character and behavior most often be described as "love, joy, peace, patience, kindness, goodness, faithfulness, gentleness and self-control"*? If these qualities do not most often describe his habitual lifestyle and behavior, then he is either not saved or he is walking in disobedience. Since one of the "jobs" of the indwelling Holy Spirit is to cause us to walk in obedience to God's Word, these named "fruit" will be evident in most of his behavior. I guess this a good time to ask ourselves the same question!

It seems too often to be true that the person one is dating is putting forth his best behavior to make an impression that in reality does not accurately represent his true character and habitual behavior. If you are truly seeking the Lord's guidance in choosing His mate for you, He will reveal to you the true nature of his character and spiritual condition. I am convinced that this focus is the most important challenge every woman must master before a covenant of marriage is entered into.

Also, God's Word commands that every believer "not be unequally bound together." Look again with me at 2 Corinthians 6:14-16, this time in greater detail. We need to examine not only what this passage means but how it is to be applied to every believer's life.

> [14]Do not be bound together with unbelievers; for what partnership have righteousness and lawlessness, or what fellowship has light with darkness? [15]Or what harmony has Christ with Belial, or what has a believer in common with an unbeliever? [16]Or what agreement has the temple of God with idols? For we are the temple of the living God; just as God said, "I will dwell in them and walk among them; And I will be their God, and they shall be My people." (2 Corinthians 6:14-16)

There are several things we need to learn from the first sentence in verse 14. I am anything but a Greek scholar. In fact, I can't even quote the Greek alphabet correctly. But what I do have available to me are some really wonderful Greek resource materials. *Thank You, Lord, for those who do know Greek and Hebrew and have obeyed your leading to put together resources that help give us much insight into the original languages.* These original language meanings, including their verb tenses, give us much greater information that leads to more accurate interpretation, understanding, and application.

The verb phrase *do not be* is the English translation of a Greek verb tense that is described as "present imperative with a negative." First, the present imperative verb tense represents a command for on-going, continual action. Second, the negative aspect can either be *stop doing* the action or *be careful not to start* the action. In my opinion, this verb could be either or both, but I'm more inclined toward *don't start doing it* here in this context. This Greek verb *heterozugeo* that is translated "bound together" is describing a yoke that many of you are familiar with: wooden devices that couple two oxen together—that is the idea here. This Greek word is defined as "to be yoked unequally; as with pagan idolaters and by extension, particularly in marriage"[7] To paraphrase 2 Corinthians 6:14, "Do not under any circumstances or for any reason be joined together/be legally partnered with an unbeliever."

Let us understand from God's intended purposes regarding marriage that God commands every believer *not to marry an unbeliever*. The command in verse 14 is not limited to just marriage, but as I mentioned earlier, also forbids any formal, legal partnership between a Christian and any unbeliever, such as business partners, etc.

James 1:5-6 promises each believer, "But if any of you lacks wisdom, let him ask of God, who gives to all generously and without reproach, and it will be given to him. But he must ask in faith without any doubting, for the one who doubts is like the surf of the sea, driven and tossed by the wind." God's wisdom does give us what we need to be enabled to walk in obedience to Him. The scripture also tells us that "spiritual things are spiritually discerned." First Corinthians 2:14 (CSB) states, "But the person without the Spirit does not receive what comes from God's Spirit, because it is foolishness to him; he is not able to understand it since it is evaluated spiritually."

Let us consider that discovering another person's true spiritual condition—that is, whether they are saved or not—can most often be a very difficult task, but especially for a young woman as it concerns the person she believes could be her future husband. Most of the time it is not our jobs to determine the true spiritual condition of another person. However, there are times when it is absolutely necessary to discern this, and choosing a marriage partner is the most important of all. Please hear my heart when I say that many, many choices young ladies make regarding a future mate are made based on what can often be described as lies or deception. But be encouraged, the Holy Spirit's fruits of righteousness cannot be counterfeited for any length of time.

Even though there are many deceivers out there, there are also those who are being deceived. Again, Jesus said to us, "You will

---

7 *The Complete Word Study Dictionary: New Testament*

know them by their fruit"—their habitual, continual lifestyles and devotions. So my earnest advice and sincere warning to everyone who is contemplating marriage is to make sure that the person's habitual character and behavior exemplifies the presence of the Lord Jesus Himself. Our God will reveal to you that understanding if you ask and patiently wait for His answer. The consequences of marrying a man who is not saved is being unequally yoked together, and heartbreaking years of disagreements and arguments and many hard times lie ahead. I can tell you that within the past week of this writing, two precious ladies have confidentially told me about how miserable life is in their living with an unbelieving husband's self-consumed life. He most often totally disregards her personal needs, and his disrespectful and hateful behavior toward her is extremely hurtful.

Let me end this chapter by saying to those whose heart is aching to be married, that it is incalculably worse to be married to the wrong person than it is to remain single. In fact, look closely at 1 Corinthians 7:32-35:

> [32]But I want you to be free from concern. One who is unmarried is concerned about the things of the Lord, how he may please the Lord; [33]but one who is married is concerned about the things of the world, how he may please his wife, [34]and *his interests* are divided. The woman who is unmarried, and the virgin, is concerned about the things of the Lord, that she may be holy both in body and spirit; but one who is married is concerned about the things of the world, how she may please her husband. [35]This I say for your own benefit; not to put a restraint upon you, but to promote what is appropriate and *to secure* <u>undistracted devotion to the Lord</u>.

Since God created marriage to be the foundational unit of all civilization, He has the sovereign right and the responsibility to set the rules for marriage, period. His designed institution of marriage *always* works best when we look to Him for guidance and wisdom. The clay cannot tell the potter how to design the clay vessel according to Romans 9:21. What we can know and trust in totality, without reservation, is that "for it is God who is at work in you, both to will and to work for *His* good pleasure," according to Philippians 2:13. To Him belongs all honor, praise, thanksgiving, and obedience!

CHAPTER 3

God's Primary Role for a Wife

When I began to put the messages in this book on paper, I was, and still am, convinced that our God wants all of His children to clearly and accurately understand His Word. As I am sure you are already well aware, unless His Word is accurately understood, there will be no God-intended application to our lives. Some of you may find what I am about to share with you to be very foreign. I do not hear the major subject of this chapter taught or discussed in most Christian circles. Somehow all too much of our Christian community in America today has fallen prey to and has embraced much of what the world believes and practices regarding marriage—many disregard what our God clearly reveals in His Word regarding His designed role for a wife.

Please know that I have not been unaffected myself. Lee and I married in 1959, and our daughters were born in 1964 and 1966. I tell you this to give context to my younger years as a wife and a mother. For some of you, you are unaware that these were years where the women's equal rights movement was gaining steam. I was not immune to its influences.

GOD'S PORTRAIT OF A "RIGHTEOUS WOMAN"

Let me digress. I haven't as yet shared with you my testimony of salvation by faith and God's grace. I am one of many who cannot remember the actual *moment* I was saved. When I was about six years old, a neighbor invited my sister and me to go with them to a gospel tent revival. My sister actually got saved that night. And even though I walked the aisle with her, I was not saved at that time and place.

Because my sister did truly get saved that evening, she regularly took us to church. We first attended Idewild Presbyterian Church in Memphis because it was close enough for us to walk. A few years later, we rode a bus to Bellevue Baptist Church. I clearly remember being around fifteen when God convicted me that I was not genuinely born again, and He led me to confess my sins to Him and acknowledge my need of a Savior. This is the time I sincerely surrendered my life to the Person and the work of the Lord Jesus Christ. And soon after, I was baptized (a second time) in a genuine act of obedience as a new born-again Christian.

You may notice that there are only some scant details of this portion of my life for which the reasons will become obvious. I was raised in a home where my mother was saved but was treated harshly and abused by my father (the word *father* is even hard for me to say concerning him, much less put in print). Even though I have never experienced personally being treated harshly by a husband, for which I praise God, I witnessed it personally year after year as I grew up.

In much grief, later it was revealed to me that he was a child molester. My sister was his victim. Honestly, I believe it was by God's grace and mercy that I can recall very few details of my childhood—not very much at all. I genuinely believe this is a grace gift from my ever-faithful and gracious heavenly Father. I remember wonderful summers with my grandparents in Holly Springs, Mississippi, and sweet times with two different sets of next-door neighbors. I can vividly remember times when I would dream of Christ Jesus taking me up in the clouds to meet Him. There are no words to express how healing, protective, and inspiring those occasions were to me then, and still are today as I remember them.

Be assured that I know that I didn't live a sin-free life after salvation, but the Lord always kept me close. He always convicted me of my sins and graciously forgave me and drew me close to Him in sweet fellowship. It was about this time that the Lord brought me to the place where I was to meet my future husband. We were

3: GOD'S PRIMARY ROLE FOR A WIFE

high school sweethearts and were married during Lee's junior year at Georgia Tech in Atlanta, Georgia.

At that time of my life, I did not know that God's Word clearly states that His children are not to marry non-believers. But again, in His grace and mercy, God led me to a young man who was from a truly godly home. His mother was a Bible teacher and made sure she taught her sons the ways of our Lord and our God. Lee was saved at the age of eight and was not only raised in a godly home but was also nurtured in a Bible-believing, Bible-teaching church from infancy. I never cease to thank our God for such grace and mercy and recognizable love He manifested to me through this wonderful young man, by whom I have been privileged to be loved, honored, and cherished these past sixty-plus years of marriage.

OK, back to the late 1960s, at the flaming start of the women's equal rights movement. I remember vividly the exact words I told my husband at that "temptation" time in my mid-twenties. I said, "I deserve to be as successful as you are in the working world." Later, I recall, with much consternation and sorrow, looking at Lee and saying, "Lee, this is just not working." Yes, you are right. I meant our marriage. I can hardly believe this myself, because this was at a time when our two girls were still in grammar school.

At this time, I was working with an international charity, and as Satan would orchestrate, I became very successful in the fundraising arena. I had acquired a high position of management, and my primary focus was this work. It was not the work that the Lord had called me to—that is, to manage my own household well. I was not concentrating on providing a peaceful, nurturing, and safe place for my young girls and my husband. Let me add, I was deceived into thinking I was doing the Lord's work. I did have a spiritual influence, and I bragged about it to others. My flesh was so fed that I couldn't recognize that what I was doing was the devil's plans to keep me from fulfilling my most important job—managing my own household well. It would be many, many years into our marriage until I came to understand that God's Word has clearly defined the primary role for wives: to be the manager of their own households. I'll get to the biblical confirmation a little later.

As you would probably expect, our all-loving, all-compassionate, and all-merciful God did not leave me alone to my own devices. Let me preface the next statement by saying that I have never heard the audible voice of God speaking to me. However, I do believe He does speak audibly when it is needed and profitable for His children and for His kingdom to advance. About a year prior to the event I am about to describe, I unmistakably heard the Lord tell me to resign from working with this charity, but I had not obeyed. Then one day, and I remember even the place this happened, God asked me, *Do you want to know what will happen to your girls if you do not obey Me and resign from this "charity" work?*

My response was immediate! I said "No!" I never asked Him to tell me because I didn't want to know. I then resigned within twenty-four hours. Honestly, it was so astonishingly scary to me that I did take action immediately. I later confessed to my husband and my girls how selfish I had been for seven years. I asked their forgiveness for my ungodly behavior in neglecting their welfare in many cases, because I had been so intoxicated with the fleshly desires, accolades, and awards I was receiving in abundance.

All of this leads to one of the reasons God told me to write this book. "There is a way *which seems* right to a man, but its end is the way of death" (Proverbs 14:12, 16:25). There is another truth I would like to add regarding this time in my life. It was about this time that our church began a community discipleship ministry by organizing a community-wide home Bible study initiative. There were about nine classes sprinkled around the city for neighbors, relatives, and friends to be offered an opportunity to study God's Word and be transformed by its inherent power (to those who believe) into the image of God's Son, Christ Jesus.

This large undertaking started in January 1977, and my always faithful and gracious God led me to join one of these first neighborhood Bible study classes. This was in the early years of Precept Ministries, International's writing and publishing their Precept Upon Precept Bible study materials. I have continued to use their materials to this day. They now offer various formats, and I have consistently used them in the discipleship ministry God has called me to, beginning in 1979. This is still God's call on my life as I teach a multi-generational women's Sunday school class and as I lead a weekly "Precept" Bible study in my local church. In my Sunday school class I almost always use one of the Precept Ministries Bible study formats for them to study from and for me to teach from. I have never deviated in my weekday Bible study from using Precept

Upon Precept Bible study materials. I have said on occasion that I see no reason for me to reinvent the wheel; they do a far better job than I could ever do.

There is a reason for mentioning this particular subject. Every woman, married or not, can't afford *not* to be an intentional and continuing student of God's Word, whether in a formal setting or in individual discipline. Christian wives especially need to be alert to the fact and occasionally warned that to live in obedience to God's declared purposes for fulfilling our role of a righteous wife requires that we know our God intimately and trust Him completely to provide everything we need to fulfill the role of managing our own household well. The power and perseverance required comes only through the deliberate feeding on just who the Jehovah God of the Bible is; who Jesus Christ, the Nazarene is; who we are in our Lord Jesus Christ; and how we are to live life in faithful obedience to His instructions and commands.

The message is clear. It is God's living Word that equips each of us for "every good work" He has foreordained that we should walk in. This truth is clearly seen in Ephesians 2:10 which states, "For we are His workmanship, created in Christ Jesus for good works, which God prepared beforehand so that we would walk in them." Look with me at 2 Timothy 3:16-17. I pray the Lord will deposit these seeds of truth deep within your hearts and that it will bear much fruit in your continuing walk with Christ by the power of the Holy Spirit.

> [16]All Scripture is inspired by God and profitable for teaching, for reproof, for correction, for training in righteousness; [17]so that the man of God may be adequate, equipped for every good work. (2 Timothy 3:16-17)

You probably have noticed that I emphasize words in some of the scripture passages in order to help us focus on specific truths related to what I believe our God wants us to pay particular attention. When Paul used the words *all Scripture* in verse 16, he was speaking of the Old Testament at that time which had already been compiled and established as God's Word. By the time of Jesus' earthly ministry, the Old Testament as a whole had been completed and authenticated as God's written revelation. All four Gospels of the New Testament record Jesus referring to and quoting Old Testament passages. I will address the writings of the New Testament a little later.

Next, I want us to notice the word *profitable*, which in the Greek (*ophelimos*) means "advantageous, useful, helpful."[8] Now let's focus on the specific things for which God says, "all Scripture" is "profitable"—advantageous, useful, helpful:

- *For teaching:* Most interpret this to refer to instruction in what is right doctrinally.
- *For reproof:* Declaring what is being done that is wrong.
- *For correction:* Instruction in how to make right what is wrong.
- *For training in righteousness:* Bringing up/training a person in what is right; many refer to this process as being equivalent to the child training process.

This passage gives us the reason we need God's Word to accomplish the four aforementioned benefits—so that the people of God will be made *adequate*. The Greek word *artios* is translated "adequate," which means "completely qualified, sufficient."[9] Then Paul uses the Greek word *exartizo* translated "equipped," which means "competent, proficient, adept or capable."[10] So, to paraphrase this immeasurably important truth, let me put it this way. In order to be competent, enabled to do God's work God's way, each of us must know, understand, believe, trust, and obey God's Word. Yes, and it certainly includes a wife being able to manage her own household well.

The resounding answer to, "I just don't have time to study God's Word," is, YOU CANNOT AFFORD NOT TO. I am convictional that our empowering to do God's appointed purposes victoriously and effectively totally rests on our willingness to be guided by His Word and to walk by faith and not by sight. By walking by His Spirit, we are empowered not to fulfill the desires of our flesh. Very few Christians get it right most of the time, much less all of the time, without God's divine guidance and provision. It is God's Word that makes it possible for us to do God's work God's way, even part of the time.

---

8 *The Complete Word Study Dictionary: New Testament*
9 *The Complete Word Study Dictionary: New Testament*
10 *The Complete Word Study Dictionary: New Testament*

3: GOD'S PRIMARY ROLE FOR A WIFE

There is a promise of God that I pray back to Him often, and I'm pretty confident that for some of you it is one you rely on as well. It's found in Romans 8:28, but rarely is verse 29 added. Look with me at Romans 8:28-29 for the full picture of this promise:

> ²⁸And we know that God causes all things to work together for good to those who love God, to those who are called according to *His* purpose. ²⁹For those whom He foreknew, He also predestined *to become* <u>conformed to the image of His Son</u> so that He would be the firstborn among many brethren.

Please never be caught quoting Romans 8:28 to anyone other than those whom you believe are truly born again. It clearly doesn't apply to anyone other than those who love God, those who are called according to His purpose. This promise of verse 28 is part of the way God works directly for His children so that they are "conformed to the image of His Son," our Lord and Savior, Christ Jesus.

Now that we have laid a foundation to focus on the primary role of a "righteous wife" to manage her own household well, let's look at this biblical mandate found in two specific New Testament passages: Titus and 1 Timothy. First, let's observe Titus 2:3-5 to understand the context. I want to focus on a few phrases describing how the older women are to encourage the younger women, stated within a group of exhortations:

> ³Older women likewise are to be reverent in their behavior, not malicious gossips nor enslaved to much wine, <u>teaching what is good</u>, ⁴so that they may encourage the young women <u>to love their husbands</u>, to love their children, ⁵*to be* sensible, pure, <u>workers at home</u>, kind, being subject to their own husbands, so that the word of God will not be dishonored. (Titus 2:3-5)

This phrase <u>"workers at home"</u> represents the translation of the Greek word *oikouros* and is best translated "one who looks after domestic affairs with prudence and care."[11] I'll come back later to "love their husbands," which is the encouragement in verse 4. However, now it is sufficient to point out the "love" mentioned here

---

11 *The Complete Word Study Dictionary: New Testament*

in English, the Greek word *philandros,* which represents a friendship type of love. I like to add here that this phrase is intended to instruct wives to manage their own homes in a way that their husband will want to be at home with his wife and family more than to be in any other place, because his wife has made it a place of respite, peace, and safety. She has become his best friend. His home is a place of respect, acceptance, and appreciation, and he is given the benefit of the doubt. Wives and mothers are to create a home atmosphere where this is true of your husband and your children (the same Greek word is also used here regarding children). I surmise this task is undoubtedly not a natural human response because the wives are to be taught and encouraged to establish such a home atmosphere. It is of great importance that we specifically note the reason that is stated here for these admonishing instructions given in Titus 2:3-5—it is "so that the word of God will not be dishonored."

Let's read 1 Timothy 5:14, which also identifies this specific role of women and wives. In this case I prefer the Christian Standard Bible for its most accurate translation, in my opinion.

> Therefore, I want younger women to marry, have children, <u>manage their households</u>, and give the adversary no opportunity to accuse us. (1 Timothy 5:14 CSB)

The phrase "manage their households" as translated in the CSB is where I get the instruction that wives are to be the managers of their own household. The phrase "manage their households" is the English phrase taken from the single Greek word *oikodespoteo*. It is interesting that the English word *despot* comes from this Greek word. Webster's Dictionary defines a despot as one who is an absolute ruler. This Greek word *oikodespoteo* is defined by my two main Greek dictionaries to mean "the master of the house." *The Complete Word Study Dictionary: New Testament* goes on to say the person represented by this Greek word is "the master of a house exercising authority, with the emphasis on absolute rule; to govern or manage a household or the domestic affairs of a family."

Some of you may recall two passages in God's Word that list the qualifications of an *overseer* (which my denomination calls a *pastor*) and a *deacon*, which include that these men are to be the managers of

3: GOD'S PRIMARY ROLE FOR A WIFE

their own homes. I want you to consider two verses in 1 Timothy 3 to clarify any concern that might develop.

> ⁴*He must be* one who <u>manages</u> his own household well, keeping his children under control with all dignity. . . . ¹²Deacons must be husbands of *only* one wife, *and* good <u>managers</u> of *their* children and their own households. (1 Timothy 3:4, 12)

Even though most translations translate this Greek word "manage/managers," it is very important to note that the English words in 1 Timothy 3:4, 12 are translated from a Greek word that is entirely different from that of 1 Timothy 5:14, which speaks of wives/widows. This Greek word in 1 Timothy 3:4 and 12 is *proistemi,* which means "to be over, to preside over, to rule." There is no contradiction here in the same letter that Paul wrote to Timothy in 1 Timothy 3:4 and 12 regarding overseers and deacons and in 1 Timothy 5:14 regarding wives.

The scriptures state clearly that the husband is the "head of the wife." The husband has all final rule and authority over his own wife. However, the wife's defined primary role, according to God's Word, is to be the manager of her own household. I understand clearly that the husband is the overseer of all that concerns his family and that he is commanded in scripture to provide for his family. First Timothy 5:8 states it this way: "But if anyone does not provide for his own, and especially for those of his household, he has denied the faith and is worse than an unbeliever."

My husband spent most of his career in positions of executive management in manufacturing. I learned well that in his field of work there are those who oversee the company as a whole to assure that their product continues to be made according to their directions, specifications, and qualifications. There were also plant managers who managed a facility where the product was made. These plant managers were given the authority to run their plants as they believed best yet were always responsible for and accountable to those in leadership positions over the whole company. However, those who effectively oversaw the entire company did not interfere and/or micromanage the day-to-day overall management of the individual plants as long as the products they produced met their specific qualifications.

GOD'S PORTRAIT OF A "RIGHTEOUS WOMAN"

As one understands the workings in the business world of manufacturing, a better understanding of the role of a wife seems to become more evident. My husband knows and wholeheartedly believes in the arrangement God has set before us. I have heard him say on many occasions that he is so grateful to have a wife that "manages his family's everyday needs well" and that he has given me the authority and backing to do so. He adds that providing for his family spiritually and materially is all the job he wants. He can't understand why men would want to micromanage their wives and is grateful he has not been given that job as well.

Before we go any further into this subject, please listen to my words carefully. There is no place in scripture that states that the husband is a superior being because God has sovereignly appointed him to be the head and leader of his wife and family. Yes, God has declared specific roles for the husband and for the wife, but their designated roles in no way declare or imply any degree of superior value. In fact, in God's kingdom there is no "male" nor "female," according to Galatians 3:28: "There is neither Jew nor Greek, there is neither slave nor free man, there is neither male nor female; for you are all one in Christ Jesus."

In order for me to clearly state my conviction about what I believe scripture reveals about the primary role of a wife and the relationship she is to have with her husband, I want us to look at a few other instructions from God's Word. Look with me in 1 Timothy 2:11-12:

> [11]A woman must <u>quietly</u> receive instruction <u>with entire submissiveness</u>. [12]But I do not allow a woman to teach or exercise authority over a man, but to <u>remain quiet</u>.

The words *quietly* and *quiet* here are the same Greek word *hesuchia* and can refer to silence but also can refer to tranquility, peace, and/or not causing any disturbance, according to several Greek resources to which I frequently use for research. I realize this passage doesn't use the word *wives* or *husbands*. However, it must be assumed that these instructions do clearly include the parameters of a wife's role in her own household. Every wife's role as manager of her own household should include her receiving instruction from her husband with peaceful tranquility. But also, every wife has an equally important but different role than her husband in their marriage. She frequently has information that her husband often needs in order to make good final decisions. I am of the strong opinion that she is not to be silent but should peacefully share any vital information needed in order for her husband to have accurate and sufficient information to make the right decisions.

As mentioned before, I have found no place in God's Word where a husband is given the role to "make his own wife submit" to his authority or headship. But God's Word does clearly command that a wife is to *voluntarily* submit to the authority of her own husband. In fact, there are two such passages which come to mind. Let's look at these together:

> Wives, <u>be subject to your husbands</u> as is fitting in the Lord. (Colossians 3:18)

As you are already well aware, I use both Greek and Hebrew word studies and their verb tenses for my better understanding, which gives me a more accurate interpretation and application. The Greek verb *hupotasso* that is translated "be subject" means "to place oneself under the ranking authority of someone." The Greek verb translated "be subject" also is a present imperative verb (i.e., a command that is contentious), and in English it can accurately be translated, "as a habit of your life, you wives must subject yourself under the authority of your own husband as is fitting in the Lord."

Ephesians 5:24-25 says the same. You will note that these following verses have included a command for both the husband and the wife, whose stated example is Christ Jesus:

> [24]But as the church is subject to Christ, so also the wives *ought to be* to their husbands in everything. [25]Husbands, love your wives, just as Christ also loved the church and gave Himself up for her. (Ephesians 5:24-25)

Let me paraphrase these two verses a bit. "Husbands are to love their wives sacrificially and unconditionally, meeting her needs, just like Jesus did and does for us, His church. Whenever and/or wherever it is needful, the husband is to give up his own personal, fleshly desires for his wife's well-being and ministry as Christ did for the church. And as the church is under the authority of Christ, wives

GOD'S PORTRAIT OF A "RIGHTEOUS WOMAN"

should voluntarily place themselves under the authority of their own husbands."

The statements here are not only foreign to most females today but are hated, strongly opposed, and refused by many. Also, I must repeat that our Jehovah God of the Bible created the institute of marriage, and He is the only one who has the sovereign authority to make the regulating requirements and commands.

Because God's rules govern the institution of marriage, His rules will always work best and bring about the most spiritually profitable relationships and results. That is the overriding principle we learn from scripture. God blesses obedience and many times must discipline disobedience. God's revealed way is always the *best way*! ALWAYS!

In addition to placing oneself under the authority of one's own husband, God's Word tells us it is to be done "without fear." Fear of him making irreparable mistakes in his leadership and other areas that affect the family is such a common fear for many wives. First Peter 3:6 and 1 Peter 2:23 speak to this clearly.

> Just as Sarah obeyed Abraham, calling him lord, and you have become her children if you do what is right <u>without being frightened by any fear</u>. (1 Peter 3:6)

> And while being reviled, [Jesus] did not revile in return; while suffering, He uttered no threats, but <u>kept entrusting Himself to Him who judges righteously</u>. (1 Peter 2:23)

There is one more passage in God's Word that I believe is paramount to our biblical relationship to one's own husband. Look with me at Ephesians 5:33 which states, "Nevertheless, each individual among you also is to love his own wife even as himself, and the wife must *see to it* that *<u>she respects her husband</u>*."

In our world, culture, and ministry, this instruction to "respect her husband" is a major issue among many wives. They say, and rightly so in some cases, that their husband's behavior deserves anything *but* respect. My opinion is that even though the husband personally is truly not worthy of respect, reverence, or honor, the God-given position your husband holds demands it. Remember, you entered voluntarily into this covenant of marriage that has rules. That is why I made such a conscious effort to warn all women who are contemplating marriage to make certain that they carefully and closely inspect the lifestyle of their potential husband, both moral and spiritual. A man who is sold out to living for and honoring God in all his words and behaviors is one who will be empowered to love, honor, and cherish his wife in the way God commands him.

Sadly, over the years I have known of husbands who consistently disobey their personal responsibilities as a husband. They don't love or honor or cherish their wives as they are commanded to do. First Peter 3:1-2 tells us, "In the same way, you wives, be submissive to your own husbands so that even if any *of them* are disobedient to the word, they may be won without a word by the behavior of their wives, as they observe your chaste and respectful behavior." We will look at this passage in greater depth later.

Have you ever considered that when the circumstances tempt you to not trust God to work His will through your husband, and you are tempted to do what you believe to be the best action anyway, that your actions could place you in a very dangerous position. First, not trusting God to fulfill His promises is walking by sight and not by faith, disobeying one of God's clear instructions according to 2 Corinthians 5:7: "For we walk by faith, not by sight." That would make your actions sinful. Second, it is true that one may choose disobedience, but they are never permitted to choose the consequences of their disobedience. As I heard Dr. Charles Stanley say many years ago, "Sin will take you further than you ever intended to go. It will cost you more than you were ever willing to pay. And it will keep you longer than you ever planned to stay."

I have also heard it said, and I believe that scripture supports it, "One is never safer than when one is obediently in the center of God's will." All this to say, I may not fully understand the reason behind God's divine plans, but I know wholeheartedly and without reservation that what He has told me to do His will always turn out in the end to be the very best. God's plans always produce in us more and more blessings and grace and will bring about in us more and more transformation into the image of the Lord Jesus Christ and will bring Him the greatest glory.

As this chapter closes, I want you to know that I have tried to convince you through God's Word to believe that a wife's primary role is to *manage her own household well under the headship and authority of her husband*. We must believe as to obey with full confidence that any other way is foolish, is dangerous, and will result in major, unintended consequences. But obedience always brings God's blessings and supernatural intervention in our circumstances that produces far greater benefits than we could ever imagine. Yes, it may take years and difficult trials, but the rewards always outweigh the costs. To our God be glory, honor, praise, and thanksgiving!

It is worth repeating at the end of this chapter what I have just mentioned earlier—very important truths that I have learned from my forty-plus years of concentrated biblical study of the God who created the institution of marriage. The scriptures make the designated roles of both the husband and the wife crystal clear, and there is no inference that the husband's ability, worth, or usefulness in God's kingdom work is superior to that of his wife's ability, worth, or usefulness in God's kingdom. In fact, there is also no gender stipulation or specification in any of the spiritual gifts (which are given to each individual believer at the time of their personal salvation).

When sin entered God's created perfect and sinless world, the institution of marriage required different designated roles to function as God had intended. By God's providence, He designed the male to be best equipped to lead a family, to become the final authority in all decisions. God also in His providence designed the woman to be the best equipped to be the manager of the home and the best qualified to nurture children in holiness and obedience in the home she manages. So the male is not superior in quality, value, or importance because he is the designated head of the family. The husband also has a head to whom he is to submit and is accountable; his head is Jesus Christ Himself to whom someday he will give an account. Also, the female is not inferior to her husband because he is the head and she must submit to his authority; God has simply declared the most suitable and best operating roles for both the husband and the wife, which in concert create the framework for the most spiritually profitable family unit.

Human nature in our time and culture categorically rejects that these above-mentioned roles are best for the family's welfare and that they work best for the furtherance of sound and profitable relationships and community. However, *in God's kingdom*, there is no higher calling than being exactly who He created us to be, male or female. As a woman, you have, are, and will continue to be the person who is equipped by God both physically and emotionally to give birth to, nurture, and train up the future generations for God's glory and purposes. Yes, the roles are separate and distinct, but they are equally important roles as God has designed them. How do we know that the role of a husband to lead and provide for his family and for his wife to manage their household well works best? Honest and true observation and evaluation of how best a family thrives proves it. But the most important reason is because God designed it, revealed it to us through His Word, and empowers us by His Spirit to do His work His way. In other words, *because God said so!* The rewards of obedience are eternal and incalculable. Hallelujah, what a God and Savior we worship and serve. To Him be all glory, honor, praise, and thanksgiving!

CHAPTER 4

God's Primary Responsibilities for a Wife

There are two passages from God's Word that I need to repeat because they are absolutely essential to doing marriage God's way. The following phrase will be repeated over and over during these chapters: *God always blesses obedience.* But also, because God loves us too much to leave us in sin (disobedience *is* sin), He disciplines us with the specific purpose of getting His children to a "godly sorrow that leads to repentance" (2 Corinthians 7:10)—that is, obedience. Disobedience/sin is extremely damaging to each of us spiritually but also to our witness as Christ-followers. So our Lord God just won't allow His children to stay there too very long; He simply loves us too much to do so.

It is commonly understood that a person will not completely trust someone that they do not know. It is because of that principle that this book is purposefully filled with God's Word. The primary goal of all scripture is to reveal who the sovereign Creator God is—His character and His ways along with His relationship with and promises to all those who put their faith and trust in His Son, our Lord Jesus Christ. In the reading of, studying, believing, and obedience to the Jehovah God of the Bible, He opens our hearts and spirits to the point of our knowing Him intimately and trusting Him explicitly, wholeheartedly, and without reservation.

Since our culture and its deception regarding marriage is so diametrically opposed to biblical truth, I am addressing specific scripture passages that I pray will increase your understanding about biblical marriage. But more than that, how I pray these pages will give you the vehicle through which you are ever increasing in the knowledge of God Himself, thus increasing your faith exponentially. I am asking the Holy Spirit to move powerfully in all the hearts and lives of those who will encounter the Word of God and the God of the Word within these pages!

It is very wise and eternally profitable for each of us to make the decision to continually strive to live our lives in a way that manifests Jesus' character and ways in and through us. The absolute truth is that the unsaved people you encounter are listening to what you say, watching what you do, and being influenced by how you relate to other people. Each one of us may be the only "letter of Christ" some non-believers see or know (2 Corinthians 3:2-3). Examine carefully God's promises below which are found in both the Old and the New Testaments:

> All these blessings will come upon you and overtake you <u>if you obey</u> the Lord your God. (Deuteronomy 28:2)

> But He said, "On the contrary, blessed are those <u>who hear the word of God and observe it</u>." (Luke 11:28)

One of my highest goals for writing this book is *not* to give those who read it a long list of *dos and don'ts;* my intent is for all women, those who are married, those who are not married, and those who desire to be married, to know their God well enough to trust Him and obey what He tells us through His Word. As I'm sure many of you are well aware, biblical Christianity is *not* a legalistic approach to try to make God love us by trying to obey a list of dos and don'ts. It is primarily a relationship with the true and living God Who wants to draw you close to Him so He can manifest His love, blessings, protection, and provisions in fullest measure toward each and every one of us.

My heart's desire for us all is to be ever increasing in our experiential knowledge of our all sovereign and loving God. This brings about a more meaningful and effective worship of and service to God—all for the glory of His great name and the greater expansion of His kingdom. Our God will complete the good work He has begun in each of us. It may be through our receiving and obeying God's instructions with joy, or it may be that we are led to obedience through God's discipline. The latter begs us to be alerted to what Hebrews 12:5-11 reveals to us:

> ⁵And you have forgotten the exhortation which is addressed to you as sons, "My son, do not regard lightly the discipline of the Lord, nor faint when you are reproved by Him; ⁶For those whom the Lord loves He disciplines, and He scourges every son whom He receives." ⁷It is for discipline that you endure; God deals with you as with sons; for what son is there whom *his* father does not discipline? ⁸But if you are without discipline, of which all have become partakers, then you are illegitimate children and not sons. ⁹Furthermore, we had earthly fathers to discipline us, and we respected them; shall we not much rather be subject to the Father of spirits, and live? ¹⁰For they disciplined us for a short time as seemed best to them, but He *disciplines us* for *our* good, so that we may share His holiness. ¹¹<u>All discipline for the moment seems not to be joyful, but sorrowful; yet to those who have been trained by it, afterwards it yields the peaceful fruit of righteousness.</u>

Look with me also at Hebrews 5:11-14. This passage gives a sharp contrast to the assumption of many who think it is within their own power to decide when and what they will believe and obey in God's Word. As you read the following, remember that the author of Hebrews is speaking to genuine believers.

> ¹¹Concerning him [Melchizedek] we have much to say, and *it is* hard to explain, since you have become dull of hearing. ¹²For though by this time you ought to be teachers, you have need again for someone to teach you

the elementary principles of the oracles of God, and you have come to need milk and not solid food. ¹³For everyone who partakes *only* of milk is not accustomed to the word of righteousness, for he is an infant. ¹⁴But solid food is for the mature, who <u>because of practice</u> have their senses trained to discern good and evil. (Hebrews 5:11-14)

The truth which you have just observed in the previous passage is speaking of Christians who have listened to sermons and accurately heard life-changing biblical truth but have become "dull of hearing" because they didn't practice the truth of God's Word that they had heard. These believers not only don't have the capability to retain the spiritual truth they have heard, but over time it becomes impossible to even remember "the elementary principles of the oracles of God." The saying, "if you don't use it, you lose it" is clearly applicable to God's Word. In fact, a Christian can even get to the point of becoming unable "to discern good and evil" as well as not being "accustomed to the word of righteousness." What a sobering thought and important warning this should be to all of us who claim to be Christ-followers.

Hebrews 5:11-14 seems to beg the following question for everyone who claims to have been born again through faith in Jesus Christ: *Am I one who has been under the teachings of the truth of God's Word and yet don't understand the "elementary principles of the oracles of God?"* Look with me at what God describes as elementary teachings in the following passage:

> ¹Therefore leaving the <u>elementary teaching about the Christ</u> let us press on to maturity, not laying again a foundation of repentance from dead works and of <u>faith toward God</u>, ²of instruction about washings and laying on of hands, and the resurrection of the dead and eternal judgment. (Hebrews 6:1-2)

If Hebrews 6:1-2 accurately describes your present spiritual condition, you need to again be taught these elementary truths. If that is true about you, you are an *infant* in your spiritual walk with Christ Jesus, and God says that you are unable to discern good and evil and are not accustomed to/experienced in the word of righteousness. Also, if you are still an *infant in Christ*, regardless of the number of years you have been saved, you are not now able to discern good

4: GOD'S PRIMARY RESPONSIBILITIES FOR A WIFE

and evil. Could it possibly be that you are *not* walking by the Spirit but by the desires of your flesh? Usually most do not even know it because they are "dull of hearing" from God. Look with me at Galatians 5:16-17: "But I say, walk by the Spirit, and you will not carry out the desire of the flesh. For the flesh sets its desire against the Spirit, and the Spirit against the flesh; for these are in opposition to one another, so that you may not do the things that you please." The encouraging truth is that once anyone acknowledges this condition and asks God's forgiveness and determines to be a "doer of the Word, and not merely a hearer who delude themselves" (James 1:22), our always good and faithful God meets them there and gives them the ability to hear and understand Him speaking through His Word and gives them the divine power to obey.

A believer's loss of "faith toward God" in Hebrews 6:1 can be equally interpreted as the loss of trust toward God. This loss of faith (not saving faith, but sanctifying faith) which results in a loss of trust, in my opinion, is the greatest loss of all. But thanks be to God, the opposite is true of those who are walking in faith and obedience to those things the Lord has revealed to them and through that obedience are continually growing in their spiritual maturity. None of us "live life" in perfect obedience to our always good and faithful God. However, as we continue to study God's Word and believe it to the point of obedience, we are being transformed more and more into the image of Christ Jesus and are being enabled to live victoriously by the power of the Holy Spirit in and through all circumstances that we encounter. These individuals are those who have been saved by grace—they have believed in the person and work of Jesus Christ, the Son of God, who died on a cross to pay their sin debt, was buried, and was raised bodily from the dead on the third day. Of first importance, they have confessed their sins and their need of a Savior, they have repented of their personal sins, and they have surrendered their lives to Christ Jesus as Lord, according to Romans 10:8-10.

> ⁸But what does it say? "The word is near you, in your mouth and in your heart"—that is, the word of faith which we are preaching, ⁹that if you confess with your mouth Jesus *as* Lord, and believe in your heart that God raised Him from the dead, you will be saved; ¹⁰for with the heart a person

believes, resulting in righteousness, and with the mouth he confesses, resulting in salvation.

Does this Romans passage describe your relationship with Jesus Christ? Some of you may be wondering why I am asking you to evaluate your own spiritual condition. It is commanded that we do so in 2 Corinthians 13:5: "Test yourselves *to see* if you are in the faith; examine yourselves! Or do you not recognize this about yourselves, that Jesus Christ is in you—unless indeed you fail the test?" Romans 8:16 states, "The Spirit Himself testifies with our spirit that we are children of God." We can be confident that the Holy Spirit Himself makes His presence known to each and every Christian. If you are not sure of your salvation, ask the Holy Spirit to make His presence known to you. If all you receive from Him is the conviction of sin, then you know that this is the time in which you need to confess your sins, repent of them, and surrender your life to the lordship of Jesus Christ.

What I have been leading up to in this chapter is the examination of what God says is one of the primary responsibilities of a righteous woman/wife. As I have mentioned several times before, the biblical foundation is found in Ephesians 5:22: "Wives, *be subject* to your own husbands, as to the Lord." The truth is that in order for any wife to walk in obedience—she must submit herself to the leadership and authority of her husband. She needs to know that it is the power of the indwelling Holy Spirit in all believers that enables her to be obedient to God's instructions. She also needs know for certain that she has become a child of God by grace through her faith in Jesus as her Lord and Savior, who has given to her the permanent indwelling of the Holy Spirit, according to Romans 8:9: "However, you are not in the flesh but in the Spirit, if indeed the Spirit of God dwells in you. But if anyone does not have the Spirit of Christ, he does not belong to Him." An undeniable truth is that no one is able to habitually live according to God's "right ways" without being saved and living by the power of the Holy Spirit.

Let's observe two life-changing truths from God's Word related to obedience. John 17:3 is where Jesus' high priestly prayer is recorded. Every Christian needs to be reminded how Jesus describes eternal life. It's interesting that *knowing* the only true God is an eternal journey.

4: GOD'S PRIMARY RESPONSIBILITIES FOR A WIFE

"This is eternal life, that they may know You, the only true God, and Jesus Christ whom You have sent." (John 17:3)

The following passage of 2 Peter 1:2-4 contains some of my favorite verses because they give us the road map regarding how to know our God more intimately, live life victoriously, and become recipients of these promises when trusting and obeying. We will probably go over this passage several more times as this book continues. It is that important to building our faith!

²Grace and peace be multiplied to you in the <u>knowledge of God and of Jesus our Lord</u>; ³seeing that His divine power has granted to us everything pertaining to life and godliness, <u>through the true knowledge of Him</u>, who called us by His own glory and excellence. ⁴For by these He has granted to us His precious and magnificent promises, so that by them you may become partakers of *the* divine nature, having escaped the corruption that is in the world by lust. (2 Peter 1:2-4)

Look again at the promises of God proclaimed in these three verses.

- God's grace and peace are multiplied to believers through the true knowledge of God and our Lord Jesus Christ.
- God's divine power grants to believers everything pertaining to life and godliness through the true knowledge of Himself.
- God calls us by His own glory and excellence.
- God has granted us His precious and magnificent promises by His own glory and excellence.
- We become partakers of God's divine nature by His precious and magnificent promises.
- We are enabled by His divine nature to escape the corruption that is in the world by lust.

For a simple example of how verse four has impacted my life: Many, many years ago I was often in the presence of a church leader. One evening, my eyes caught his, which created an emotional reaction for me. I sensed the same from him. Because I knew of the danger of my flesh, from that day forward I consciously and intentionally never allowed myself to be in his presence alone. In so doing, I "escaped the corruption that is in the world by lust . . . through the true knowledge of God and Jesus our Lord." This is just one example. There are many more. The principle and promises of 2 Peter 1:2-4 have been my road map for many years, for which I am eternally grateful. God's Word is true. His promises are "yes and amen." He continues to prove Himself faithful in all things! Hallelujah, what a God and Savior we worship and serve.

The mostly unperceived benefits of becoming a diligent student of God's Word (with the purpose of getting to know more and more about the one, true, and living God and living in obedience) is capsulized in these three verses. The heartbreaking fact is that most of us rarely continue to live life with the constant awareness that God is always at work in a believer's life to transform them more and more into the image of Jesus Christ. Look with me at several passages of scripture that should encourage and motivate every Christ-follower to focus on growing in the true, experiential knowledge of God and Christ Jesus.

> But we all, with unveiled face, beholding as in a mirror the glory of the Lord, are being transformed into the same image from glory to glory, just as from the Lord, the Spirit. (2 Corinthians 3:18)

Our living God uses His living and active Word to behold His glory whereby our transformation continues.

> For it is God who is at work in you, both to will and to work for *His* good pleasure. (Philippians 2:13)

If you are genuinely a child of God, God Himself is continually at work in you, giving you the desire and the power "to work for His good pleasure."

> Sanctify them in the truth; Your word is truth. (John 17:17)

As I have mentioned, often in ministry, *sanctify* means to be consecrated by God—made holy and set apart by God to do His will in His right ways. This passage tells us that God continually uses His living and active Word that has inherent power to make us holy.

There is another passage in God's Word that we must be aware of. As with the other verses discussed in this book, this scripture will

4: GOD'S PRIMARY RESPONSIBILITIES FOR A WIFE

not profit anyone who does not embrace and apply them in faith to their belief system and habitual behavior. Hebrews 4:2 makes this clear:

> For indeed we have had good news preached to us, just as they also; but the word they heard <u>did not profit them</u> because it was not united by faith in those who heard.

Let me repeat: when I married my husband, I was a prime example of a woman who was neither aware nor desirous of this one primary aspect of God's assigned responsibilities for a wife—to submit yourself to the authority of your own husband. I personally describe myself as strong willed and opinionated. Those who know me well enough would say a hearty *amen*! I have told my husband, Lee, and many others that he was the only one who could have lived with me. He did so by loving me into willing submission.

If any of you ladies can describe yourself the same as I have, I want to encourage you by the truth the Lord gave me. These characteristics of being strong willed and opinionated, when under the control and power of the Holy Spirit, can be very positive traits and can be used by God to benefit His kingdom and equip His children for the work of service.

I now want to address the hardest part, at least for most, of becoming God's design for a righteous wife. Remember Genesis 2:18: "Then the Lord God said, 'It is not good for the man to be alone; I will make him a <u>helper suitable</u> for him.'" God's Word names this suitable helper, "wife." The following is the best interpretation I have ever found of Genesis 2:18-24:

> Adam was *alone* and that was *not good;* all else in Creation was good (cf. 1:4, 10, 12, 18, 21, 25). As man began to function as God's representative (naming the animals [2:19–20] represented his dominion over them; cf. 1:28), he became aware of his solitude (2:20). God therefore put him to sleep (v. 21) and created Eve from his *flesh* and *bone* (vv. 21–23). God had decided to *make a helper suitable* (lit., "a helper corresponding to him," or "a corresponding helper") for the man (v. 18). "Helper" is not a demeaning term; it is often used in Scripture to describe God Almighty (e.g., Pss. 33:20; 70:5; 115:9,

where it is trans. "help" in the NIV). The description of her as "corresponding to him" means basically that what was said about him in Genesis 2:7 was also true of her. They both had the same nature. But what man lacked (his aloneness was not good) she supplied, and what she lacked he supplied. The culmination was *one flesh* (v. 24)—the complete unity of man and woman in marriage. Since Adam and Eve were a spiritual unity, living in integrity without sin, there was no need for instruction here on headship.[12]

The Hebrew and Greek languages are alike in that their languages have the same word for *woman* and *wife*. As is the case in many Greek and Hebrew words, the context of the passage determines if it is speaking of a woman in general or a married woman in particular. First Corinthians 7:34 begins to address the woman who is unmarried, then it addresses the woman who is married by using the phrase "one who."

> The woman who is unmarried, and the virgin, is concerned about the things of the Lord, that she may be holy both in body and spirit; but one who[13] is married is concerned about the things of the world, how she may please her husband. (1 Corinthians 7:34b)

When I got married, I wasn't consciously aware of the fact that God had instructed me to place myself under the headship, leadership, and authority of my husband. That didn't, however, exempt me from my obligation and responsibility to do just that. Look with me again at 1 Corinthians 11:3:

> But I want you to understand that Christ is the head of every man, and the man is the head of a woman, and God is the head of Christ.

Now go with me to examine Ephesians 5:15-33. This passage covers more than just God's instructions for wives; it contains much

---

12 John F. Walvoord & Roy B. Zuck, *The Bible Knowledge Commentary*, from Logos Bible Software (Bellingham, WA: Dallas Theological Seminary).
13 "a woman"

4: GOD'S PRIMARY RESPONSIBILITIES FOR A WIFE

about the husband and wife relationship and responsibilities for each. My point is that there is more to marriage than the wife voluntarily living under the headship and authority of her husband.

> [15]Therefore be careful how you walk, not as unwise men but as wise, [16]making the most of your time, because the days are evil. [17]So then do not be foolish, but understand what the will of the Lord is. [18]And do not get drunk with wine, for that is dissipation, but be filled with the Spirit, [19]speaking to one another in psalms and hymns and spiritual songs, singing and making melody with your heart to the Lord; [20]always giving thanks for all things in the name of our Lord Jesus Christ to God, even the Father; [21]and <u>be subject to one another in the fear of Christ</u>. [22]Wives, *be subject* to your own husbands, as to the Lord. [23]For the husband is the head of the wife, as Christ also is the head of the church, He Himself *being* the Savior of the body. [24]But as the church is subject to Christ, so also the wives *ought to be* to their husbands in everything. [25]Husbands, love your wives, just as Christ also loved the church and gave Himself up for her, [26]so that He might sanctify her, having cleansed her by the washing of water with the word, [27]that He might present to Himself the church in all her glory, having no spot or wrinkle or any such thing; but that she would be holy and blameless. [28]So husbands ought also to love their own wives as their own bodies. He who loves his own wife loves himself; [29]for no one ever hated his own flesh, but nourishes and cherishes it, just as Christ also *does* the church, [30]because we are members of His body. [31]For this reason a man shall leave his father and mother and shall be joined to his wife, and the two shall become one flesh. [32]This mystery is great; but I am speaking with reference to Christ and the church. [33]Nevertheless, each individual among you also is to love his own wife even as himself, and the wife must *see to it* that she respects her husband. (Ephesians 5:15-33)

GOD'S PORTRAIT OF A "RIGHTEOUS WOMAN"

It is significant that this Ephesian passage on the husband-wife relationship begins by instructing them both. Both the husband and the wife are to . . .

- be careful how they walk (live life); be wise, not foolish (v. 15, 17).
- understand what the Lord's will is (v. 17).
- continually be filled with the Holy Spirit (v. 18).
- be subject to one another in the fear of Christ (v. 21).

Wives are to be subject to their *own* husband. Why? Because God says a husband is the head of his wife (v. 23). How? As the church is subject to Christ—in everything (v. 24). Wives must respect their husbands (v. 33).

There are probably many of you who were like I was when Lee and I married. It took many years for me to understand why it is *so hard* for most women to willingly place themselves under the headship of their own husband. I have already mentioned that Genesis 1:28 tells us clearly that God gave both the male (Adam) and female (Eve) the command to "rule over" His newly created earth and all its contents. In other words, women were created by God to rule; God has placed it in our DNA. Go back with me to Genesis 3:16 because it gives us the reason why, for the most part, most women "fight" the instruction to willingly submit to the authority of their own husband.

> To the woman He said, "I will greatly multiply your pain in childbirth, in pain you will bring forth children; yet your <u>desire</u> will be for your husband, and <u>he will rule over you</u>." (Genesis 3:16)

Look with me closely at this verse in which God reveals His punitive discipline for Eve's disobedience to God by eating the forbidden fruit of the tree of the knowledge of good and evil. Keep in mind we are not told how long it was from the day of their creation to this event of their disobedience. Honestly, I am of the opinion that we do not have any biblical basis to even speculate. Nonetheless, let's speculate that Eve had enjoyed for some time her God-given role of co-rulership with Adam over the whole earth and the living beings He also had created and placed there.

4: GOD'S PRIMARY RESPONSIBILITIES FOR A WIFE

There are many who interpret the desire mentioned in this verse to be a *sexual* desire. The context here seems to require another interpretation. The phrase "your desire will be for your husband" is contrasted with "he [her husband] will rule over you," which is revealed by both phrases containing reference to the husband. I am convinced that part of the consequences of Eve's sin was that from that point forward, she (and thus all future wives) would no longer be a co-ruler with her husband, but that when she marries, he would "rule over her."

God did not remove the DNA for the ability to rule from women. Women continue to be very capable and effective leaders. What did change was she now would desire to rule over her husband and would not be content with nor in some cases willing to submit to her husband's authority. I am one of these women who has a strong natural ability to lead as well as the spiritual gift of leadership. It has been a struggle for me over the years to recognize when I am nearing the boundary or overstepping it, while trying to manage my own household well and still remain under the authority of my husband. I suspect I am not the only one here with the same issue.

There is a parallel passage in Genesis 4 that gives us additional insight into what similarly had occurred in Genesis 3:16. This passage uses the same Hebrew word *tesuqah* translated "desire" with similar, though not identical, circumstances of what can follow disobedient, sinful behavior.

Read closely this Genesis 4:6-7 passage. The context is that God had accepted Abel's sacrificial offering to Him but had not accepted Cain's. There is much to say about this event in history, but this is neither the time nor the place.

> ⁶Then the Lord said to Cain, "Why are you angry? And why has your countenance fallen? ⁷If you do well, will not *your countenance* be lifted up? And if you do not do well, sin is crouching at the door; and its desire is for you, but you must master it." (Genesis 4:6-7)

Note that God spoke to Cain and questioned his response to His (God's) rejection of Cain's sacrificial offering. I believe God had told them both, most likely through Adam, exactly how God was to be worshipped—it was through an animal sacrifice. Cain had determined he would bring the works of his hands, not the blood of an animal as Abel had in following God's requirement.

It is enlightening to know God's revealed truth about blood. It is found in Hebrews 9:22: "And according to the Law, *one may* almost *say*, all things are cleansed with blood, and without shedding of blood there is no forgiveness." That was truth in the beginning with Adam and Eve. It was true in the Law of Moses through the continual animal sacrifices, and is true today through Jesus' blood which was sacrificed for the payment of the "sin debt"—*once* for all people, for all times, as the sufficient payment for all sins, for all people, for all times. Hallelujah, what a great salvation we have been given!

Here in Genesis 4:7, God first told Cain how to please God with His designated offering, "If you do well." "Doing well" here was Cain bringing the sacrifice God ordered—an animal sacrifice. Then God warned Cain, as we should be warned today, "If you do not do well, sin is crouching at the door and its (sin's) desire is for you, but you must master it."[14]

As it is true for all even today, when we refuse to worship God God's way, it is sin. Sin's greatest desire is to rule over us, to be sovereign over our lives, to make us go our own way and not God's. But we must master that temptation to sin. Thus, it would be Eve's struggle as well as. All females that would be born after Adam and Eve sinned have the inborn DNA to seek to fulfill the "desires of their own flesh"—which is sin. For married women, it is a great temptation to try to rule over our own husbands. God says that because sin had entered into the human's DNA, the marriage union from that day forward was to have a single designated ruler, and it is not the wife. It is to be her own husband. Every wife is to learn how to master her own temptation to rule over her husband by the power of the Holy Spirit within her.

Perhaps some of you are wondering why I have not included the instructions for the husband yet. The reason is simple. The Lord has led me to speak specifically to women in this book, not to men. However, I have a close male friend in the Lord who has been a husband for many years. He said to me recently, "I realize that it is far easier for a wife to submit to a husband who loves her unconditionally

---

14 Worship God God's way, not in a way of your own choosing.

4: GOD'S PRIMARY RESPONSIBILITIES FOR A WIFE

and sacrificially." I agree this is very, very true. What is so hard for many to understand and obey is that wives are to honor, respect, and submit to their own husband, even if he doesn't submit to Christ Jesus' headship and authority over him and is personally not due honor nor respect. However, it is the position he holds by way of the covenant of marriage you voluntarily entered into that God demands your obedience to regardless.

When a husband has not submitted himself to the lordship of Jesus Christ, he is incapable of loving his wife as Christ loves His bride, the church. So it becomes harder indeed for the wife to fulfill her role, but nonetheless, the commands remain the same for that wife. And as scripture promises, God's grace is sufficient for all things, according to these 2 Corinthians passages:

> And God is able to make all grace abound to you, so that always having all sufficiency in everything, you may have an abundance for every good deed. (2 Corinthians 9:8)

> And He has said to me, "My grace is sufficient for you, for power is perfected in weakness." Most gladly, therefore, I will rather boast about my weaknesses, <u>so that the power of Christ may dwell in me</u>. (2 Corinthians 12:9)

First Peter 3:7 uses an interesting verb as a warning to all husbands who consider themselves as having been given the role of *dictator* rather than a benevolent master of his home and a servant leader. Look at the following verse and understand there are consequences for any husband who doesn't live in obedience to God's clear instructions given for the position of leadership authority over his wife:

> You husbands in the same way, live with *your wives* in an understanding way, as with someone weaker, since she is a woman; and <u>show her honor as a fellow heir of the grace of life</u>, so that your prayers will not be hindered. (1 Peter 3:7)

It is necessary that we understand what a wife's command to submit to and obey the leadership of her husband does *not* mean. A Christian is *never* to obey anyone, including her own husband, who has told her to do something that is sinful. According to Acts 5:29,

"But Peter and the apostles answered, 'We must obey God rather than men.'" Just a word of warning: if a wife decides that she is not going to obey her husband's clearly stated direction, she should be sure she has biblical support for not doing so. The husband will be reminded that his wife's final authority lies solely within the realm of the sovereignty of the God Whom you worship and serve.

You might be considering the idea that God would understand and even approve of you not living up to your obligations of His covenant instructions if your husband (who professes to be a Christian) in no way lives up to his. I've already mentioned the absolute truth that God *blesses obedience* and *disciplines disobedience*. He doesn't turn a blind eye to any of our deliberate disobedience.

First Corinthians 7:16a states, "For how do you know, O wife, whether you will save your husband?" I believe there are times when God's spiritual work on an unbelieving husband is hampered and possibly even delayed in order to discipline his believing wife for her disobedience to her husband's God-given authoritative leadership. A sobering thought to consider, isn't it? I encourage you to meditate on just how God might be using your obedience to Him in following your husband's leadership to manifest His loving presence in and through you. This can be used mightily by God to bring a husband to repentance and salvation. A sobering, but now greatly encouraging thought to consider, isn't it?

Some wives correctly say that their own husbands have abdicated their responsibilities as the spiritual leader of their home. They then believe that they are now to step into the vacuum and become the spiritual leader of the home themselves. However, there is no such permission given to them by God. I want to state that even though you have mighty and equally important responsibilities in the marriage, becoming the leader in your marriage in any form is disobedience. We've already talked about God loving us too much to leave us in sin, so He disciplines us to realize our sin and to lead us back into the blessings of obedience. Each of us wives are to remember that we are given the responsibility to manage our own households well, which includes much training in all areas of our children's lives, which obviously includes spiritual training. However, that does not include being the spiritual leader/head of the family.

There is another aspect of this subject of obedience/submission that I have not touched. That is the subject of the fear of the Lord. Let

4: GOD'S PRIMARY RESPONSIBILITIES FOR A WIFE

me first say that there are differences of opinions in how Christians interpret this Greek word *phobos* translated "fear." An example of early believers is revealed in Acts 9:31: "So the church throughout all Judea and Galilee and Samaria enjoyed peace, being built up; and <u>going on in the fear of the Lord</u>, and <u>in the comfort of the Holy Spirit</u>, it continued to increase."

Many say they are obedient to this command to "fear God" in 1 Peter 2:17, which states, "Honor all people, love the brotherhood, <u>fear God</u>, honor the king." However, their definition of this word *fear*, that they are saying they are obeying, could be very different from someone else's definition.

Translating *fear* from Greek into English is not an easy task. However, all of us need to know what God actually means when He tells us that He is to be feared. First, it cannot be that God is to be feared because He is sitting in heaven looking for ways to pour out His wrath on us. Romans 5:9 says to us, "Much more then, having now been justified by His blood, we shall be <u>saved from</u> the wrath of God through Him." And 1 Thessalonians 5:9 tells every believer, "For God has not destined us for wrath, but for obtaining salvation through our Lord Jesus Christ."

The fear of the Lord also cannot be that we think God is just waiting for us to mess up so He can punish us for sinning. God's Word clearly states that we are clothed with God's righteousness—that we have been declared righteous and justified through the blood of Jesus Christ when we surrendered our lives in faith to Jesus as Lord and Savior. Carefully observe the following New Testament passages.

> He made Him[15] who knew no sin *to be* sin on our behalf, so that we might become the righteousness of God in Him. (2 Corinthians 5:21)

> . . . and may be found in Him, not having a righteousness of my own derived from *the* Law, but that which is through faith in Christ, the righteousness which *comes* from God on the basis of faith. (Philippians 3:9)

> . . . being justified[16] as a gift by His grace through the redemption which is in Christ Jesus. (Romans 3:24)

---
15 The *He* is God the Father, and the *Him* is Christ Jesus.
16 "declared righteous"

> Such were some of you; but you were washed, but you were sanctified, but you were justified in the name of the Lord Jesus Christ and in the Spirit of our God. (1 Corinthians 6:11)

What is revealed to us about our relationship with God is that He does pay close attention to our behavior, not to condemn us but to allow the (potential) consequences of our disobedient behavior to be recognized by us as sin and to cause us to experience a "godly sorrow that will lead us to repentance." Again, our God is good and faithful and loves His children too much to allow us to continue in sin. Read carefully these two verses in 2 Corinthians 7:

> ⁹I now rejoice, not that you were made sorrowful, but that you were made sorrowful to *the point of* repentance; for you were made sorrowful according to *the will of* God, so that you might not suffer loss in anything through us. ¹⁰For the sorrow that is according to *the will of* God produces a repentance without regret, *leading* to salvation, but the sorrow of the world produces death. (2 Corinthians 7:9-10)

According to the Old Testament Hebrew, the definition of the word *fear* carries with it a positive quality when used as the "fear of God." It is described as the fear that acknowledges God's intentions. All this to say, when many Christians parallel the "fear of God" with a simple reverence of God, they are most likely diluting this command beyond its intended meaning. It is a positive quality for every believer to hold our Sovereign, Creator, all-loving God as the all-powerful and all-sovereign Ruler over all His creation. Because we know that God's will is always best for us, we should genuinely fear behaving in a way that does not bring Him pleasure or results in disobedience to Him. Our fear is never of condemnation because of Romans 8:1: "Therefore there is now no condemnation for those who are in Christ Jesus." But our fear of God should be anchored in our deep desire to never displease Him, to always bring Him pleasure and glory by our lives, but also that we not miss the blessings God has prepared for us. When we walk in the fear of the Lord as mentioned above (inadequately for sure), we also are spared His necessary discipline to draw us back into being useful, fruitful, and righteous vessels in His kingdom.

4: GOD'S PRIMARY RESPONSIBILITIES FOR A WIFE

The nuances of this "fear of God" go way beyond a simple reverence or high esteem. Proverbs 14:27(CSB) is translated this way: "The fear of the LORD is a fountain of life, <u>turning people away from the snares of death</u>." Yes, each of us should hold a great reverence for our Father God, but we also must continually be clearly and consciously aware that the Jehovah God of the Bible is a sovereign, holy God, and I am not. I have heard it put this way: "There is a God, and it is not me." And yes, God loves us with an everlasting love, but His holiness and love for us demands that He correct us to the point of repentance and life change for our good and His glory.

My hope is that I have not led you too deeply into muddy waters but that, in a way, we all "fear the Lord" to such a degree that we will be compelled to walk in obedience as best we know how and appropriate His all-sufficient grace and available power of the Holy Spirit to do so.

Let me summarize very briefly the major truth I have desired and earnestly tried to convey here in this particular chapter. God has laid out a specific order of authority in the marriage union ever since sin entered into the world. God commands and expects every human He creates to walk under His sovereign authority by their personal obedience—there are blessings for obedience and many times discipline for disobedience. The same is true in the covenant of marriage. God has clearly commanded and expects each and every wife to voluntarily place herself under the authority of her own husband. Let me state again that under no circumstance are we ever to obey anyone, including our own husband, who tells us to do anything that God categorizes as sin.

And of course, God has clearly commanded and expects each and every husband to love his wife *(to meet her needs sacrificially and unconditionally)* as Jesus loved the church and gave Himself up for her. The husband also has a head—it is Christ Jesus Himself. Both the husband and the wife are individually responsible and accountable to God. It is a sobering realization that each one of us will give an account for every word we have spoken and every deed we have done. More about the "judgment seat of Christ" later. But suffice it to say now, those who are saved will not be judged for our sins, because Jesus paid for them all with His blood on Calvary's cross and in His subsequent resurrection. However, we will be judged for what we did or did not do with what God has given to us as stewards as it relates to our own personal rewards or loss of rewards.

A few last scripture passages to meditate on:

> [36]But I tell you that every careless word that people speak, they shall give an accounting for it in the day of judgment. [37]For by your words you will be justified, and by your words you will be condemned. (Matthew 12:36-37)

> So then each one of us will give an account of himself to God. (Romans 14:12)

> Watch yourselves, that you do not lose what we have accomplished, but that you may receive a full reward. (2 John 8)

> But thanks be to God, who always leads us in triumph in Christ, and manifests through us the sweet aroma of the knowledge of Him in every place. (2 Corinthians 2:14)

> "Behold, I am coming quickly, and My reward *is* with Me, to render to every man according to what he has done." (Revelation 22:12)

Amen and amen!

CHAPTER 5

God's Instructions for Becoming a "Righteous Wife"

We have covered pretty thoroughly the instructions for becoming a righteous wife, according to God's definition: "submission to one's own husband's authority of leadership." One thing I know for sure is that a wife is never responsible nor accountable for what a husband does or does not do. Neither is a husband ever commanded to "make his wife submit" to his God-given authority in their marriage. It is so very important for us to remember that the husband and the wife will individually answer to God for their own behavior and not that of their spouse.

This chapter will most likely be the hardest to study, believe, and obey for the majority of readers who desire God's absolute instructions to be understood within the covenant of marriage. I'm sure you have noticed I continue to use the phrase *covenant of marriage*, because whether or not you knew it, this union you entered into (or may one day enter into) with your husband was a holy covenant agreement instituted by the Jehovah Creator God of the Bible. That *is* what marriage is—a covenant agreement.

Over the years, I have experienced wives who were extremely distraught that their husbands would not allow the family to tithe their family income. Many have felt, at the very least, they were walking in disobedience, and some have felt the extreme—shame. I believe scripture is clear that our God understands the desires our hearts. Therefore, I have advised on occasion that in this instance there is a way for them to feel at perfect peace about their family not tithing.

If this is your situation, I highly suggest you address the issue with your husband *only* when there is no other issue of disagreement or controversy within your marriage. Pick a time when he is not otherwise concerned about another issue. If your husband is saved, or professes to be, I suggest that you say something similar to the following (but *not* if he is unsaved):

> *I truly understand your decision that we will not tithe our income and that you understand my desire that we do tithe our income to God's work. I want to tell you that before God, I am walking in obedience to my Lord because He knows my heart's desire is to be obedient to give a tenth of our income to God's work. However, you should know that it is you and you alone that will give an account to God for robbing Him of His portion of our income. You alone are accountable to and responsible for your decisions to withhold what is God's alone. I promise I will not mention it again. I do want to ask your permission to tithe the money that I earn, however [that is, if you have income yourself].*

As I am sure you have already noticed, I am usually pretty direct in dealing with the things of the Lord and His revelations in His Word. However, when I introduced this example, I said to say "something similar." You know best how to communicate difficult subjects with your husband. I don't. But I wholly believe the principles stated in this illustration are valid and useful for husbands who are saved, but again not for unsaved husbands. If, after speaking similar words, your husband says "no," it is accounted to you by God

5: GOD'S INSTRUCTIONS FOR BECOMING A "RIGHTEOUS WIFE"

as an obedient giver, in my opinion, because of your desire and also because of your obedience to your husband's instructions.

An event happened many years ago that I recall vividly of a lady who was married to an unsaved man. She had been in my Precept Upon Precept Bible study classes for several years. We had witnessed God moving in supernatural ways to make a way for her to participate in many Christian activities, for which we praised God. This particular time, there was something this lady truly believed that she was supposed to do, but her husband said, "no." She told me about her disappointment and said that she was going to do it anyway. I looked at her with shock and said, "You mean to tell me you are going to deliberately disrespect your husband, when we have seen God work faithfully on so many occasions to change your husband's mind to allow you to participate? Rest assured that if God doesn't change your husband's mind about this, it will be because He is closing the door at this time for whatever reason that might be." I believed that wholeheartedly then, and I am convictional of the same principle today. I don't find in scripture where God says, "submit to your unsaved husband's authority, except when he doesn't agree with what you want to do." I will address later in this book how I suggest a wife may handle disagreements in opinions of what they should or should not do.

God does move in mysterious ways to accomplish His divine purposes and plans for our individual lives, for each family, and for individual churches and the universal church. That brings me to another critically important passage of scripture that is essential for every woman who is married to an unsaved husband to know. There are some incredibly important truths in God's Word that will give us a more complete understanding of just how to navigate this union with God's power, God's guidance, and God's blessings. Previously we observed the 1 Corinthians 7:16 passage that asked the question, *How do you know that God won't use you to bring your husband to salvation?* There is another passage that addresses how to live life with and walk in obedience to an unbelieving husband. Look with me at 1 Peter 3:1-4:

> ¹In the same way, you wives, be submissive to your own husbands so that even if any *of them* are disobedient to the word, they may be won without a word by the behavior

of their wives, ²as they observe your chaste and respectful behavior. ³Your adornment must not be *merely* external—braiding the hair, and wearing gold jewelry, or putting on dresses; ⁴but *let it be* the hidden person of the heart, with the imperishable quality of a gentle and quiet spirit, which is precious in the sight of God.

Let's start with trying to answer the question from the first phrase of verse 1: *In what way* are wives to be submissive to their own husbands? We need to go back to 1 Peter 2:18-25 to learn the correct way to live in obedience to the command of 1 Peter 3:1. This is the very key to correctly interpreting and applying the instructions in 1 Peter 3. Since it's necessary to understand 1 Peter 2:18-25, let's observe these verses before we go back to 1 Peter 3:1-4. This is another place where the man-created chapter divisions can be a hindrance to accurate interpretation and application. So let's pretend that there is no chapter division at the end of 1 Peter 2:25:

> ²:¹⁸Servants, <u>be submissive</u> to your masters with all respect, not only to those who are good and gentle, <u>but also to those who are unreasonable</u>. ¹⁹For this *finds* favor, if for the sake of conscience toward God a person bears up under sorrows when suffering unjustly. ²⁰For what credit is there if, when you sin and are harshly treated, you endure it with patience? But if when you do what is right and suffer for it you patiently endure it, this *finds* favor with God. ²¹For you have been called for this purpose, since Christ also suffered for you, <u>leaving you an example for you to follow in His steps</u>, ²²who committed no sin, nor was any deceit found in His mouth; ²³and while being reviled, He did not revile in return; while suffering, He uttered no threats, but kept entrusting *Himself* to Him who judges righteously; . . . ³:¹<u>In the same way</u>, you wives, be submissive to your own husbands so that even if any *of them* are disobedient to the word, they may be won without a word by the behavior of their wives. (1 Peter 2:18-23; 3:1)

Please bear with me as we go deeper than normal into our interpretation of these verses because it is necessary in application to know some of the verb tenses and Greek word meanings. In both 1 Peter 2:18 and 1 Peter 3:1, the English translation of "be submissive" is translated from the same Greek word *hupotasso,* and both are present tense verbs meaning an ongoing habit of behavior.

Verse 18 is addressing "servants," which was a very common condition in those times of the early church. There were many new believers who had been sold into slavery. Others were indentured servants, working off some kind of debt. In whatever case, a servant, according to this passage, would have been under the authority of his or her "master." Also, verse 18 gives no exceptions by explicitly stating, "but also to those who are unreasonable." Continue to keep in mind that in order for us to accurately interpret and apply "in the same way" (3:1), we must remember the truths given to us in these illustrations in 1 Peter 2:18-23.

The Greek word translated "unreasonable" is *skolios.* The medical condition *scoliosis of the spine* gets its name from this Greek word. Vines Expository Dictionary of Biblical Words states its meaning this way: "Is used of crooked, tyrannical or unjust masters."[17] *The Complete Word Study Dictionary: New Testament* describes this Greek word to originally mean "perverse, unjust masters." Thus, "the same way" that wives are to submit to their own husbands includes the same way a servant must be submissive to his or her "master," even if they are crooked, unjust, or a tyrannical task master. However, submission *never* includes obeying a command that would be a sin in God's revealed, inerrant Word.

We see in verses 19-20 such submission to authority "finds favor with God" (i.e., when His children patiently bear up under sorrows when treated harshly and when suffering unjustly). We now must conclude that "in the same way" includes wives who suffer unjustly and are harshly treated as they submit to the authority of an unsaved husband. Verses 21 goes on to say that we believers have been called for this purpose—to patiently endure harsh behavior against us "since Christ also suffered for [us], leaving [us] an example for [us] to follow in His steps."

So, a wife is to submit even to her unreasonable husband, not only because this finds favor with God but also because Jesus left us an example to do this very thing. In our culture and time,

---

17 *Vines Expository Dictionary of Biblical Words* (Nashville, Tennessee: Thomas Nelson Publishers, 1985).

these instructions from God's Word are often not only scoffed at but ridiculed. In my mind, living victoriously under these circumstances requires believing God's promises to be true and trusting our God's faithfulness to empower us through it for His glory and for our transformation into the image of His Son, our Savior, Jesus Christ. Only those who genuinely know their God and are committed to obedience to His instructions—whatever it takes—will always be divinely enabled by God to victoriously pass the test of "submitting to the authority of an unreasonable husband."

One of the sad truths about those who give into their own reasonings and their self-proclaimed justifiable excuses to disobey God's specific instructions, is that they will never know the incredible results of how God would have used them for His divine purposes and glory, or the invaluable, incalculable spiritual blessings they would have received. I'm sitting here writing, feeling certain that so many of you have never heard of this passage, much less have had it explained or had any idea that the Word of God said such a thing.

So let me continue. Verse 23 tells us that Jesus "kept entrusting Himself to Him who judges righteously." And that is what we all must do in all circumstances of life. The question we all need to ask ourselves and then answer from time to time is, *Do I know my God well enough to trust Him implicitly and then entrust myself to Him in each and every circumstance in my life?* We are most always *not* told what blessings are ours for obedience to a tyrannical task master, but we must know our God well enough to trust that they are worth any temporary suffering.

I repeat, I believe it to be true that no one will trust someone they don't know well and believe in. Our faith in God as our Father and that His ways are always for our highest good is absolutely essential to our obedience to Him, especially when we have no clue as to the outcome. Not only are we not told what the blessings for obedience are, but neither are we told what the consequences of our disobedience will be. The depth of our obedience to trust God in very difficult times and circumstances is a true indicator of the depth of our faith in and trust of our always faithful and good God. I have heard it said, and I heartily agree, "We do have the choice of whether or not we will obey God, but He never gives us the choice of what the consequences of being disobedient will be."

5: GOD'S INSTRUCTIONS FOR BECOMING A "RIGHTEOUS WIFE"

Look with me again at 1 Peter 2:21-23, remembering Christ left us an example to follow. We need to keep in mind these verses do give us His example while suffering unjustly. We are told that we "have been called for this purpose." For what purpose have we been called, we must ask? The answer given to us is, "since Christ suffered for [me]," I am to follow His example in suffering so that I will be seen and known as a follower of Christ.

> ²¹For you have been called for this purpose, since Christ also suffered for you, leaving you an example for you to follow in His steps, ²²who committed no sin, nor was any deceit found in His mouth; ²³and while being reviled, He did not revile in return; while suffering, He *uttered no threats*, but kept entrusting *Himself* to Him who judges righteously. (1 Peter 2:21-23)

We are trying to understand 1 Peter 3:1, which tells wives in "what way" we are to be submissive to our own husbands. Let's look separately at each of Jesus' examples that is stated in this passage of God's Word. While being treated harshly or suffering unjustly . . .

- *Do not sin.* One way most of us are tempted to sin is by taking revenge. Yet God tells us that revenge taking is God's role, not ours (or anyone else's for that matter), according to Romans 12:19: "Never take your own revenge, beloved, but leave room for the wrath *of God*, for it is written, 'Vengeance is Mine, I will repay,' says the Lord."
- *Don't be deceitful in your response,* as 1 Peter 2:1 instructs, as well as many other passages: "Therefore, putting aside all malice and all deceit and hypocrisy and envy and all slander. . . ."
- *Do not revile in return.* This word *revile* isn't a common, everyday part of our regular English vocabulary. The meaning of this Greek word *loidoreo* during the early days of Christianity is "abusive speech."
- *Utter no threats.* Perhaps this last point given to us of Jesus' example is among the most common area in which a believer is tempted. My high school *Webster's New Collegiate Dictionary* (1958—yes, I still have mine, and I use it) defines *threats* as "the expression of an intention to inflict evil or injury on another."

We are to keep entrusting ourselves to God who judges righteously.

Please understand that I am not saying nor in any way implying that following the examples of Jesus given above is easy. I am convinced that it takes the supernatural power of God's Spirit working in our lives to follow Jesus' example in suffering. But I do believe unconditionally and without hesitation that God also *always* provides us with sufficient power to walk victoriously in any and all circumstances that He allows into our lives. As we noticed in verse 23 above, by following Jesus' example we are "entrusting ourselves to God who judges righteously."

Over the years I have been taught much from God's Word about this subject. The following came to me as I was trying to better understand 1 Peter 3:1b. We have already discovered the answer to *how* we are to follow Jesus' example when suffering unjust, harsh treatment. At first, I didn't understand what it meant by, "so that even if any of them are disobedient to the word, they may be won without a word by the behavior of their wives." Look with me again at these first 2 verses in 1 Peter 3:

> ¹In the same way, you wives, be submissive to your own husbands so that even if any *of them* are disobedient to the word, they may be won without a word by the behavior of their wives, ²as they observe your chaste and respectful behavior.

There are those, and I am among them, who believe that "disobedient to the word" is a description of a husband who is not yet saved. I believe this because of the Greek verb tense used here: it is in the present tense, which indicates the action is a continual and ongoing behavior, and it is also in the indicative mood which means it is absolutely true. I use the phrase *habitual lifestyle.*

Again, I don't want to get too technical, but Greek verb tenses can be the very key that unlocks the true meaning of many passages in God's Word, thus giving us correct application. I am of the opinion that this described husband is not saved, because a genuine follower of Jesus Christ has been transformed into a new creation who cannot live in habitual sin, according to 1 John 3:9 which we looked at earlier. Living in habitual sin is a characteristic of the unsaved.

5: GOD'S INSTRUCTIONS FOR BECOMING A "RIGHTEOUS WIFE"

We are also told in 1 Peter 3:1, "so that . . . they may be won without a word by the behavior of their wives." We see by this explanation in verse 1, the *behavior* of the wife can be a primary vehicle God can use to bring her husband to salvation. As I understand this passage, it will not help (and may even be a hinderance) if you continually confront your husband with the gospel (e.g., I know of wives who have left sticky notes with Bible verses on the bathroom mirror). Knowing and following Jesus' examples given to us in 1 Peter 2 is so critically important.

First Peter 2:23-24 gave us four examples of what our behavior as wives is *not* to be and one example of what our behavior *is* to be. First Peter 3:2 tells us how our habitual lifestyle should be characterized—"chaste" and "respectful." *Respectful* is a common, everyday word we can easily understand in its implications, but how about "chaste"? The Greek word *hagnos* translated "chaste" originally meant, "free from defilements or impurities, innocent, pure, blameless."[18]

So, we have observed that the life we are to live is to be in purity and holiness as we continually entrust ourselves to God. This is especially important when dealing with an unsaved husband. Living a chaste and respectful life seems to be one of the most important parts a wife can play in living obediently to God, trusting Him for every aspect regarding her husband. In my opinion, 1 Peter 3:4 seems to be one of the least understood instructions in this section of God's Word. Look with me at this verse, and let's see if I can bring some clarity to its meaning and application:

> But *let it be* the hidden person of the heart, with the imperishable quality of a gentle and quiet spirit, which is precious in the sight of God. (1 Peter 3:4)

We are told that there is to be a heart quality that motivates, inspiring a wife to obey all the instructions mentioned above regarding just how she is to navigate life with an unsaved husband, even if he treats her harshly. Let me insert this again now. These passages in 1 Peter 2-3 that we are observing and trying to understand and obey by God's grace are diametrically opposite to the most commonly held beliefs and behaviors in today's time and culture,

---

18 *The Complete Word Study Dictionary: New Testament*

whether in Christendom or in the pagan culture of the world. Not to mention our human flesh strongly rejects even the thought of it. But that can be said of many beliefs and behaviors in the American culture we now reside.

First Peter 3:4 also stated two qualities that are "precious in the sight of God." The first quality is a "gentle spirit." I am convinced that our most common understanding of the word *gentle* (often translated "meek") is not even close to what the Greek word *praus* represents. This Greek word doesn't mean in any stretch of the imagination, "weakness." In fact, this word was used in training a wild horse to be useful—one could say of a horse that has been domesticated. The horse's strength is not removed or diminished; it is bridled. So a good, understandable definition of this word *gentle* can correctly be given as "bridled strength"—strength under control. I have used the illustration of sitting on your hands and being quiet when you know what you want to say is not chaste and respectful but also humbly saying what God is impressing you to say.

The next characteristic that is to be hidden in our hearts is a "quiet spirit." This English word *quiet* is also too often misunderstood here. This Greek word in no way means total and absolute silence. We have looked at this Greek word previously. This Greek word *hesuchios* translated "quiet" actually can also mean, "tranquility arising from within, undisturbed from without, causing no disturbance."[19] I am of the opinion that because the wife is described originally by God as a "suitable *helper*," complete silence, in most cases, is not what will best help our husbands be the best, most effective leaders of their families he can be. Wives most often have the most knowledge of every aspect of the home's behavior and needs. We have already looked at Titus 2:5 where the wife is the "manager" of her own household. Yes, she is to manage the home under her husband's oversight and direction; however, the home is the place where the wife exhibits managing authority in the home.

One last thought here. Ask the Lord to lead your unsaved husband to realize that you are his helper, his biggest cheerleader, his best friend—*not* a challenger or competitor like he may often face at his workplace.

---

19 *The Complete Word Study Dictionary: New Testament*

5: GOD'S INSTRUCTIONS FOR BECOMING A "RIGHTEOUS WIFE"

As I mentioned earlier, making the best decisions requires correct and sufficient information. When it's time for major decisions to be made that affect a man's family, the wife often will have important information worth considering in making that decision. It is true that when a husband is too arrogant, proud, and domineering to include his wife in such decisions or to think her insights are too unimportant to consider seriously, he is foolish by rejecting information that is vital to coming to the most profitable conclusions. Wives who live with husbands who believe the lie that they have the God-given job of "monarchy" can often be used by God to impact their husband's erroneous belief by their chaste and respectful behavior and their heart's attitude displaying a meek and quite spirit. I believe that is the thrust of this passage in 2 Peter 2-3.

This subject gets me to some advice that I truly believe the Lord gave me through observing two separate and seemingly unrelated events in God's Word. Many wives are absolutely not like me and believe "submission" means total silence and no information shared with her husband as major decisions are being made. And other wives are like I was and many times continue in conversations over and over again about something that brings anger and frustration to her husband. The Lord taught me after many times of failure how to best communicate my evaluations of important issues because, as I've already shared more than once, you would describe me as opinionated and strong willed. The following is what the Lord taught me, and I have shared it with much conviction many times over the years: when the wife truly believes that what her husband is seriously considering doing is not the right direction, I advise her to *consider* taking the following steps:

1. When there is no unsettling undercurrent at home, when things are mainly peaceful and mostly stress free, tell your husband in an unthreatening voice tone and demeanor what you believe is wrong with his evaluations and why.

2. If he doesn't listen (that is, he doesn't agree with your advice), and when you discern that the timing is best, go to him a second time with your applicable reasonings, which I title a "reminder."

3. If he doesn't listen then, and he doesn't agree with your advice and reasonings, go to him a third time, which I title

an "appeal." It is important that you state that you know God has given him the responsibility and accountably of his decisions, not you, and you will not mention it again—AND DON'T!

4. If he doesn't listen this time, you should not approach him again on this decision. If you do, I title that behavior as "nagging." If you want to know what God says about a "nagging wife," go to Proverbs 19:13; 21:9, 19; 25:24; and 27:15.

5. If things go badly because he didn't listen to you, do not throw this up to him. He already knows.

You ask, as well you should, *Where did I come up with three and only three times to approach a decision your husband is about to make?* I'm glad you asked. It's from two separate events in the New Testament. The first one is very familiar to most every Christian—Jesus praying to His Father in the Garden of Gethsemane on the night of His betrayal. Jesus asked the Father three times to "remove this cup from Me, yet not My will, but Yours be done," as recorded in Matthew 26:36-44. I noted that Jesus asked "three" times and then didn't ask again.

Also, the Lord reminded me of Paul's thorn in the flesh. Look quickly with me at the following passage and what the Lord told Paul regarding his prayers for God to remove this "thorn in the flesh":

> [7]Because of the surpassing greatness of the revelations, for this reason, to keep me from exalting myself, there was given me a thorn in the flesh, a messenger of Satan to torment me—to keep me from exalting myself! [8]Concerning this I implored the Lord three times that it might leave me. [9]And He has said to me, "My grace is sufficient for you, for power is perfected in weakness." Most gladly, therefore, I will rather boast about my weaknesses, so that the power of Christ may dwell in me. [10]Therefore, I am well content with weaknesses, with insults, with distresses, with persecutions, with difficulties, for Christ's sake; for when I am weak, then I am strong. (2 Corinthians 12:7-10)

5: GOD'S INSTRUCTIONS FOR BECOMING A "RIGHTEOUS WIFE"

As we can clearly observe in this 2 Corinthians passage, the Lord answered Paul's request for this "thorn" to leave him. The Lord's answer was not "yes." Paul knew why this thorn was given to him, and our Lord's implicit answer was "no." I'm sure you noted that Paul stated he had asked the Lord three times. The Lord told Paul that His grace was sufficient for Paul. And I'll add that God's grace is always sufficient to enable every believer to live victoriously through any and all trials and circumstances as well. Please don't overlook our Lord's reasons for wanting the thorn to remain: Jesus' power is perfected in a believer's weakness, and it was to keep Paul from exalting himself. In our weaknesses the power of Christ dwells in us and it manifests through us.

There have been centuries of debates about just what this "thorn" actually was. The only clue we are given is that it is was a messenger of Satan to torment Paul. Most believe it was something physical; Paul alludes to some kind of eye problem in Galatians 4:15 and perhaps also in Galatians 6:11. Allow me to take my author's privilege and share with you what my sanctified imagination has discerned as one legitimate alternative to this thorn being physical. And it is not my original thought. Several years ago, a movie called *The Apostle Paul* was in town, and my husband and I went to see it. One of the lines in the movie, during a time when Paul was supposedly dictating to Luke the book of Acts, had Paul alluding to the fact that he had experienced dreams of his past persecutions of the believers which were still occurring and tormenting him. I had never heard that before, and I thought to myself, *You know, that checks all the required boxes.* I sure did chase a rabbit here. Of course, if God had intended for us to know exactly what this thorn in Paul's flesh was, He would have told us. The major takeaway from Paul's declaration in 2 Corinthians 12:7-10 is that we each should learn not what the thorn was but be encouraged that in whatever we are encountering, "God's grace is sufficient" to empower us to go through it victoriously. Romans 8:37 says exactly that: "But in all these things we overwhelmingly conquer through Him who loved us."

Back to the subject of the 1 Peter 2–3 passages on submission. I would like to complete this particular chapter on this subject with what I believe could be of great encouragement. Even though it's against the "desires of my flesh," I have learned of the great rewards of doing life God's way and some of the consequences of following the desires of my flesh. My greatest mistakes have been made when I determined I was going to do what I thought was best, even though I knew it was against the direct wishes of my husband. Sorry to say, yes, I have been guilty of doing the very thing God has told me not to do—with great regret, I might add. Hopefully I have now learned that being right and insisting on it is not what it's all made out to be, especially when it is causing you to sin against a clear instruction of God.

Another important truth I have learned is not only does obedience to God require that I submit to my husband's God-given authority, but I must do it with chaste and respectful behavior. Also, I have learned that if I believe he is wrong, and I can't change his mind, I get in God's way by continuing to correct him. All my husband will have done is make a bad judgment decision. I was the one who sinned. God tells us that bad decisions can easily be corrected by Him, according to Romans 8:28: "And we know that God causes all things to work together for good to those who love God, to those who are called according to His purpose." However, God will discipline me because He loves me too much to leave me in sin, which harms both me and my witness.

There is another aspect here that I believe is important to add to the conversation. If (better said, *when*) we are confronted with a very difficult decision of whether we will walk in obedience or not, we might think we will be taking the easy way out and just not obey God. Be forewarned that deliberant disobedience to God's revealed instructions will never turn out to be the easy way out. It makes all the difference to know that God has placed you in this trial for a particular spiritual reason that, at the time, only God Himself knows. But there is a passage that covers every kind of trial. Look with me at Romans 5:1-5 for the great benefits of our choosing to go through trials with God's power, not doing everything possible we can do to remove ourselves from this circumstance that is so very difficult:

> [1]Therefore, having been justified by faith, we have peace with God through our Lord Jesus Christ, [2]through whom also we have obtained our introduction by faith into <u>this grace in which we stand;</u> and we exult in hope of the glory of God. [3]And not only this, but we also exult in our tribulations, knowing that tribulation brings about

5: GOD'S INSTRUCTIONS FOR BECOMING A "RIGHTEOUS WIFE"

perseverance; ⁴and perseverance, proven character; and proven character, hope; ⁵and hope does not disappoint, because the love of God has been poured out within our hearts through the Holy Spirit who was given to us. (Romans 5:1-5)

When we decide to believe the truths contained in this passage, we take on a new and life-changing opinion about our trials and tribulations that Jesus told us we will encounter in this world. Look with me again at John 16:33: "These things I have spoken to you, so that <u>in Me you may have peace</u>. In the world you have tribulation, but take courage; I have overcome the world."

Most likely there is not a single Christ-following wife who does not want her husband to be saved. On occasion, I believe that her earnest desire may not primarily lie in her deep desire that he not spend eternity in hell in torment and absent of God's presence. If the truth be known, some may simply want to have a husband that loves them just as Christ loves the church and gave His life for her, and to stop treating her as a doormat and occasionally, and perhaps even many times, treating her harshly. I am not at all saying that it is a bad desire not to have to suffer his harsh treatment. However, when a wife's primary desire and focus is that her husband be saved so he will spend eternity in heaven with God and also enjoy His presence and provision in this life, that wife's outlook, focus, and priorities seem to change significantly. All of a sudden, she will want to be a primary vehicle through whom God brings salvation to her husband. I have known some of the former and some of the latter.

It could be as much as thirty-plus years ago when the Lord put on my heart to search the scriptures to locate passages that wives could claim were applicable prayers they could pray for their husbands. Many items of prayer listed below are perhaps not yet true of your husband at this time, but you are praying in faith that it will be so at some future time. I am sharing this with you now in hopes that it will help some of you to be encouraged to pray back to God some of His truths and promises in His Word.

God loves to hear His words sent back to Him from one of His children who is seeking Him and basing her requests on His declared truth—His Word. Below, consider inserting your husband's name where designated. I have not identified the biblical addresses in the prayer itself, but they are collected and listed at the end:

"A Prayer for Your Husband"

Father, I come to You in the name of Jesus on behalf of my husband, _____. I thank You that I am bone of his bone and flesh of his flesh—that he left his father and mother, and that he finds contentment in me.

I ask You, Lord, that _____ will love me as Christ loves the church and will give himself up for me. I pray, Father, that he will abide faithful as the head of me, his wife, as Christ is head of the church . . . that he will dwell with me according to knowledge and give honor to me. I pray, Father, that _____ will not provoke our children to exasperation but will bring them up in the discipline and instruction of the Lord, and he will teach our children diligently your commandments, statues, and judgements.

Almighty God, in the name of Jesus, I ask that today, _____ will seek Your kingdom and Your righteousness first—that he will fear the Lord my God to keep Your statutes and commandments—that he will love the Lord my God with all his heart, with all his soul, and with all his might.

I pray, Father, that _____ will be skilled in all learning and wisdom, and that he will be brought before important people, and that his labor will produce profit. I ask, in the name of Jesus, that whatever he does will prosper, that he will honor the Lord from his wealth and give You the first of all his increase. I thank You, Father God, that _____ does not put his trust in riches, but will continuously trust in You who shall supply all our needs according to Your riches in glory in Christ Jesus—that he would know that the kingdom of God is not eating and drinking, but righteousness and peace and joy in the Holy Spirit.

Father, I pray in the name of Jesus, that no evil formed against _____ will prosper and that _____ will not be deceived with empty words of the sons of disobedience nor be

5: GOD'S INSTRUCTIONS FOR BECOMING A "RIGHTEOUS WIFE"

partakers with them, but that You, Almighty God, will protect him from the strange women who flatter with their words—that he will walk as a child of light . . . kind, tenderhearted, and forgiving.

Oh, Holy God, I pray that _____ will not look at things which are seen, but at the things which are not seen, for these are eternal—that he will be anxious for nothing, but with all prayer and supplication with thanksgiving will make his requests known to You—that he will trust in the Lord with all his heart and not lean on his own understanding, but in all his ways will acknowledge You and You, Oh Father, will make his paths straight.

Father, I pray that today _____ will not be drunk with wine, wherein is excess, but he will be filled with the Holy Spirit and that the fruit of the Spirit will be his character—that he will understand what the will of the Lord is for his life and work, always giving thanks for all things in the name of our Lord Jesus Christ to You, God our Father.

Now, Almighty God, in the name of Jesus, I thank You for hearing my prayer and thus giving me the desires of my heart—that _____ will have fullness of joy and will continue to be transformed into the image of Christ Jesus. To You be all glory, honor, praise, and thanksgiving.

In the precious and powerful name of Jesus I pray. Amen and Amen.[20]

---

20 Scripture references are in the King James and the New American Standard Bibles: Genesis 2:23; Deuteronomy 6:2, 5, 6; Psalms 1:3; Proverbs 2:16; 3:5, 6, 9; 5:15; 11:28; 14:23; 22:29; Isaiah 54:17; Daniel 1:17; Matthew 6:33; Romans 14:17; 2 Corinthians 4:18; Ephesians 4:32; 5:6-8, 17-23; 6:4; Philippians 4:29; 1 Timothy 6:17; 1 Peter 3:7.

CHAPTER 6

Some Miscellaneous Relevant Biblical Insights

Ladies, I want you to be aware of the fact that God does not leave you by yourself with no repercussions while you are married to a non-compliant, ungodly husband. We have observed 1 Peter 2-3 at least twice before in this book, which gives us a possible outcome of an unbelieving husband being saved through influence of his wife's chaste and respectful behavior. Also, this passage instructs the wife that her heart attitude and actions are to be found with "an imperishable" quality of a gentle (I prefer *meek* to *gentle* for the reason I have already shared) and quiet (doesn't mean in all cases absolute silence but can also mean a controlled, peaceful behavior) spirit, which is precious in the sight of God.

There are stated consequences that every husband who claims to be a Christ-follower will experience when he acts in harsh and abusive ways toward his wife. If a believing husband does not show his wife honor as a fellow heir of the grace of life, or he does not live with his wife in an understanding way, his prayers may be hindered. We have seen before that 1 Peter 3:7 clearly states this: "You husbands in the same way, live with *your wives* in an understanding way, as with someone weaker, since she is a woman; and show her honor as a fellow heir of the grace of life, <u>so that your prayers will not be hindered</u>." However, even though this may be true in someone's marriage, whether or not her husband grants her the position of honor she is biblically due, his sinful behavior does not allow for the wife to consciously decide not to follow what God instructs her to do.

Again, I clearly want to say that it must be so very, very difficult to walk in obedience in many such cases. Jesus knows that. Yet He has told us to follow His example in suffering unjustly. However, I also want us all to remember that trusting and obeying God releases His divine power in us to live victoriously in any and all circumstances—with the trial always comes God's power to endure difficult situations according to 1 Corinthians 10:13: "No temptation has overtaken you but such as is common to man; and God is faithful, who will not allow you to be tempted beyond what you are able, but with the temptation will provide the way of escape also, so that you will be able to endure it."

One of the sincere, ongoing concerns of mine over the past decades is not only a probability but is an actual, all-too-often occurrence: that men in the church are being elected to high positions of authority and leadership while I know that they are not husbands who "live with their wives in an understanding way"—they do not show their wives honor in their homes, much less cherish and love them as Christ loved the church and gave His life for it. Consequently, there are churches which have men in leadership roles who, by what God says, may be having their "prayers hindered."

So, ladies, if you are living in a marriage with a husband who fails to live in a godly way, please know and trust that our always good and faithful Lord does not leave him faultless but can work on him in ways that only our God knows. Your husband is not accountable nor responsible *to you* for his behavior, but better still, he is responsible and accountable to our Father God, and he will "reap the harvest from the seeds he has sown." What I have learned over the decades is that when a wife gets so upset with the sinful behavior of her husband that she disregards God's instructions for her, God then has to discipline her. Such behavior by the wife often interferes

6: SOME MISCELLANEOUS RELEVANT BIBLICAL INSIGHTS

with God's "corrective" work He is doing in regard to her husband. In other words, wives need to remember to stay out of God's way as He deals with a disobedient and/or an ungodly husband.

It is interesting to note that just following God's message to both husbands and wives, He gives some instructions. Look with me now at 1 Peter 3:8-15, where instructions are given not only to husbands and wives but to all followers of our Lord Jesus Christ. But I want us at this time to concentrate only on what scripture is saying to wives:

> [8]To sum up, all of you be harmonious, sympathetic, brotherly, kindhearted, and humble in spirit; [9]not returning evil for evil or insult for insult, but giving a blessing instead; for you were called for the very purpose that you might inherit a blessing. [10]For, "The one who desires life, to love and see good days, must keep his tongue from evil and his lips from speaking deceit. [11]He must turn away from evil and do good; he must seek peace and pursue it. [12]For <u>the eyes of the Lord are toward the righteous</u>, and <u>His ears attend to their prayer</u>, but the face of the Lord is against those who do evil." [13]Who is there to harm you if you prove zealous for what is good? [14]But even if you should suffer for the sake of righteousness, *you* are blessed. And do not fear their intimidation, and do not be troubled, [15]but sanctify Christ <u>as Lord</u> in your hearts, always *being* ready to make a defense to everyone who asks you to give an account for the hope that is in you, yet with gentleness and reverence. (1 Peter 3:8-15)

Pay special attention to verses 10-12. Notice in verse 12, your prayers are also in jeopardy if your behavior is not evaluated by God as righteous, and God's face is against those who do evil (practice sin). I am especially drawn to verse 10 by a statement that gets to the heart of our desires. Our Lord God is telling each of us if we desire *life,* which I believe is referring to a life that God blesses, if we desire to *love* (love as God loves), and if we desire to see good days, we must keep our verbal communication from evil and deceit. Also, verse 11 tells us that we must turn away from evil and do good; we must *seek peace and pursue it.*

This command, and it *is* a command, that I am to seek peace and pursue it, has taken on recognizable changes for me during the years of our marriage. As with most couples, my husband and I faced times when we disagreed on certain ways in which an issue was to be settled. It took me years to come to the realization that my continued conversation in trying to make him understand just what I was saying made things worse. I finally realized I was trying to justify my position, which was actually not justifiable. I have learned better how to "seek peace and pursue it," rather than just get my way. Peace is wonderful; contention is not!

Look with me at verse 15 where we are told to "sanctify Christ as Lord in your hearts." This command (yes, it is an imperative tense verb) is for us to set apart (that is what *sanctify* means) our hearts to Jesus Christ as Lord and master—owner of our lives, our time, our possessions, and our talents—and always be ready to share the hope that is within us. We each need to ask ourselves, *What is the hope that is within me?* If there has been a time in your past where you have come to understand that you are a sinner in need of a Savior, if you have sometime in the past confessed and then repented of your sins and surrendered your life to the work and Person of Jesus Christ as Lord, the gospel of Jesus Christ *is* your hope. Hope is a Person; His name is Jesus. We are to always be ready to give an account of that hope—that confident assurance you have that Christ Jesus is going to return for His bride, His church. And when He does, He will give each of us a new, glorified, eternal body and take us all to be with Him in glory forever and ever and ever and ever. Let me say again: I believe that our Father God is on the threshold of sending His Son, our Savior Jesus Christ, back for His bride! But whether or not it is this year, next year, or the next decade or beyond, we must all be ready to meet Him in obedience and anticipation. Come, Lord Jesus, come!

No, we can't save anyone. However, the gospel of Jesus Christ contains inherent power to save all who will believe, according to Acts 10:43: "Of Him [Jesus Christ] all the prophets bear witness that through His name everyone who believes in Him receives forgiveness of sins." One of the basic truths that we don't mention much is that just sharing the circumstance regarding when you got saved, without the two essential components of the gospel, is not sharing the gospel. It is true that this is your testimony, and it truly may cause a reaction in their hearts. Some of our testimonies can truly be inspiring.

6: SOME MISCELLANEOUS RELEVANT BIBLICAL INSIGHTS

However, no one ever gets saved without hearing that Jesus, the Son of God, died on the cross for their sins, and that He was raised bodily from the grave (death) for their justification (being declared by God to be righteous), according to Romans 4:25.

Let's look at salvation through the lens of Romans 10:8-11.

> ⁸But what does it say? "The word is near you, in your mouth and in your heart"—that is, the word of faith which we are preaching, ⁹that <u>if you confess with your mouth Jesus *as* Lord</u> and <u>believe in your heart that God raised Him from the dead, you will be saved</u>; ¹⁰for with the heart a person believes, resulting in righteousness, and with the mouth he confesses, resulting in salvation. ¹¹For the Scripture says, "Whoever believes in Him will not be disappointed."

Yes, you caught me. I am compelled to continually remind us that there is only one way to God—to live eternally in the presence of our Father God, our Lord Jesus Christ, and the Holy Spirit. It is stated clearly in Romans 10. The indescribable truth is also that our eternal life with our God and our Savior begins the instant we are saved. Because that is true, which was never true of us before we surrendered our lives to Christ Jesus, we now have the power within us by the Holy Spirit to live victoriously in obedience to God's instructions in His Word in whatever circumstances we are in now or will be in the future. Hallelujah, what a Savior and God we now worship and serve.

One of the most important issues we face as mothers is the watch-care over our children. The culture and time in which we live today propels our children (and grandchildren, etc.) to accept immoral behavior as right, natural, and acceptable. Many fall prey to believing these lies of Satan and are themselves participating in them. These are the circumstances which some mothers and wives face today, while they are committed to raising their children in the discipline and instruction of the Lord (Ephesians 6:4).

What if I told you there is a sure way for you to evaluate your children's spiritual condition? It is found in Ephesians 6:1-3:

> Children, obey your parents in the Lord, for this is right. Honor your father and mother (which is the first

commandment with a promise), so that it may be well with you, and that you may live long on the earth.

If any of your children are living in recognizable rebellion to your instructions, you can know for sure they are living in sin, and their rebellion is against God Himself. For children to obey and honor their own parents is not just a suggestion—God commands it. If your child(ren) is habitually not obeying your instructions, they are habitually sinning against God's clear command. No one who is habitually in rebellion against their parents is in a right relationship with God.

Since we are focused on children at this point, there is a very dangerous pitfall many parents fall into today. That is, many parents have a *friendship* relationship with their children. Some parents today seem to want to please, and in some cases appease, their child(ren) rather than train them to live godly, righteous lives, which we all agree is so very, very difficult in the culture and time we live. These children many times grow up with little or no concept of respecting those in authority, many times believing that they are free to live in any way they desire with no consequences or retributions.

Many, many decades ago, when our girls were infants, I heard Dr. James Dobson teach that disciplining one's children, which consists of training them in what is good and acceptable behavior, is actually what gives a child a sense of well-being and safety. Even though they usually balk at being required to obey the family's set of rules, these boundaries assure them of the loving care of their parents. It establishes boundaries by which they most often get comfort and security, even if just subconsciously. My husband has told me that the Lord would remind him when he faced a temptation that his parents had clearly taught him not to be involved in such behavior, which caused him to obey. However, he does admit to the fact that there were times when he "weighted the cost" and did it anyway. But also, he remembers using his parents' rules as a good excuse and an easy way out when he knew that he shouldn't participant in certain activities.

Of course, there were, are now, and will continue to be children who go beyond these boundaries, but causing them to reap the consequences of disobedience helps to prepare them for life when they are on their own and must choose for themselves whether or not

6: SOME MISCELLANEOUS RELEVANT BIBLICAL INSIGHTS

to walk in obedience to our Jehovah God of the Bible. As many have said before me, correcting mistakes when a child is small means the consequences of their mistakes are relatively small. Choosing wrong/sinful behavior as a young teen or an adult usually brings with it greater and longer-lived consequences.

Let me encourage you with this—there is a time for really sweet friendship with your children, but it comes later. But we all need to be reminded that our children don't need a compliant friend as a parent during their childhood development years. They need parents who know Proverbs 13:24: "He who withholds his rod hates his son, but he who loves him disciplines him diligently."

A little side note here: the book of Proverbs is not necessarily a book of promises. Proverbs are given to us to know that if we do what the proverb instructs, there will most likely be that stated outcome. Such is true regarding the oft-quoted Proverbs 22:6: "Train up a child in the way he should go, even when he is old, he will not depart from it." God doesn't promise us that if we raise our children in a Christian home and teach them the ways of the Lord that they will never depart from how we raised them. What God's Word is saying here is that if we do train up our children in the way they should go, it is most probable that they will continue to live godly lives. We are never able to make them get saved. As we all know and understand, that is the Lord's job and His alone. But when we raise them in the instruction and discipline of the Lord, they learn who God is, that He loves them, and how He expects them to live. These truths explained clearly to them will prepare their hearts for the conviction of the Holy Spirit for their sin and the drawing of God to Himself through the work and Person of our Lord Jesus Christ—that is, salvation.

I have mentioned previously that I have been anything but perfect in completing my roles as both wife and mother. The Lord has been gracious, merciful, and kind in His intervention to use my mistakes to cause His good works to overshadow and to re-do many things that I did wrong. Words are not capable of expressing my eternal thanksgiving and gratitude to our Lord God.

I would like to refer back to Proverbs 22:6 and share two observations I now understand from this passage. First, it's in the understanding of the phrase "in the way he should go." We have carefully observed the fact that our responsibilities include the training of our children in God's righteous ways through Christ Jesus—a given from God's Word. However, I am told that this particular phrase in Proverbs has another connotation. It refers primarily to our examination of each individual child to determine the "bent" of our children's personality, natural talents, strengths, and interests. In other words, for instance, if your child shows an interest and ability in music, you should begin to make an effort (if possible) to provide opportunities for this child to be involved in musical activities until a place of aptitude and success is determined. Likewise, if there is perceived interest in and propensity toward athletic activities, you can move that child towards sports until it is observed he or she has found something they can enjoy and be successful in. If there is an observable bent toward things of the mind such as reading, searching out details of special subjects, we should research things for them to do that would increase and satisfy their curiosity in learning.

Helping your children locate and participate successfully in the things that use their God-given natural abilities should be a major part of training them "in the way they should go." Because of God's all-knowing and sovereign power, you can be assured that when your children come to faith in Christ, the spiritual gifts that they receive then will complement the natural abilities God infused into their DNA at conception. There are some parents who fall into the trap of trying to make a child do what they did (in sports, business, etc.) or what they wish they could have done. Obviously, this goal takes the focus off of the "way that their child should go." Helping your children discover their God-created bent for the future God has ordained is one of the most God-honoring duties you can ever do for your children and for God's kingdom.

The second observation I have from Proverbs 22:6 is that there is an area of child raising, I must confess, in which I was a total failure. I was not wise enough to recognize that you do not necessarily raise/train/discipline each child the same way. Our first child was one who had the tendency to not like obeying our rules. She jokingly (and in her mind, maybe not so jokingly) has said that she doesn't expect to live long on the earth because she was one who was inclined to disobey her parents, using Ephesians 6:1-3 as her basis. As a footnote, in our God's magnificent and lavish grace and mercy, our daughter has grown up to be one of the most godly women I have ever had the privilege of knowing. Thank You, Jesus. You indeed take my lemons and make wonderful lemonade. I have always been comforted and grateful for the truth given to us in Joel 2:25a which states, "Then I will make up to you for the years that the swarming locust has eaten."

Our second child, also a girl, was a very compliant child. I did not know that what had helped us keep our first daughter somewhat under control was sometimes not needed and too harsh for our second. I didn't recognize that until she was married and away from home. Again, in our God's great mercy and grace, she too is one of the most godly women I have ever had the privilege of knowing. First John 1:9 makes all believers this promise: "If we confess our sins, He is faithful and righteous to forgive us our sins and to cleanse us from all unrighteousness." Our God continues to accomplish His promises of Romans 8:28 regarding all my many failures. Again, thank You, Jesus.

Again, let me say, we all need to be well aware and reminded that it is only God who can change hearts and lives. It is only God who can save. As wives and mothers, when we know God's revealed principles and use them in raising our children, He can and does prepare their hearts and minds to be more receptive to God's righteous behavior and become less likely to be involved in things that are destructive and dangerous to their health and well-being of both body and soul.

The next point I'd like to address with you is that of consistency of discipline. Somewhere in my early years, I learned to count to three when asking a child to either do what I asked them to do or to stop doing what they were doing or else they would reap the consequences. I mentioned earlier that the Lord brought to me in my very difficult growing-up years two sets of neighbors who loved me and spent much time with me, bringing my heart some sense of joy and safety. I can even see in my mind's eye where I was in their house when I heard this neighbor say, "I knew my mother always did what she said she intentioned to do. If she had ever said she was going to kill me if I did *so-in-so*, I honestly believed then she actually would have." Maybe she was somewhat exaggerating.

That conversation became a goal of mine for my girls. I wanted them to look forward to a promise becoming reality and to believe that if I gave a consequence for misbehavior, it was sure to come if they misbehaved. So, I learned to count, but when "three" came, the consequence became reality. There were times I had wished I hadn't started the count, however. I witness all the time people using the "one, two, three" count method. But I rarely see the parent making good on the consequences of getting to "three." All these children learn is that they, not the parent, determine if and when they are going to obey.

Now a *not so critically important* tip. We tried to major on the major issues and not major on the minor ones. Our younger daughter turned out to be our most style-conscious daughter, but that is not how she began. From kindergarten through the second and probably the third grade, I told each of her teachers to pay no attention to how she was dressed. Being color and pattern coordinated was not my priority—she did go to school with some really funny combinations. So, to us, modesty was a sword to fall on. I would send Lee with the girls to choose their bathing suits each year. Yep! It worked really well. They also were told that they could wear nothing with any gang related or Satanic implied words or symbols.

My best advice is to carefully choose the hills you are willing to die on. It seems to be very profitable to try to rearrange your mindset to say "yes" as often as possible, while always keeping the welfare of your children the top priority, but to be very flexible regarding your own preferences of styles, haircuts, etc.

There seems to be a pattern that Christian parents are so often prone to follow. That is, doing whatever they can do to keep their disobedient children from experiencing the just consequences of their bad choices. Let me illustrate what I mean by sharing personally what I know to be true. I had an uncle by marriage who was a widower and had married my aunt who was also widowed. They enjoyed some wonderful times in their advanced ages. Both loved, worshipped, and served the Lord faithfully. My new uncle had an adult son who habitually abused drugs and alcohol. And because of his chosen lifestyle, he was always in need of money for bail, for food, for transportation, etc. By the time this precious widower and my aunt married, he had given his wayward son all of his savings. While my aunt was still living, she would intercept her husband's son from reaching his dad because she knew he would send him whatever money he was in need of. His intent was compassion, but it never brought about his son's suffering to the point of repentance.

When parents continuously interfere and prevent their children from experiencing the consequences of their bad/ungodly behavior, I am strongly of the opinion that we contribute to the continuation of

6: SOME MISCELLANEOUS RELEVANT BIBLICAL INSIGHTS

their sinful and destructive behavior. But more than that, especially because we don't want our children to suffer, we can literally interfere with God's work to get them to a place of desperation so that they have no alternative but to recognize that becoming a Christ follower is a thousand times better than "eating the pigs' food in a hog pen." (Of course, my illustration is of what is commonly known as "The Parable of the Prodigal/Lost Son" recorded in Luke 15:11ff.)

However, it is always so very important that parents continue to diligently try to maintain a relationship with any wayward children. There is no influence without a relationship—a wise man once told me. I have personal experience here as well. This year we had the indescribable joy of a rebellious family member being saved. I am convinced it is partially based on this principle. She knew she was loved and cherished during these very difficult years because the relationship continued, but she also knew that her lifestyle was ungodly and destructive according to God's Word and would not be financially supported.

Often I hear parents admit that they continue to bail their children out of the difficult circumstances caused by their children's own decisions. On occasion I hear of some wise parents who believe that their children should experience the results of their own bad choices or behaviors to teach them responsibility and accountability. The same would be true for both *good* decisions or behaviors. Again, I am of the opinion that those of us who are genuine followers of Jesus Christ may be the worst offenders because many of us know by experience what difficult circumstances can be caused by bad choices and behaviors—we just want to spare them pain. Maybe that is a compassionate thought and intention, but it results many times in hindering and sometimes even damaging their road to correction.

Let me touch on a subject that is so very difficult for some who are reading this book. Perhaps you have desperately desired to have children but as yet have not been successful. I personally know of years when Lee and I tried and tried, but I didn't conceive. By God's grace, our first daughter was born just before we celebrated our fifth wedding anniversary. My monthly disappointments didn't last very long compared to some of you who are reading this book. Scripture is clear to tell us that life and death are in God's power alone. God is the only one who can create life, and He is the one who determines the day that physical death occurs, according to Deuteronomy 32:39:

GOD'S PORTRAIT OF A "RIGHTEOUS WOMAN"

"See now that I, I am He, and there is no god besides Me; It is I who put to death and give life. I have wounded and it is I who heal, and there is no one who can deliver from My hand."

It is a fact that our Lord God hears every prayer of the righteous, according to Proverbs 15:29: "The Lord is far from the wicked, but He hears the prayer of the righteous." What we humans have trouble with at times are some of His answers. Our God demonstrated His unconditional, sacrificial love toward us by sacrificing the life of His own Son in order to pay our own personal sin debt, which is death. So the death Christ died was our substitutional death in order that we might have eternal life through Him. We are told nothing can separate us from God's love, according to Romans 8:38-39: "For I am convinced that neither death, nor life, nor angels, nor principalities, nor things present, nor things to come, nor powers, nor height, nor depth, nor any other created thing, will be able to separate us from the love of God, which is in Christ Jesus our Lord." We can be absolutely certain that since God did not spare His own Son, He will not withhold any good thing from us.

Carefully observe with me Romans 8:32 which states, "He who did not spare His own Son, but delivered Him over for us all, how will He not also with Him <u>freely give us all things?</u>" This is God's declaration of love to all of us who are Christ followers—it is totally true and completely reliable. We can be absolutely confident that God never withholds *anything* from us that we need to live out the good works that were prepared beforehand for us to walk in, according to Ephesians 2:10: "For we are His workmanship, created in Christ Jesus for good works, which God prepared beforehand so that we would walk in them."

It is of great importance that all of us who are Christ followers understand, believe, and trust that God hears and answers *every one* of our prayers. Again, because the answer is not always what we wanted it to be, some are inclined to believe God has never heard or that He is unwilling to answer. Actually, that is true for the non-believer. God does not hear the prayers of a sinner, but He does hear the prayers of those who do His will, according to John 9:31: "We know that God does not hear sinners; but if anyone is God-fearing and does His will, He hears him."

God answers His children in three categories: (1) "yes," in which He usually answers quickly; (2) "not yet," where His answer is "yes, but not now;" (3) and also "no, because I have better plans for you." Even if the answer is "no" to your cry for children, and you are a genuine born-again child of God, He tells us through His Word that it is only because He has better plans for you and your husband that do not at this time include your own birthing of children. Believe it! Trust it! God is always performing and developing your circumstances for your good and His glory, according to Romans 8:28. God loves you too deeply to withhold your ability to bear children, unless His predetermined plans for you at this time require that you are not able to personally bear a child.

The next thing I would like to share with you is something that you may or may not be able to accomplish. That is, having a consistent agreement with your husband regarding the discipline to be undertaken for your children's rule breaking. Having developed a unified front with your husband makes it very hard for your children to manipulate you and bring division between the two of you. Manipulation of parents is sometimes a perfected art form by children. I was very fortunate that our girls knew they could not play one parent against the other. However, I am afraid that many children in today's culture and time are masters of doing just that. My advice to those of you who do not have a husband who agrees with you regarding the raising and discipline of your children, is to do the best you can by God's grace, continually asking for His wisdom and discernment. Then by faith, leave the rest to our faithful and good God to "always be about working all things out for good to those who love God and are called according to His purpose" (Romans 8:28).

In chapter two, I took you through what God declares about His creation of the heavens and the earth. I didn't comment much on the fact that God created two specifically different humans—one was absolutely male; the other was absolutely female. In the time in which we live, some are so deceived that they will not allow their eyes to determine the gender/sex of their child at the time of their physical birth. However, the DNA of a person will always accurately reveal the gender/sex given them by God, even though many today believe and accept that a person can determine what gender they are by their own doing. The truth is that drugs and surgery today can mutilate and change sexual physical configuration, but no one can change a person's DNA, which is God's imprint as to how He

Himself created, formed, and determined that person's gender/sex and multiplied millions of other characteristics.

There is no human procreation without a male sperm penetrating a female egg (ovum). I don't want to get too deep into science, because I don't know enough to even do so. But from what I have learned, the medical treatment for pre-puberty gender/sex change (which seems to be more common than one could ever have imagined) is done by giving girls testosterone and boys female hormones that will halt their puberty and will make them sterile for life.

I am convinced that this evil and destructive transgender movement and the acceptance of it as a legitimate choice is one of the most dangerous, if not the most dangerous and destructive issue facing our children and youth today. As I mentioned in an earlier chapter, when God created the institution of marriage between one male and one female, He also created the family unit to be the moral foundation for all civilizations. God told Adam and Eve to "be fruitful and multiply and fill the earth." Those who have tried to become another gender and go through the physical mutilation and hormone therapy required render themselves incapable of participating in one of God's original commands. As you are probably well aware, no matter how a person might mutilate their bodies to try to become physically the opposite sex of their birth, their DNA will always continue to read the "male" or "female" of their physical birth.

There have been a number of times when a mother has come to me in tears just having learned her child is now professing to be a homosexual. I have talked with two women who have homosexual professing daughters. God makes it clear in His Word that any type of homosexuality is an abomination to Him, according to Leviticus 18:22: "You shall not lie with a male as one lies with a female; it is an <u>abomination</u>." In fact, God's Word declares that someone who has a lifestyle characterized by homosexuality has not as yet been saved according to Revelation 21:8 and 1 Corinthians 6:9-10:

> But for the cowardly and unbelieving and <u>abominable</u> and murderers and immoral persons and sorcerers and idolaters and all liars, their part *will be* in the lake that burns with fire and brimstone, which is the second death. (Revelation 21:8)

6: SOME MISCELLANEOUS RELEVANT BIBLICAL INSIGHTS

⁹Or do you not know that the unrighteous will not inherit the kingdom of God? Do not be deceived; neither fornicators, nor idolaters, nor adulterers, nor effeminate, nor <u>homosexuals</u>, ¹⁰nor thieves, nor *the* covetous, nor drunkards, nor revilers, nor swindlers, will inherit the kingdom of God. (1 Corinthians 6:9-10)

This whole LGBTQ movement is straight from the devil's kingdom of darkness. And he knows well how to best cultivate, manipulate, and deceive our vulnerable youth. I do so pray each of you will be encouraged to strictly guard your children's access to all the different forms of social media. It has also been revealed publicly that some of our local school boards have covertly inserted teaching materials that inform and influence their students, your children, toward homosexual, transgender, and other ungodly, destructive behavior. So now it has become even more essential that parents not only carefully monitor their child's access through social media, etc., but also the things they are secretly being taught in school. Hopefully, you most probably well know, "You are from God, little children, and have overcome them; because greater is He who is in you than he who is in the world," according to 1 John 4:4.

This is the best advice I can give to any Christian parent who has received the news that their child has chosen to adopt this ungodly lifestyle. I would make sure that your child has heard the full gospel of Jesus clearly and knows what God's Word says about this chosen lifestyle. To be sure that they understand the eternal consequences, I highly recommend that you show them in your Bible Revelations 21:8 and 1 Corinthians 6:9-10. Literally read to them from your Bible to make certain that they understand the eternal consequences that are revealed in God's Word, which is true whether or not they believe it. As I have mentioned several times, our words do not carry with them any divine power to change anyone's heart or life, but God's Word does!

If your children have seen clearly what God says, and they tell you they don't care, then you can know you have done what you needed to do. They now know that you are aware they are sinning against a Holy God, and they are in dire danger of someday receiving God's judgment—an eternity away from God's presence in hell, which is also referred to as "the lake of fire." After this, my best advice is to not shun nor shame them. They now know exactly what you know to be true about their chosen lifestyle (because God said so). Your continued expression of a mother's unconditional love will hopefully be recognized by them as God's love for them as well.

The mothers I recently mentioned saw to it that their girls were raised in the church and heard the gospel taught and preached many times since childhood. Do not think that you can change their lifestyle through shame and condemnation. Homosexuality is *not* their real problem. Their problem is being a sinner in need of a Savior, and there is only One who can save anyone out of the slave market of sin. His name is Jesus Christ, the Son of God. The Bible teaches that homosexuality is just one kind of immorality.

There is something else that I would like to point out regarding this subject. Most of you would not allow your daughter (or son) to bring home a partner of the opposite sex and allow them to share the same bedroom in your house. Of course, the same should be true if the partner is of the same sex. Love, communicate, and fellowship with your son or daughter who has chosen this lifestyle. And keep on praying! We never know when our good and faithful God will move in miraculous ways in the lives of our children. What we do know is that His timing is always perfect and rarely agrees with ours.

We all need to be alert to the fact that our children have likely been brainwashed by their schools, their friends, etc.—by the evil culture in which they live today. Be prepared for the possibility of their trying to convince you that homosexuality is a viable personal choice for anyone or that they have been made by God to be a homosexual (or any other lifestyle that is under the immoral umbrella of sin). Understand that they do believe "these lies which are of Satan himself." We are warned by John 8:44b: "He [the devil] was a murderer from the beginning, and does not stand in the truth because there is no truth in him. Whenever he speaks a lie, he speaks from his own *nature*, for he is a liar and the father of lies."

It needs to be repeated what I have been told and I now believe to be true, that transgenderism is our children's greatest evil temptation in our current culture. I have repeated several times that God says, "You shall know the truth and the truth will set you free." God is the only one Who has the power to set anyone free from the bondage of sin. Primarily, God grants freedom from the stronghold/

6: SOME MISCELLANEOUS RELEVANT BIBLICAL INSIGHTS

slavery to sin through His truth—that is, His Word that is believed and obeyed.

I taught middle schoolers and high schoolers before God called me to disciple adults. It seems to be a continuing fact that one of the hardest things for these young people to believe is found in 1 Corinthians 15:33: "Do not be deceived: 'Bad company corrupts good morals.'" My advice for you mothers is to declare a non-negotiable! Tell your children they can pick their friends, but you will always have the veto power—based on this passage. The oversight of our children's friends is one of the hardest, most important aspects of parenting teenagers today. Peer pressure, schools, and social media are relentless invaders on God's truth. I heard a pastor recently give an invaluable instruction, and I totally agree, that parents must be the primary disciplers of God's truth for their children. Parents today cannot afford to relinquish this most important job to anyone else, including your local church or any organization. Our churches should play an important part in their spiritual training, but I want to reinforce your belief that your oversight and primary role of discipleship regarding your children is given to you as parents by God Himself.

The following is one of the things I did. You may choose to or not. I gathered my two teenage girls on one of our beds and looked them square in the eye and said (as best as I can remember exactly), "I know that each one of us, including myself, is capable of sinning sexually. Our flesh is just too weak at times to overcome the temptation." I told them how I keep from that temptation is "to never put myself in a place of temptation." Perhaps your children will heed your advice, but if they don't, you know you have told them the truth, according to Matthew 26:41: "Keep watching and praying that you may not enter into temptation; the spirit is willing, but the flesh is weak." Also observe with me again the truth as recorded in Galatians 5:16-17: "But I say, walk by the Spirit, and you will not carry out the desire of the flesh. For the flesh sets its desire against the Spirit, and the Spirit against the flesh; for these are in opposition to one another, so that you may not do the things that you please."

Over the years, many have asked me, *How can you be sure you are walking by the Spirit and not the desires of your flesh?* As I think you would agree—that is a very good question. The following is the way I understand this principle of walking/living by the Spirit's control and not giving into what my flesh desires. Of great importance, it's to know/believe that you have the Holy Spirit permanently dwelling within you. This is true for every Christian, according to Romans 8:9: "However, you are not in the flesh but in the Spirit, if indeed the Spirit of God dwells in you. But if anyone does not have the Spirit of Christ, he does not belong to Him." One of the major job assignments of the Holy Spirit is to guide believers into all truth, according to John 16:13a: "But when He, the Spirit of truth, comes, He will guide you into all the truth."

Scripture tells us that it is the Holy Spirit's job to guide a believer into all truth. Nothing can stop Him from doing the job Jesus has sent Him to do *but me . . . but you*. God's Word commands us not to quench the Holy Spirit in 1 Thessalonians 5:19. Scripture also commands us not to grieve the Holy Spirit in Ephesians 4:30. So, what do I do that grieves the Holy Spirit? Glad you asked. One grieves the Holy Spirit by doing/behaving in ways scripture has stated and He has guided that you are *not* to do. Also, you ask, how does one quench the Holy Spirit? Again, glad you asked. A believer quenches the Holy Spirit by refusing to do what He is guiding you to do. I am of the belief that if I walk closely to the Lord, and as best as I am able to listen to the Holy Spirit's prompting me, His power is released in me to control my flesh's temptations and trials.

Frequently I pray that I will hear the Spirit's still small voice behind me saying, *This is the way; walk in it*, according to Isaiah 30:21: "Your ears will hear a word behind you, 'This is the way, walk in it,' whenever you turn to the right or to the left." It is not a principle of trying to convince the Holy Spirit to guide you, to reveal His truth, to intercede for you, etc. It is to be understood that the Holy Spirit will do His job unless I grieve Him or I quench Him. So it is not my job to persuade Him to do His job; it is my job to *not* prohibit Him from doing His job in and through me. I am commanded to continually be filled by the Holy Spirt, according to Ephesians 5:18: "And do not get drunk with wine, for that is dissipation, but be filled with the Spirit." This Greek word *pleroo* is a present tense command that is passive. This Greek verb tense reveals it is not me who does the filling of the Spirit. I am commanded to continually allow the Holy Spirit Himself to fill/control me. A great prayer to pray often is, *Lord, I am totally surrendered to You today, and I am asking You to continually fill me with Your Holy Spirit and power.* The best and surest

6: SOME MISCELLANEOUS RELEVANT BIBLICAL INSIGHTS

way to accomplish this is not to grieve Him (that is, I must *not* do what I know I should not do). Also, I must not quench Him (that is, I must do what I know God by His Spirit tells me to do). Easy? Not at all, but it is not only possible but probable as you learn to listen to His "still small voice." The rewards are eternal. I promise you that the Holy Spirit's "still small voice" becomes louder and more easily recognizable as you obey this command in Ephesians 5:18.

God will train your ears to recognize the voice of the Holy Spirit as He does His work in you as you trust and obey Him. Aren't you grateful for God sending the Holy Spirit on the Day of Pentecost, fifty days after Jesus had been bodily raised from the grave, to permanently indwell and empower each and every believer? Again, hallelujah, what a Savior!

Some people find it helpful and enjoy using other materials taken from God's Word to prompt them about God's promises and then pray them back to Him. Others do not. The following is a scriptural prayer for your children. I believe that all can profit from being reminded of God's promises through praying scripture back to Him. This prayer covers many issues. As the Lord prompts your heart to pray, consider choosing the area that most relates to your circumstances with your child(ren).

"A Scriptural Prayer for Your Children"

Father, in the name of Jesus, I come before You this day on behalf of my child, _____. I pray, and as I pray, I believe that _____ will incline their hearts toward You and in all their ways will acknowledge You and You will direct their paths. That they will not submit or consent to any evil thing or be occupied in any deed of wickedness with boys or girls, men or women that work iniquity. I pray that they will not partake of the unbelievers' ways or lifestyles. I ask You, Father, that You will keep _____ from any trap which has been laid for them by the snares of evildoers. I pray that these wicked people will fall together into their own nets and that my child shall pass over them and escape from wickedness.

I pray that _____ will not be deceived or misled! I pray that they will not have evil companionships or communion or associations with corrupt and depraved people. I pray that

GOD'S PORTRAIT OF A "RIGHTEOUS WOMAN"

_____ will have good manners and good morals, and that they will be of good character. I ask that they will always awaken from any drunken stupor, addiction to drugs, or sexual deviations, and they will return to a sober sense and their right mind. I pray that _____ will depart from all known sin and choose to seek Your kingdom and Your righteousness first. I pray that _____ will not love or cherish the world or the things in this world. I ask that the lusts of their flesh and the cravings for sensual gratification and the lust of their mind's eye and the greedy longings of their hearts be banished from them in the name of Jesus.

I ask that _____ will be victorious over the wicked one, the devil, and that _____ will be strong and courageous. I pray that Your Word will always dwell richly in _____'s heart. I ask that _____ will keep in their heart what they first heard about Jesus, will grow in wisdom and the knowledge of You, will enjoy perfect confidence and boldness in You, and will not have to shrink back from Jesus at His coming!

Father, I ask that _____ will be and remain in communion and obedience to You; that they will not deliberately nor knowingly habitually commit or practice sin. I pray that no one will be able to deceive _____ and lead them astray, for I ask that they will practice righteousness! I pray that _____ will conform their life to Your divine will, in purpose, thought, and deed; that they will live a consistently conscientious life and be righteous, even as Jesus is righteous.

Father, Your Word says, "The Son of God appeared for this purpose, that He might destroy the works of the devil." So right now, I ask in Jesus' name that You thwart Satan—his principalities; his powers; his master spirits who rule the darkness; his spiritual wickedness in heavenly places—and squelch/destroy any assignments against _____ this day in the name of Jesus. Lord, I ask You to sever his relationship in the spirit world and in this natural world with _____! Please make _____ off limits to him and his kingdom of darkness. I proclaim that Satan has no authority in my child's

6: SOME MISCELLANEOUS RELEVANT BIBLICAL INSIGHTS

life, for I am a member of Your family, seated with Christ Jesus at the right hand of the You, Majesty on High.

Now, Father, I pray for _____'s salvation. According to Your Word, because of my relationship with You through faith in Jesus, _____ is sanctified to You (set apart, cleansed). I'm so grateful. I know that doesn't mean _____ is saved by my faith but that they are the recipient of Your favor, blessings, and protection. I ask and believe that the Holy Spirit will convict _____ of sin, righteousness, and judgment, and reveal to _____ that Jesus is also able to save them from the penalty of their own sin debt. That they will surrender their life to the fact that Jesus is God and that You raised Him from the dead as proof that His spotless blood satisfied/paid in full their sin debt that was owed to You.

Therefore, Father, I ask and believe by faith that _____ will continually be filled with the knowledge of Your will in all spiritual wisdom and understanding. That You will strengthen them with all power according to Your glorious might for the attaining of all steadfastness and patience, joyously giving thanks to You, Father, who has qualified us to share in the inheritance of the saints in light.

Father, I ask that _____ will become a disciple, taught by You and obedient to Your will, and that great shall be their peace and undisturbed composure. Because I have believed You have heard my prayers, I thank You for hearing me and thus will give me the desires of my heart: that _____ will walk in obedience to Your perfect will for their life and have fullness of joy.

It is in the matchless, all-powerful name of Jesus that I pray. Amen and Amen.[21]

---

21 Scripture references: Psalm 141:4, 9, 10; 1 Corinthians 7:14; 15:33-34; Colossians 1:11-12; 1 John 2:3, 4, 15; 3:6-9; Isaiah 54:13.

CHAPTER 7

What "Works" When It Isn't Working

(PART 1)

Our God has compelled me to address a subject that is so very painful for those who have been wounded by divorce. As I started writing this book, I titled it, "First Things First." In chapter two, I covered the God-established institution of marriage. Again, especially concerning such a long-term heartache subject for so many, I want to basically go to God's Word and try to guide you to a deeper understanding, interpretation, and application of the basics of what God intended when He "breathed" these recorded words through men He chose to be the vessels through whom He would speak. As I have mentioned on several occasions, John 8:32 promises, "and you will know the truth, and the truth will make you free."

Most of us are aware that there are varied and vastly different opinions regarding the subject of divorce and remarriage among Christians who are devoted followers of Jesus Christ as Lord and also among established preachers and teachers of God's Word. We go to the same passages and we interpret them differently, which often causes uncertainty, heated debates, and even division about exactly what God's instructions are on this critically important subject. Again, I want to clearly state that I have not been immune from having to give counsel and loving care to a family member who faced this very issue, namely a sister. I want to also admit that my understanding in some cases is not the majority opinion. I will give my biblically researched opinion, along with the "majority opinion." As best I know how, I will give you biblical support for why I believe what I believe. I earnestly ask you to read this chapter completely—to get the precise revelation in God's Word clearly seen and to know its location.

There is a statement I have heard spoken by many that I want to discuss. Many say something similar to, "That circumstance *[and they vary]* is biblical grounds for divorce." That statement spoken to or by a Christian truly needs to be researched and determined by chapter and verse whether or not God clearly states that He is giving permission for a believer to initiate divorce proceedings. It is my practice to use a specific process to investigate such controversial statements—a process that I have used for my own personal study of God's Word since 1977. This study method is called *inductive* by many and is based on observation, interpretation, and application on the basic principle that context rules all interpretation. Yes, this process may sound very familiar to many of you but especially to those who are acquainted with Precept Ministries. I have been blessed to have been associated with this ministry and have used their Bible study materials for over forty years, for which I will be eternally grateful.

We will, in this chapter and the next, be observing every passage in the New Testament that addresses the subject of divorce and the subject of remarriage. There is relatively much for us to study, consider, and reason. If you have gotten this far in the book, my request for you is to try to consider each passage in its context with the goal of understanding exactly what God is saying and not be influenced by what you have been taught previously.

In writing this book, specifically this chapter and the next, I have prayed often that the order of my presentation of specific passages of God's Word would be logical and easy to follow. You will see some passages of scripture that we have previously covered; I believe that looking at them again and evaluating and reasoning

7: WHAT "WORKS" WHEN IT ISN'T WORKING

them all together will help us be reminded of or introduced to what God's Word says regarding marriage.

As is my habit when I am trying to better understand a subject, I first look in my Greek or Hebrew dictionary to discover what pertinent words meant in their original language and how it was used in the Old Testament (Hebrew, for the most part) or the New Testament (Greek). God's Word speaks of marriage many times in the Old Testament. As always, context determines the meaning of any word used in God's Word. For instance, what is true about some of the Hebrew words translated "marriage" (as is true of many Hebrew words) is that they are filled with varying meanings beyond the marriage covenant. For instance, one Hebrew word baal is often translated "marriage" but also is used to describe a quality, attribute, or characteristic like anger or refers to a Canaanite deity or a generic term for lord.

Since the Hebrew words translated "marriage" have multiple usages and meanings, they were not helpful for me to determine a concise definition through one specific Hebrew word. So, in order for me to create a biblical definition for marriage, I am going to use the accepted Hebrew meaning of "covenant," and it's mentioned in Malachi 2:14: "Yet you say, 'For what reason?' Because the Lord has been a witness between you and the wife of your youth, against whom you have dealt treacherously, though she is your companion and your wife by covenant." The definition I have landed on for marriage is, "the conscious, intentional choice made by one male and one female to enter into a lifelong, binding covenant agreement exclusively with one another as husband and wife until death separates them."

As I clearly mentioned in chapter two, God Himself established the institution of marriage on the sixth day of Creation. This marriage covenant from the beginning was God's idea in creation, and He purposed that marriage is to be the foundational unit of all civilization.

Let me take a sidebar here to again explain why I will not be going to the Old Testament for instructions regarding the subject of marriage, divorce, and remarriage. Most of you who are reading this book probably agree that both the Old Testament and the New Testament are equally God's revelation. I am unapologetically of the opinion that God's Word makes it clear that the laws of the Old Testament have been fulfilled in the Lord Christ Jesus and are no longer applicable for giving new covenant believers laws and instructions on how we are to live under the new covenant of grace through faith. The Old Testament is incalculably valuable for us to study and believe. It gives us incredibly important and necessary information for us to know who our Jehovah God is—His character and His ways. In addition to that fact, the Old Testament contains life-changing truths we must know and believe about how God relates to His creation, especially to those whom He has created in His own image—the human race.

However, Christians are not instructed by God to go to the Old Testament to look for laws and commands regarding how to live righteously in the new covenant of grace, inaugurated by Jesus' blood sacrifice and His supernatural bodily resurrection from the dead and ascension into heaven. As I explained in chapter one, Christ followers are not under the Laws of Moses and the instructions of the prophets as recorded in the Old Testament. However, I wanted to repeat this issue as I take you only to the New Testament passages to examine what "the laws of Christ" inform, instruct, and guide us regarding marriage, divorce, and remarriage.

Below are scripture passages that clearly state that there is great value in the Old Testament laws for believers to be aware of and understand. Pay close attention to the following Romans 7 passage as it explains what one of the primary purposes the Old Testament law accomplishes today. The Old Testament law reveals *sin*. As this verse will tell us, God Himself reveals what behavior, even the thoughts that one might dwell upon, He has determined to be unholy and unrighteous—*sin*. Just to remind us again, since God has created all things and has sovereign rule over all things, He is the only one who has the right and authority to determine what is *sin*. Read Romans 7:7:

> What shall we say then? Is the Law sin? May it never be! On the contrary, <u>I would not have come to know sin except through the Law</u>, for I would not have known about coveting if the Law had not said, "You shall not covet."

The following passages in Romans 3:19-20 and Galatians 3:19-25 give us insight and reasoning why the Law was given even though it never had the power to forgive sin.

7: WHAT "WORKS" WHEN IT ISN'T WORKING

> [19]Now we know that whatever the Law says, it speaks to those who are under the Law, so that every mouth may be closed and all the world may become accountable to God; [20]because by the works of the Law no flesh will be justified in His sight; for through the Law *comes* the knowledge of sin. (Romans 3:19-20)

> [19]Why the Law then? It was added because of transgressions, having been ordained through angels by the agency of a mediator, until the seed [Jesus] would come to whom the promise had been made. [20]Now a mediator is not for one *party only*; whereas God is *only* one. [21]Is the Law then contrary to the promises of God? May it never be! For if a law had been given which was able to impart life, then righteousness would indeed have been based on law. [22]But the Scripture has shut up everyone under sin, so that the promise by faith in Jesus Christ might be given to those who believe. [23]But before faith came, we were kept in custody under the law, <u>being shut up to the faith which was later to be revealed.</u> [24]Therefore <u>the Law has become our tutor</u> *to lead us* <u>to Christ</u>, so that we may be justified by faith. [25]But now that faith has come, <u>we are no longer under a tutor</u>. (Galatians 3:19-25)

Galatians 3:23 gives the termination date for obeying the Law of Moses: until Christ Jesus (the seed) would come. It also clearly states an additional work of the Old Testament law now in the age of the new covenant of grace. It is a "tutor" intended to bring a person to Christ. It's the Law that reveals to every person that they are sinners in desperate need of a Savior and leads them to the only one who is able to forgive them of their sins—the Person, Christ Jesus. We who have been saved by faith in Christ Jesus are no longer under the Law, the tutor. The Law has already accomplished its work as a tutor on those who have put their faith and trust in Jesus. Hallelujah, what a Savior!

I have added these passages to encourage you and me that Christ Jesus has fulfilled the laws of the Old Testament. Man cannot keep them. They bring condemnation as they are broken. *But God!* The incredible truth of the gospel is that Jesus Christ gave us the gift of the Holy Spirit to permanently indwell every Christian, not only to guide and guard us but also to enable every believer to walk obediently in the laws of Christ and not the Law of Moses.

It is so very needful, in my opinion, that when we are trying to understand how to endure extremely difficult circumstances, that we know where to look in God's Word for directions on how we are to walk victoriously in and through them.

I personally know of people who have given and continue to give advice on how to live through circumstances today as a Christian. But on occasion, that advice came from the Old Testament law and turned out to be not only not helpful but in some cases harmful.

Let me repeat a passage I earlier mentioned because its truth is the foundation of living a life that is pleasing to the Lord—but it also gives us hope in how we can be confident in knowing how to live righteously in Christ Jesus. You guessed it; it's 2 Peter 1:3-4. Examine now again these two verses:

> ³Seeing that His divine power has granted to us everything pertaining to life and godliness, <u>through the true knowledge of Him</u> who called us by His own glory and excellence. ⁴For by these He has granted to us His precious and magnificent promises, so that by them you may become partakers of *the* divine nature, having escaped the corruption that is in the world by lust.

As I mentioned before, both the understanding of the original language and many times the tense of the verbs can be necessary to come to a deeper understanding of a passage. In this case, the verb tense of "has granted" is *perfect, passive*. A perfect tense verb tells us that the *stated fact or action* was given to the addressed person (*passive*) at some time in the past but that it continues to be true and active in the present time.

So, to paraphrase, our Father God of the Bible has given His children everything that we need to live everyday life, in every moment, victoriously in every circumstance. However, this divine power is manifested to us only through the Truth and the promises He gives to us as recorded in the New Testament. There is another aspect of 2 Peter 1:3-4 that we cannot miss—this divine power exclusively comes to us through a specified declared conduit. God's divine power

7: WHAT "WORKS" WHEN IT ISN'T WORKING

is given to each follower of Jesus Christ through the true, experiential knowledge of God. God's true, experiential knowledge can only be found in His Word. His divine power to live life in righteousness and godliness is activated in a person's life through the knowledge of, belief in, and obedience to the Truth as revealed in and through God's Word.

My goal for the remainder of this chapter is to examine closely the scriptures in the New Testament that directly speak to or directly relate to the subject of divorce and/or remarriage. And you now understand why there will not be a single Old Testament passage used for any instructions or commands regarding these subjects.

For the correct definition of *marriage*, we look to the definition God gives and not man. All the verbs and the nouns that are translated "marriage" or "marry" are from the same Greek root, *gamos*.[22] The Greek word *gamos* is a noun and is defined as "the actual joining of a husband (referring exclusively to a male) and wife (referring exclusively to a female) and is used also of the wedding festivities."[23]

When researching a subject in God's Word, one needs to try to discover if there is anything related to *time* that is mentioned. Romans 7:2 says, "For the married woman [a singular feminine noun] is bound by law to her husband [a singular masculine noun] while he is living; but if her husband [a singular masculine noun] dies, she is released from the law concerning the husband [a singular masculine noun]." The Greek word translated "married" here is *hupandros* and is defined as "under a husband, married; spoken of a wife."[24] As you have just clearly noted, this passage states the length of time the marriage covenant lasts. It is until one of the spouses dies.

We have defined marriage to be one male and one female consciously and intentionally entering into an exclusive covenant agreement to be for as long as both are living. This covenant is part of the law of Christ, according to Romans 7:2, which I referred to in the previous paragraph.

The next scripture passage we should address is found in Matthew 19:3-8. There are several statements in this passage that I want to clarify. We need to carefully observe this passage in its context. The Pharisees had come to Jesus with the specific

---

22 Strong's reference number: 1062 from Logos Bible Software (Bellingham, WA).
23 *The Complete Word Study Dictionary: New Testament*
24 *The Complete Word Study Dictionary: New Testament*

intent to test him. There were among the Jewish leadership totally contradictory opinions on divorce. They intended that their question would trip Jesus, and His answer would cause at least some Jews to stop following Him—hoping His answer on divorce would alienate many Jews.

> ³*Some* Pharisees came to Jesus, testing Him and asking, "Is it lawful *for a man* to divorce his wife <u>for any reason at all</u>?" ⁴And He answered and said, "<u>Have you not read</u> that He who created *them* from the beginning made them male and female, ⁵and said, 'For this reason a man shall leave his father and mother and be joined to his wife, and the two shall become one flesh'? ⁶So they are no longer two, but one flesh. What therefore God has joined together, <u>let no man separate</u>." ⁷They said to Him, "Why then did Moses command to give her a certificate of divorce and send her away?" ⁸He said to them, "Because of your hardness of heart <u>Moses permitted</u> you to divorce your wives; <u>but from the beginning it has not been this way</u>. (Matthew 19:3-8)

Look again at verse 3. As I mentioned before, it was the Pharisees who came up to Jesus for the sole purpose of testing Him regarding the controversial subject of divorce among the Jews. They wanted Jesus to agree or disagree with one side or the other. The Pharisees controlled the synagogues and were the teachers of the Law. The Pharisees thought they could cause many to rise up against Jesus by attempting to persuade Jesus to make a statement on divorce that they would disagree with. So, they asked Jesus, "Is it lawful for a man to divorce his wife for any reason at all?" When Jesus uses the phrase "have you not read" in verse 4, He is referring to the Old Testament. Jesus' answer was "from the beginning it *[divorce]* has not been this way."

It is extremely important that we closely observe just what this passage says and what it does not say. As was the common practice of Jesus during His earthly ministry, He answered a question with a question. Their question in verse 7 was based on Jesus' response in verse 6: "What God has joined together, let no man separate." They then asked, "Why then did <u>Moses command</u> to give her a certificate of divorce?" Since the Pharisees were the teachers of the Law, it was

7: WHAT "WORKS" WHEN IT ISN'T WORKING

certainly a legitimate question for them to ask. However, their claim upon which their question was based was not altogether true. Many Christians research the Pharisees' question here in verse 7 by going to Deuteronomy 24:1, which is part of the Law of Moses. Deuteronomy 24:1 states that "<u>When</u> a man takes a wife and marries her, and it happens that she finds no favor in his eyes because he has found some indecency in her . . . <u>he writes her a certificate of divorce</u> and puts *it* in her hand and sends her out from his house." What is stated in all of Deuteronomy 24:1-4 (which we'll closely observe soon) is an action with the stated consequences—*not* a command that gives permission to divorce. Their answer was correct as it referred to Moses but not correct that God Himself had given the command (permission) for divorce in the Law.

God does clearly declare His opinion regarding divorce in Malachi 2:13-16. Look closely with me at this passage in God's Word:

> [13]This is another thing you do: you cover the altar of the LORD with tears, with weeping and with groaning, because <u>He no longer regards the offering or accepts</u> *it with* <u>favor from your hand</u>. [14]Yet you say, "For what reason?" Because the LORD has been a witness between you and the wife of your youth, against whom you have dealt treacherously, though she is your companion and your wife by covenant. [15]But not one has done so who has a remnant of the Spirit. And what did *that* one *do* while he was seeking a godly offspring? Take heed then to your spirit, and let no one <u>deal treacherously against the wife of your youth</u>. [16]"<u>For I hate divorce</u>," says the LORD, the God of Israel, "and him who covers his garment with wrong," says the LORD of hosts. "So take heed to your spirit, that you do not deal treacherously." (Malachi 2:13-16)

This passage in Malachi 2 reveals several things about divorce. First, GOD HATES IT! Second, divorce is described here as "dealing treacherously against his wife." Third, the consequences here are dire under the Law; God would no longer have regard for his offering nor would accept his offering with favor. That meant under the law his sins would not be covered.

GOD'S PORTRAIT OF A "RIGHTEOUS WOMAN"

Let me insert the following before we continue to observe the Matthew 19 passage. It is true that divorce is mentioned on several occasions in the Old Testament, but there is no specific passage in the Old Testament that says, "For this reason you are permitted to divorce your wife." I don't want to muddy the waters here, but I don't want anyone to reject the point I am trying to make about what the Old Testament says about divorce. I am aware that God declares He has given Israel a certificate of divorce because of all of her adulteries (Jeremiah 3:8; Isaiah 50:1), but He has specific and declared plans to bring her back (Jeremiah 3:14). This is significant because, as I mentioned earlier, we will deal with a New Testament passage about adultery in a marriage later. Also, 1 Corinthians 7:10-11 addresses remarrying your wife: "But to the married I give instructions, not I, but the Lord, that the wife should not leave her husband, but if she does leave, she must remain unmarried, <u>or else be reconciled to her husband</u>, and that the husband should not divorce his wife."

Point of clarity: Because of my mention of God's giving Israel a certificate of divorce, there is something I must clarify before I continue: *God does indeed hate divorce.* God's reason for the divorce was to reveal to Israel the consequences of continued adultery. However, God's intent was and is to remarry her later, according to Jeremiah 3:14. The New Testament contains the same principle—God disciplines His children to bring us to repentance and reconciliation. There may be times when a wife is compelled to divorce her husband for adultery, but to be obedient to God's command in 1 Corinthians 7:10-11 and to follow God's example in Jeremiah 3:14, the intention of one's heart should be forgiveness and reconciliation. The Lord makes it clear that He never contradicts Himself, according to 2 Timothy 2:13: "If we are faithless, He remains faithful, for He cannot deny[25] Himself."

Over the years the Lord has revealed much wisdom and insight by reasoning God's actions in the Old Testament with the commandments and details given to us in the New Testament. For instance, Genesis 15:6 says, "Then he [Abram] believed in the Lord; and He [God] reckoned it to him as righteousness." This passage isn't clear just what Abram believed about God. However, Galatians 3:8 and 16 (which we observed earlier) tells us exactly what Abram

---

25 This Greek word can also be translated "contradict."

7: WHAT "WORKS" WHEN IT ISN'T WORKING

believed. His belief that brought salvation to him is the same as it always has been. Before Christ came, one was saved by believing God's promise of a coming Savior, as Adam (Genesis 3:15) and Abram did. Today, after the death and bodily resurrection of Christ Jesus, we are saved by believing that Jesus Himself was indeed the *promised Messiah*. Just to refresh our memories from chapter one, look with me again at Galatians 3:8 and 16 and rejoice, because the best interpreter of scripture is scripture itself:

> [8]The Scripture, foreseeing that God would justify the Gentiles by faith, preached the gospel beforehand to Abraham, *saying*, "All the nations will be blessed in you." . . . [16]Now the promises were spoken to Abraham and to his seed. He does not say, "And to seeds," as *referring* to many, but *rather* to one, "And to your seed," that is, Christ. (Galatians 3:8, 16)

Now back to Matthew 19, and we'll begin here with addressing verse 7 again:

> [7]They said to Him, "Why then did Moses command to give her a certificate of divorce and send *her* away?" [8]He said to them, "Because of your hardness of heart <u>Moses permitted</u> you to divorce your wives; but from the beginning it has not been this way. [9]And I say to you, whoever divorces his wife, except for immorality, and marries another woman commits adultery." [10]The disciples said to Him, "If the relationship of the man with his wife is like this, it is better not to marry." [11]But He said to them, "Not all men *can* accept this statement, but *only* those to whom it has been given. [12]For there are eunuchs who were born that way from their mother's womb; and there are eunuchs who were made eunuchs by men; and there are *also* eunuchs who made themselves eunuchs for the sake of the kingdom of heaven. He who is able to accept *this*, let him accept *it*." (Matthew 19:7-12)

Matthew 19:8 needs to be carefully looked at. In verse 8 Jesus says, "Because of the hardness of your heart <u>Moses</u> permitted you to divorce your wives." Jesus clearly stated here that it was Moses, not

God, who permitted divorce. But the main answer Jesus gave them is found in the remaining words of verse 8, which says, "He said to them, '<u>but from the beginning it has not been this way</u>.'" In other words, divorce was never God's way. The "from" implies that it wasn't God's way in the beginning and it isn't God's way now either.

Actually, Mark 10:5 records it this way: "Because of your hardness of heart <u>he</u> [Moses] <u>wrote you</u> this commandment." The truth is, because Jesus says it, undoubtedly Moses did permit and did write a commandment that "permitted a man to write a certificate of divorce." However, it was never a commandment of God—that is, it is not included in the written Word of God nor agreed to in scripture. To state it this way, nowhere in God's Word is it written, "God did permit and did write a commandment that permitted a man to write a certificate of divorce."

Summary: Divorce was never God's way from the beginning. Undoubtedly, somewhere else Moses must have physically written that commandment. We just don't know when or where because it was not a commandment God gave him—that is, it cannot be found in God's Word. Again, Deuteronomy 24:1-4 is not a command to divorce. It just states the consequences if a person did divorce.

As is Jesus' habit on many occasions when teaching or answering questions, Jesus quotes scripture. Jesus didn't answer the question they asked, per se. He told them what God said about divorce (in Matthew 19:6) which was, "What God has joined together, let no man separate." Look with me closely again at Matthew 19:8: "He said to them, 'Because of your hardness of heart <u>Moses permitted</u> you to divorce your wives; <u>but from the beginning it has not been this way</u>.'" In essence, Jesus was saying, "I am aware that Moses gave you [the Jews] permission to divorce and wrote it down somewhere, but it was never recorded in scripture—that is, it was never part of God's written revelation."

Then Jesus warns them of the consequences. I believe His disciples, as mentioned in verse 10, understood the full impact of Jesus' declaration here: if you choose to divorce your wife, you are to know you can never marry another woman. But if you choose to divorce your wife and then marry another woman, you are committing adultery. Jesus' disciples understood the full impact of Jesus' teaching here because none of them wanted to be declared an adulterer. As Jesus' disciples would have already been taught by

Jesus, and an unnamed writer would later write in Hebrews 13:4, "Marriage *is to be held* in honor among all, and the *marriage* bed *is to be* undefiled; for <u>fornicators and adulterers God will judge</u>."

There are other places where God's Word addresses divorce, but strangely enough most of them deal specifically with remarriage. We will deal with all of these passages in the next chapter.

There is so much to read, understand, and apply here. So let me encourage you to meditate on and digest what you have seen in God's Word in this chapter before you go to the next. My earnest desire for this chapter is to set the biblical foundation for what God says about marriage, divorce, and remarriage. We will build upon these truths and instructions in detail in the next chapter and hopefully address the questions that you still have. Please hang in there; there is much encouragement to come as well.

CHAPTER 8

What "Works" When It Isn't Working

(PART 2)

Let's get back to the Greek word *gameo* that is translated "marry, marries, marriage." This Greek word is mentioned in the following places in the New Testament in addition to the Matthew 19:3-12 and Romans 7:2 passages we observed in the previous chapter: Matthew 22:25-32; Mark 6:17, 12:25; Luke 14:20, 17:27; and 1 Timothy 5:11, 14. These passages don't concern the topic we are discussing now, but I wanted to list them all to encourage you to continue in your own search for truth within the context of these verses.

In 1 Corinthians, Paul's first letter to the church in Corinth, there is a long passage that deals with the full gamut of marriage and moral behavior. It is in chapter 7. This chapter contains the most comprehensive instructions given to us in the New Testament regarding marriage, divorce, and remarriage. That suggests it is vital that we explore this chapter in detail. Carefully observe these verses as we go through them in segments, because they contain critical information every believer needs to know and trust as to obey. Most of 1 Corinthians 7 will be discussed—I'll only omit the verses that I believe are not pertinent to the subject at hand.

The book of 1 Corinthians was written sometime between 52–56 AD. Paul had first gone to Corinth about 50 AD and had stayed there for eighteen months. The first part of this letter, chapters 1–6, deals primarily with things that had been reported to him by "Chloe's people" (1 Corinthians 1:11). You will see that in 1 Corinthians 7, Paul is now turning his focus to answer the questions these Corinthians have asked of Paul.

Paul is being very inclusive in most aspects of marriage because he knew that this young church membership was made up primarily of Gentiles who had previously been idol worshipers. Their previous worship was in the Temple of Aphrodite, which was on the top of a mountain that was close to and visible from the city of Corinth. Much of their idol worship there was expressed sexually with temple prostitutes. They had much to learn now that what had been encouraged and good before was now immoral, sinful, and prohibited. They were now, as believers in Christ Jesus, forbidden to practice their past heathen behavior. So Paul begins at the starting place: a man was not to touch (in a suggestive way) a woman who was not his wife. Let's begin our study of 1 Corinthians 7 with the first few verses in the chapter:

> ¹Now concerning the things about which you wrote, it is good for a man not to touch a woman. ²But because of immoralities, each man [singular masculine] is to have his own wife [singular feminine], and each woman [singular feminine] is to have her own husband [singular masculine]. (1 Corinthians 7:1-2)

Paul begins addressing the issue of immorality by explaining to Christians (both male and female) how they are to deal with the sexual desires that God has placed within us. Because of the implanted DNA for the desire for sexual intimacy, a Christ follower is to carefully guard their behavior so that their desires are under control and they don't involve themselves in immoralities (v. 2). So the first answer as to how *not* to participate in immoralities was not to touch a woman in any suggestive ways. The second was that they

8: WHAT "WORKS" WHEN IT ISN'T WORKING

should get married—each man to one woman and each woman to one man.

Please look with me now at 1 Corinthians 7:3-5:

> ³The husband must fulfill his duty to his wife, and likewise also the wife to her husband. ⁴The wife does not have authority over her own body, but the husband does; and likewise, also the husband *does* not have authority over his own body, but the wife *does*. ⁵Stop depriving one another, except by agreement for a time, so that you may devote yourselves to prayer, and come together again so that Satan will not tempt you because of your lack of self-control.

Generally speaking, according to my observation, not only is 1 Corinthians 7:1-4 not considered to be "true" in the time and culture we find ourselves living in, but it is ignored and treated as totally irrelevant now. Sexual activity among both unmarried women and unmarried men in our modern world is acceptable by oh too many and often expected as a normal part of dating. All too many believe, even if they do not say it publicly, any form of sexual activity outside of marriage is simply a social activity to be enjoyed by all. It seems that in our culture and time, many seem to be actively involved in sexual immorality or agree with those who are.

It is impossible for me to know how the instructions in 1 Corinthians 7:3-5 speak to you individually. However, I know that our backgrounds in many cases affect how one addresses and obeys these commands. Both "fulfill" in verse 3 and "stop deriving" in verse 5 are *present imperative* verbs, meaning both husband and wife are commanded that it must be the habit of their lives to be intimately available to their own spouse.

Again, Paul addresses the issue of sexual desires tempting men and women to the point of losing self-control. I believe wives must take very seriously not only what our responsibility is to our own husband but be warned of the above stated possible consequences of depriving them. Clearly our husband's infidelity (sin) could possibly be a response to his wife's not being available to meet his needs, but in no way is this passage insinuating that a husband can blame his wife for his adultery. Those of us who are wives should be alert to the fact that we could unintentionally contribute to our husband's vulnerability to evil women's attentions/seductions.

On a sidenote here, I believe it is not unlikely that wives find ourselves needing to warn our husbands of women they encounter at work. For example, many years ago Lee was talking to me about his day at work, which was common. He mentioned there had been a woman who had come to his office with some issue. Honestly, I cannot remember what the issue was. But after hearing Lee tell me about his conversation with her, I had an inner sense of danger. I asked Lee to never, never allow a woman in his office with the door closed. It was not Lee's fidelity that was the issue. It was for his protection against her either making an advance on him or even saying something damaging about Lee that never occurred. Lee took the advice very seriously and to my knowledge took this precaution to heart and thereafter left his door open when a female was in his office alone.

First Corinthians 7:6-9 is saying to those who are unmarried that it is good to remain unmarried *and* it is good to be married. And again, Paul specifically addresses the subject of our inborn sexual desires. We know because Paul tells us that he was a Pharisee in Philippians 3:5. I have been told that being married was a requirement for becoming a Pharisee, so either what I have been told is in error, or Paul had by this time become a widower because he implies in 1 Corinthians 7:7 that he is unmarried. Also, I believe the "gift" that Paul mentions in this verse would most probably be the gift of celibacy (Matthew 19:11). Let's now carefully examine 1 Corinthians 7:6-9:

> [6]But this I say by way of concession, not of command. [7]Yet I wish that all men were even as I myself am. However, each man has his own gift from God, one in this manner, and another in that. [8]But I say to the unmarried and to widows that it is good for them if they remain even as I. [9]But if they do not have self-control, let them marry; for it is better to marry than to burn *with passion*.

In 1 Corinthians 7:10 and 12 Paul makes a rare statement: "I say, not the Lord." It is helpful for us to know that Paul would make it plain from whom he received what he teaches. It is found

8: WHAT "WORKS" WHEN IT ISN'T WORKING

in Galatians 1:11-12: "For I would have you know, brethren, that the gospel which was preached by me is not according to man. For I neither received it from man, nor was I taught it, but I *received it* through a revelation of Jesus Christ." So when Paul made the statement, "I say, not the Lord," he is stating that while Jesus Christ was personally teaching Paul after His resurrection and ascension into heaven, He didn't specifically say that. However, Paul does end this particular subject in verse 40b by saying, "and I think that I also have the Spirit of God."

Next, Paul begins to address the issue of divorce. When he uses the phrase "not leave," he is specifically speaking of divorce. It is made clear by verse 11 where Paul states, "she must remain unmarried." Read 1 Corinthians 7:10-11:

> ¹⁰But to the married I give instructions, not I, but the Lord, that the wife should not leave her husband ¹¹(but if she does leave, she <u>must remain</u> unmarried, or else <u>be reconciled</u> to her husband), and that the husband should not divorce his wife.

It is important to note that Paul is addressing the circumstance where both the husband and the wife are professing Christians. It is quite normal that when very important instructions (here the two underlined verbs are *imperatives* and thus are commands) are given in scripture that there is most often a warning regarding the consequences of disobedience, as in verse 11. To paraphrase, Paul is speaking to both the husband and the wife that the Lord Jesus commands you not to divorce, but if you choose not to obey Jesus, you are then commanded to remain unmarried or to remarry your former spouse. Because of the culture, many passages in God's Word will address only the male with commands or instructions, but when instructions are like these, it is needful that we assume that what is told to the husband is also true for the wife.

It is important to note that in 1 Corinthians 7:1-11, the issues being addressed were specially to the circumstance where both the husband and the wife were already saved. Starting in 1 Corinthians 7:12, Paul begins to address couples in which one of the spouses is not yet saved by using the phrase "to the rest" in verse 12. It is very safe to assume that this young church would have had many

GOD'S PORTRAIT OF A "RIGHTEOUS WOMAN"

couples in which one of the spouses was not yet saved. Since Paul is answering *their* questions now, most probably it was common for the following question to be asked: *Since my husband is not saved and is now living a pagan lifestyle, should I divorce him?* Or vice-versa. Observe 1 Corinthians 7:12-16 for Paul's answer:

> ¹²But to the rest I say, not the Lord, that if any brother has a wife who is an unbeliever, and she consents to live with him, <u>he must not divorce her</u>.²⁶ ¹³And a woman who has an unbelieving husband, and he consents to live with her, <u>she must not send her husband away</u>.²⁷ ¹⁴For the unbelieving husband is sanctified through his wife, and the unbelieving wife is sanctified through her believing husband; for otherwise your children are unclean, but now they are holy. ¹⁵Yet if the unbelieving one leaves, let him leave; the brother or the sister is not under bondage in such *cases*, but God has called us to peace. ¹⁶For how do you know, O wife, whether you will save your husband? Or how do you know, O husband, whether you will save your wife?

These five verses in 1 Corinthians 7 are critically important, so let's look at them in minute detail. The "must not send" (meaning divorce) in verse 13 is a command, not a suggestion. Several reasons are given for the believing spouse to understand the consequences of divorcing an unbelieving spouse. It is a wonderful and an extremely gracious promise for God to sanctify the unbelieving spouse while he or she remains married to a believing spouse. As we have noted before, the word *sanctify* does not speak to salvation but that the unbelieving spouse would be set apart to receive many of the same blessings and benefits from God that believers are given. Paul even says that it may be possible that God will use the believing spouse as a vessel through which He will save the unbelieving spouse.

Allow me to share a personal illustration. A sister of mine married an unbeliever who became an alcoholic. They were married for many years, and they had four children. Soon after all the children were grown and left home, my brother-in-law literally made my sister

---
26 This verb is also a command in the imperative tense.
27 This verb is also a command in the imperative tense.

8: WHAT "WORKS" WHEN IT ISN'T WORKING

leave their house. My assumption was he could no longer tolerate the condemnation from the Holy Spirit's presence being manifested through my sister's love and service for the Lord. As time went on, he never offered monetary support for my sister, even though he made a good salary and she didn't. For some reason, the Lord only knows, he also did not want a divorce.

From the beginning of their separation, my sister met with the whole family for special occasions. Not too long afterward, her estranged husband had surgery, and my sister brought him into her home and nursed him while he recuperated. During this time in which my sister was being very gracious and benevolent toward him, most Christians told her that she was crazy for doing so and should "divorce the bum."

After I talked with my sister in person about what God's Word says, I wrote her a letter (I believe she kept that letter for some thirty-plus years. She has joyfully passed into the presence of our Savior during the time in which this book is being written.) It is important for me to say that I have never given a person advice on what they should do or what they should not do regarding whether to divorce or not divorce. Those decisions should always be made by the individual person based on God's counsel to them personally. Yes, I do believe that our God does give us individual wisdom on what to do when we ask Him, based on James 1:5-6: "But if any of you lacks wisdom, let him ask of God, who gives to all generously and without reproach, and it will be given to him. But he must ask in faith without any doubting, for the one who doubts is like the surf of the sea, driven and tossed by the wind." What I did and have continued to do when asked for guidance regarding such circumstances is to give them the scriptures that speak to their issue and ask them to carefully study them and do what God tells them to do.

My sister read those Bible passages and chose not to initiate any divorce proceedings but continued her righteous and kind behavior toward him. It was in his testimony at his baptism some years later (I saw the video myself) that it was my sister's unconditional love that God primarily used to save him while watching Billy Graham preach on his television. So, ladies who are now married to an unbeliever, "For how do you know, O wife, whether you will save your husband?"

One last fact about my sister: I am convinced that because she was obedient to the Lord, God used her mightily in His kingdom during all these many years of separation. She taught Sunday school for all those years, she led a women's Bible study, and she served on major committees of her church: a pastor search committee, finance committee, and personnel committee, to name a few.

Our good and faithful God did not have to set her aside from ministry and discipline her for disobedience. He blessed and spiritually prospered her for her obedience, and she continued to be a strong witness for the gospel and God's kingdom. There is more to be said of this sister, which will come later.

Because it is extremely profitable, I repeat: God does give us the freedom to make choices whether to obey Him or not, but He does not let any of us choose the consequences of our disobedience. God does indeed discipline His children for disobedience because He loves each of us too much to allow us to continue too long in sin and its destructive consequences both to us personally and for His great name's sake.

In 1 Corinthians 7:17, where we previously left off, Paul now turns his attention to instruct the adults who had just recently been saved and are wondering what they should do. The first thing he wants them to know is in this verse. Look with me at 1 Corinthians 7:17: "Only, as the Lord has assigned to each one, <u>as God has called each in this manner let him walk</u>. And so, I direct in all the churches." The phrase "as God has called each" literally means "continue to live in the same marital circumstances you were in when you got saved." Paul will use the word "called" (i.e., *saved*) and its implications five more times (verses 20, 21, twice in 22, 24) to emphasize the importance of his instructions to "continue to live in the same marital circumstances you were in when you got saved." Paul gives examples of some of the conditions in which a new believer could find themselves. He begins with verse 18, and the first circumstance he mentions is to be circumcised or not circumcised, and he continues with these conditions through verse 24. As they don't apply directly to our subject at hand, these verses will not be discussed in detail here. But I encourage you to read them when you have time.

Second Corinthians 5:17 explains the foundation upon which Paul gives some of these specific instructions to the *new* believers. Look with me at 2 Corinthians 5:17: "Therefore if anyone is in Christ, *he is* a new creature; the old things passed away; behold, new things have come." This statement of fact is extremely meaningful

8: WHAT "WORKS" WHEN IT ISN'T WORKING

and an incalculable blessing to many people who have led a life that would be considered immoral or otherwise ungodly.

It's here I want to address 1 Corinthians 7:27-28, which contains the Greek word *gameo* and is translated "marry." Look with me at the following two verses and note how I interpret them:

> ²⁷Are you bound to a wife? Do not seek to be released. Are you <u>released from a wife</u>?²⁸ Do not seek a wife. ²⁸But <u>if you marry, you have not sinned</u>, and if a virgin marries, she has not sinned. Yet such will have trouble in this life, and I am trying to spare you. (1 Corinthians 7:27-28)

The context of these two verses is clearly that Paul is speaking the those who have recently been saved; they have been made new creatures. The old things of their life before salvation have passed away, which would include things from their previous marriage, and their divorce is now nonexistent as remarriage is concerned. God has said, "Behold, new things have come." Paul tells these new Christians they will *not* become adulterers if they should remarry. That is why Paul instructs them, "If you marry, you have *not sinned.*" Again, please keep in mind these are God's instructions for those who are saved as adults who have already experienced divorce.

There is one more verse in 1 Corinthians 7 that I want us to observe and then try to understand what God means by what He said in a previous section of 1 Corinthians 7. This particular passage brings up an issue where godly people disagree on its meaning and application. Look with me at 1 Corinthians 7:39, which states, "A wife is bound as long as her husband lives; but if her husband is dead, she is free to be married to whom she wishes, only in the Lord." Paul also repeats the same instructions in Romans 7:1-3. You may remember that I mentioned verse 2 in the previous chapter.

> ¹Or do you not know, brethren (for I am speaking to those who know the law), that the law has jurisdiction over a person as long as he lives? ²For the married woman is bound by law to her husband while he is living; but if her husband dies, she is released from the law concerning the husband. ³So then, if while her husband is living, she is

---
28 Meaning a person who is already divorced when he or she got saved.

joined to another man, she shall be called an adulteress; but if her husband dies, she is free from the law, so that she is not an adulteress though she is joined to another man. (Romans 7:1-3)

The particular verse that I want us to reexamine is in 1 Corinthians 7:15, which states, "Yet if the unbelieving one leaves, let him leave; the brother or the sister is <u>not under bondage</u> in such *cases*, but God has called us to peace." There are devoted Christ followers who interpret "not under bondage" in verse 15 to mean the believer is free to initiate divorce proceedings against the husband who left her and is also free to remarry without being declared by God to be an adulterer. The phrase commonly used is "abandonment is biblical grounds for divorce." I am *not* of the opinion that this verse can be faithfully interpreted this way for the following reasons.

1. Paul ends this segment on marriage in 1 Corinthians 7 with the clear declaration in verse 39 that "A wife is bound as long as her husband lives." Then Paul adds immediately, "if her husband is dead, she is free to be married." If Paul had intended to include that the abandoned wife was free to remarry, I am of the strong opinion that he would have clearly stated it, as he did in verse 39. *But he did not.* Paul said the wife "is no longer under bondage" in 1 Corinthians 7:15, just a few verses prior.

2. The Greek word translated "under bondage" in verse 15 is *douloo*[29] and is defined, "to be a slave, to serve, to be subject, to be subjugated to."[30] When a wife marries, she is commanded to voluntarily subjugate herself to her husband's leadership authority; she is to obey him. He has been given by God the position of being the "head" of his family, including his wife. If the husband leaves the wife, *she is freed from* (i.e., not under bondage to) *her covenant-binding command* of having to obey, honor, and respect the husband who has left her—that is, "she is no longer under bondage" to do what her husband tells her to do or to obey him in way or matter. In my strong opinion,

---

29 Strong's reference #1402
30 *The Complete Word Study Dictionary: New Testament*

8: WHAT "WORKS" WHEN IT ISN'T WORKING

she is no longer under the bondage of subjugation to his authority in any way. The husband who left her gave up his position of being the head of his household, including his former wife.

3. The Greek word translated "bondage" in verse 39 ("A wife is bound as long as her husband lives") and "are bound" in verse 27 ("Are you bound to a wife") is *deo*[31] and is defined as "to bind together."[32] Both verses 39 and 27 are in the context of the condition of being married—being joined together by the covenant in which they voluntarily entered.

Paul seemed to be very clear and precise in choosing his words here. Actually, God was very clear and precise in His delivery of His words to Paul regarding the instructions, commands, regulations, and consequences in this chapter. If God had meant in verse 15 that the wife was free to initiate divorce and be remarried, He would have inspired Paul to clearly say so as he did in 1 Corinthians 7:39. In fact, I have never found a place in God Word's where He speaks to any circumstances that free a believer to initiate a divorce and then be remarried to another. What God does clearly address is adultery as it pertains to divorce and remarriage. Remember the Matthew 19:9-10 passage where Jesus' disciples had such an extreme response to the issue of divorce, remarriage, and adultery: "The disciples said to Him, 'If the relationship of the man with his wife is like this, it is better not to marry'" (Matthew 19:10). If I have brought to your attention some parts of God's Word that you have never carefully studied, please ponder and meditate on the exact wording in this vitally important segment in scripture—1 Corinthians 7—entirely.

Now, I want us to look at the remaining passages in God's Word that contain the Greek word *gameo* and are translated into the English words *marry, marries,* or *marriage*. There is a common thread in God's Word, including in the following passages, that deals with marriage, divorce, and remarriage. When a divorced person gets remarried to someone other than their previous spouse who is still alive, there is one exception given that exempts them from becoming an adulterer.

---

31 Strong's reference #1210
32 *The Complete Word Study Dictionary: New Testament*

Keep in mind as you carefully read the following scripture passages how Jesus' disciples responded to Him in Matthew 19:3-12. In the previous chapter, we saw how Jesus responded to the Pharisees asking if it was lawful for a man to divorce his wife for any reason. Jesus responded that divorce was never intended from the beginning. He also mentioned remarriage and adultery in Matthew 19:9. As we examine these passages that use the Greek word *gameo*, let's review this Matthew 19:9 passage once more:

> "And I say to you, whoever divorces his wife, <u>except for immorality</u>, and marries another woman commits adultery." (Matthew 19:9)

Note that Matthew 19:9 does not give permission to divorce and remarry. This passage simply gives the circumstances and its consequences. The issue here is what keeps a divorced person who remarries another who is not his previous wife from becoming an adulterer. This passage and Matthew 5:31-32 clearly state under what circumstance a person who remarries another does not become an adulterer. If you are familiar with Jesus' "Sermon on the Mount" and His section of the "Beatitudes," you will recognize Jesus' use of contrasts to clarify several statements. Matthew 5:31-32 includes one of His most common contrasts: "It was said, but I say." The "It was said" refers to someone other than Jesus—in many cases the Jews followed the "oral law" more closely than the "written law" during the time of Jesus' first coming. The "I" in verse 32 obviously is Jesus speaking of Himself.

> ³¹ "<u>It was said</u>, 'Whoever sends his wife away, let him give her a certificate of divorce'; ³²<u>but I say</u> to you that everyone who divorces his wife, <u>except for the reason of unchastity</u>, makes her commit adultery; and whoever marries a divorced woman commits adultery." (Matthew 5:31-32)

In verse 31 Jesus clearly states through this contrast that what Moses had said/written is *not* what Jesus or any of God's commandments had said about divorce. This passage in Matthew 5 can be a difficult one to understand. I believe there is a twofold warning. First, the person who divorces his wife makes her commit adultery if he divorces her for any reason other than "her unchastity." The Greek

8: WHAT "WORKS" WHEN IT ISN'T WORKING

word translated "unchastity" here is *porneia*[33] and is the Greek word that is the umbrella word for any and all kinds of sexual acts outside of marriage. To my best understanding, this passage means that when a husband divorces his wife and she did not commit adultery, if she remarries another man she would become an adulteress—that is, by him divorcing her without her having committed adultery, he would be the cause of her becoming an adulterer if she remarries. Also, we see that the person who marries a woman who has been divorced and their spouse has *not* committed any kind of sexual immorality, he (or if reversed, she) then becomes an adulterer him/herself. We cannot totally understand why God makes some of these rules. He doesn't require our understanding, but He does require our obedience. The basis upon which my faith lies is that our God is always right in His given commands, even though I may not understand them at all.

I hope that you have continued to notice these passages don't give permission to divorce. These passages are stating the possible consequences of a divorced person remarrying another person—being declared by God "an adulterer." If the divorced person remarries and their spouse has not committed adultery, the consequence is that they themselves become an adulterer. However, if the divorced person marries another and her former husband has committed adultery, she does not become an adulterer. Again, Jesus does not say you are free to remarry, He only states whether or not one becomes an adulterer by their marriage to another. Mark 10:11-12 gives us yet again another scenario.

> [11]And He said to them, "Whoever divorces his wife and marries another woman <u>commits adultery against her</u>,[34] [12]and if she herself divorces her husband and marries another man, she is committing adultery."

In this passage, there is another aspect of divorce which we've not seen before. That is, if the husband who divorced his wife (who was not guilty of adultery) marries another woman, he is committing adultery against his former wife. Because of this, the consequences of the first wife marrying another have changed—in this case remarriage to another will *not* make her an adulterer because her former husband

---

33 Strong's reference #4202
34 The "her" here is of course the wife he has divorced.

had committed adultery against her by marrying another woman. Notice that verse 12 states that the same thing is true if the roles were reversed. As I read again Mark 10:11-12, it seems to me this aspect of divorce does not require this *exception* to be mentioned because this passage speaks of the adultery having been committed to the former spouse by his/her marriage to another. It may take several readings of the passage, as it does me, to understand the circumstances being described here.

Now, one last place where the Greek word *gameo* is used. Carefully observe Luke 16:18:

> Everyone who divorces his wife and marries another commits adultery, and he who marries one who is divorced from a husband commits adultery.

This passage now addresses another aspect of the circumstance in Mark 10. Everyone, this passage says, who divorces his wife and marries another commits adultery—*except* when his former wife had committed immorality. This passage also adds that the person who marries someone who has been divorced, they themselves commit adultery. I (not this verse) have added to this statement made in verse 18 that "the exception" clause applies. Even though "except for immorality" is not specifically stated here, the two mentions in Matthew 5 and 19 are sufficient for us to assume that the exception exists here as well. So, if the *former spouse* of the *divorced person they are marrying* has committed any form of immorality, then that person would *not* become an adulterer. I have wrestled with how to best paraphrase Luke 16:18 to help insert the "except for immorality" phrase. Jesus needs to say something only once to make it true. To put it another way, regarding the "exception" statement, Jesus has mentioned it twice, which makes me assume that it applies even though it has not been repeated.

Hebrews 13:4 declares God's response to adultery—God will judge adulterers. Let me add here a truth that needs to be repeated. Any sin committed before a person is saved has not only been forgiven but also been forgotten by the one true God at the point of salvation. The person who had murdered before salvation then is no longer a murderer in God's eyes, but the consequences from civil law many times continues. The same is true of a person who had committed

8: WHAT "WORKS" WHEN IT ISN'T WORKING

any act that God calls sin. When anyone gets saved through faith in and surrender to the Person and work of Jesus Christ, they are no longer guilty before God because the blood of Christ has cleansed them from all sin. And yes, that does include adultery.

> Marriage *is to be held* in honor among all, and the *marriage bed is to be* undefiled; for fornicators and adulterers God will judge. (Hebrews 13:4)

For those of you who have just discovered that in God's eyes you have committed adultery since you were saved, there is a wonderful promise in 1 John 1:9. The promise of this verse tells every believer that "If we confess our sins, He is faithful and righteous to forgive us our sins and to cleanse us from all unrighteousness."

If you divorced and remarried after you got saved, 1 John 1:9 tells you what to do as well: Confess to God that you have committed adultery and that you are grieving over your sin. Then ask the Lord to forgive you for this sin, and He promises that not only will He forgive you, but He will also cleanse you from all the unrighteous deeds you have committed. What a glorious and magnificent God we worship and serve.

According to my best understanding, 1 Corinthians 7:27-28 is addressing any person who has been saved *after* they were divorced—the context requires it. These two verses give us an example of the fact that God makes all things new. We have already observed the scripture that clearly states this in 2 Corinthians 5:17: "Therefore if anyone is in Christ, *he is* a new creature; the old things passed away; behold, new things have come."

Adultery can be forgiven and will be forgiven *when confessed*. But as I have mentioned several times, we cannot choose the consequences. But even if you are going through the consequences of past sins, our God promises "to cause ALL things to work together for good for those who love God and are the called according to His purposes" (Romans 8:28).

Hear me clearly. I am *not* saying that there is never a time when a wife should leave her husband in a righteous way. I *never* give any advice regarding whether or not a wife should leave her husband. I *always* give her the scriptures and tell her to study them and ask God what she should do. Again I repeat that James 1:5 promises,

"But if any of you lacks wisdom, let him ask of God, who gives to all generously and without reproach, and it will be given to him." God is more concerned about your welfare and future than you are! I said, "never and always," didn't I! Well, there is a circumstance when my advice would be, "leave immediately if not sooner." That circumstance is when your child(ren) is in physical danger. Get them away from their father as soon as possible. In a previous chapter we looked at 1 Peter 2:18-3:1, talking about when the wife is in physical danger. The wife must ask the Lord what she is to do and when because He will always guide her clearly for her well-being and transformation into Jesus' image, and His glory.

Throughout this chapter, we are speaking primarily of remarriage. I have personally helped close friends walk through very difficult and painful marriage issues. Some have chosen not to accept what God has revealed in His Word and were later "put on the shelf," so to speak, regarding effective Christian ministry. Others, like my sister, have chosen to obey and trust God, and He mightily used her obedience to lead her husband to salvation. And there are some friends who were divorced by their husbands and then remarried, without becoming adulteresses because of their husbands' adultery.

I am sharing personal experiences (some identified, some not) because I want you to know that I have lived what I believe to be God's clear instructions in several of the circumstances that I have addressed in this book. No experience or circumstance any believer has or will have is able to ever trump God's clear instructions regarding any subject that He has addressed in His Word. There is no such truth as, "I know I am not following God's revealed command, but I also know He will understand because I just cannot do this His way. It's just too hard." There has never been, is not now, and will never be a circumstance that comes into a Christian's life in which God has not already provided at way to victoriously endure it, according to 1 Corinthians 10:13: "No temptation has overtaken you but such as is common to man; and God is faithful, who will not allow you to be tempted beyond what you are able, but with the temptation will provide the way of escape also, so that you will be able to endure it."

I hope that you have observed my heart by now, but I feel compelled to repeat a couple of points. I have written this book because the Lord told me to do so. I have had no desire nor intention to judge what anyone else has done or has not done. That is God's

8: WHAT "WORKS" WHEN IT ISN'T WORKING

job and His job alone. I take no credit for any of the good this book might do, nor do I take on myself any condemnation for what it is not able to accomplish. My prayer is that our good and always faithful God will accomplish in and through this book all that He has set out to do through His Word. To Him and Him alone is all glory, power, honor, praise, and thanksgiving.

We have already seen many times that God's Word states that "the truth that you know will set you free." What I have discovered in my life of forty-plus years of ministry is that many, if not most, Christians make decisions based on insufficient or incorrect information. I have labored hard to bring to the light in these pages what God says about many varied subjects. Being uninformed about what God has clearly revealed in His Word unfortunately does not excuse or erase any unintended consequences of making wrong decisions that are in opposition to what God has recorded in scripture.

I want to end these previous two chapters with two important passages of scripture because I am certain that these have caused some, if not many, deep sorrow of spirit as you have read and examined God's Word. But, as Paul has told us in 2 Corinthians 7:10, "For the sorrow that is according to *the will of* God produces a repentance without regret, *leading* to salvation, but the sorrow of the world produces death." One of the greatest and most glorious gifts we have been given by our all sovereign and good God is forgiveness through which God deposits His righteousness into us. And there are so many more gifts! I have often said and I believe that it would not be good for us to worship and serve a "god" who was sovereign but *not* good. However, the sovereign Jehovah God of the Bible is not only *always good* but He is *always merciful, loving, gracious, kind, compassionate*, and so much more. And we become His children by adoption into His family upon salvation. He is indeed our heavenly Father! He is a good, good Father indeed!

God sacrificed His only Son, Jesus Christ the Nazarene, on the cross over two thousand years ago to pay in full our sin debt that we could not pay—a debt that Jesus did not owe. For those of us who have surrendered our lives to His Son in faith, we are now sons/daughters of the living God and joint heirs with God's Son, Jesus, for all eternity. We now have the Holy Spirit Who takes His permanent residence within us. He not only guides us into all truth

(John 16:13), He literally by His power causes us to obey (Ezekiel 36:27). Our glorious and magnificent God does not need to prove His love for us. God has already proven His unconditional love by what He has done on the cross.

Look with me now at Romans 5:8-11 for the best news the human race has ever been given:

> ⁸But God demonstrates His own love toward us, in that while we were yet sinners, Christ died for us. ⁹Much more then, having now been justified by His blood, we shall be saved from the wrath *of God* through Him. ¹⁰For if while we were enemies we were reconciled to God through the death of His Son, much more, having been reconciled, we shall be saved by His life. ¹¹And not only this, but we also exult in God through our Lord Jesus Christ, through whom we have now received the reconciliation.

Child of God, if the scriptures in these chapters have revealed to you a personal sin, keep in mind that complete, total, and absolute forgiveness is just one step away. Confess your sin (agree with what God has said about it), give it the name that God gives it (sin), and ask your heavenly Father to forgive you! He has never and will never turn away from your request for forgiveness, but by His great grace and mercy He will not only forgive you for that sin but will cleanse you from all unrighteousness.

If you have never been saved by grace through faith, please read Romans 5:8-11 again. With all sincerity of heart, confess your sins to Him, and put your faith and trust in Jesus Christ as your Lord and Savior, and you will be saved, according to Romans 10:9: "If you confess with your mouth Jesus *as* Lord, and believe in your heart that God raised Him from the dead, you will be saved." The gospel is simple and the rewards are more than you could ever imagine—they are eternal with the promise of living and ruling with Jesus throughout all eternity. Amen and Amen.

CHAPTER 9

Victorious, Christ-Honoring Living

Although my words may be encouraging and inspiring to some on occasion, I want to stress that they do not contain within them any power to change anyone. But God's Word does because He clearly tells us in Hebrews 4:12: "For the word of God is living and active and sharper than any two-edged sword, and piercing as far as the division of soul and spirit, of both joints and marrow, and able to judge the thoughts and intentions of the heart."

This chapter will discuss several subjects. Disclaimer: Some of the remaining content will not have "chapter and verse" connected to my words. I don't claim to be an expert in any field, but as I have walked closely with the Lord over the past fifty-plus years, and as I have been privileged to study much and teach many, I sense the Lord would have me share some practical insights that I have gained from striving to know my God more intimately and living according to His Word. With all advice, one must take it to the Lord to get confirmation as to whether or not it is to be personally applicable and should be followed, which certainly includes my own advice within these pages.

GOD'S WORD

Be blessed, encouraged, inspired, and *changed* by again looking at four passages of scripture.

> Your word is a lamp to my feet and a light to my path. (Psalm 119:105)

> [19]So we have the prophetic word *made* more sure, to which you do well to pay attention as to a lamp shining in a dark place, until the day dawns and the morning star arises in your hearts. [20]But know this first of all, that no prophecy of Scripture is *a matter* of one's own interpretation, [21]for no prophecy was ever made by an act of human will, but men moved by the Holy Spirit spoke from God. (2 Peter 1:19-21)

> Sanctify them in the truth; Your word is truth. (John 17:17)

> And you will know the truth, and the truth will make you free. (John 8:32)

The Lord has shown me over the years that not only is it the Truth of God's Word that sets one free, but it is also what one doesn't know that can cause a person much harm. John 8:32 above implies that lies and even biblical truth you don't know and/or believe can keep a person in bondage. Let me also say here that none of what I have written in this book has been intended to debate or to criticize anyone else's beliefs or interpretations of scripture. The details I have communicated in these chapters are my conclusions made from my own personal studies of God's Word over many decades. It is crystal clear to me that some of my interpretations and applications of some scripture passages do not reflect those of other believers who love God and His Word as much as I do. Daniel 11:32b tells us, "The people who know their God will display strength and take action." I simply implore each one of us to always use God's Word as our final authority for life and ministry.

PRAYER

One has no greater, effective way to pray than by praying back to God what He has given to us in His Word. It is amazing to me that so often when I am praying, the Lord will bring to my mind some words from a passage that I have studied recently. I don't always remember the location of the passage in God's Word, but I have a computer program I use to locate the passage quickly. Some people print out specific passages of God's Word on index cards and pray them back to our all sovereign, always faithful and good God. As I read them back to my Lord, it most often becomes a time of worship as well as petition. Hallelujah, what a Savior we worship and serve.

THE LOCAL CHURCH/LOCAL ASSEMBLY OF BELIEVERS

Let me add another thought for you to consider: being an active church member is immeasurably important to our churches ministering in full capacity as well as our own Christian walk, and it impacts our lives in more divinely effective ways.

> [13]For by one Spirit we were all baptized into one body, whether Jews or Greeks, whether slaves or free, and we were all made to drink of one Spirit. . . . [25]so that there may be no division in the body, but *that* the members may have the same care for one another. [26]And if one member suffers, all the members suffer with it; if *one* member is honored, all the members rejoice with it. [27]Now you are Christ's body, and individually members of it. (1 Corinthians 12:13, 25-27)

Jesus' spiritual body, which is identified in the New Testament as the "church," was created through His resurrection, His accension into heaven, and His sending of the Holy Spirit on the Day of Pentecost—the day the Holy Spirit was originally given to each person who was saved by faith to permanently indwell all believers. Every person who got saved on and after Pentecost was and continues to be supernaturally and spiritually placed by the Holy Spirit into the body of Christ (the church) as a vital and necessary member of which Christ Jesus is the Head. There is much to be said about having been placed into Christ's body, but I won't get into it now. I want every Christian to understand, as best I know how to convey it, that because each one of us is a member of His body, there are incalculable promises, benefits, and responsibilities for each of us. One of the most beneficial is found in 1 Corinthians 12:25-26 above. It works best for us to think of the different parts of the human body as we look at these two verses because Paul uses this illustration to help us understand this biblical, spiritual reality.

When any part of our physical bodies is diseased or injured, either visible or internal, the whole body is affected. For instance, when you badly stub your toe, your whole body responds in pain. Often the whole body is needed to tend to that injury. The legs may need to get you to where the ointment, bandages, or ice are. Or if the injury is bad enough, they may be needed to get you to the doctor's office. My husband had a severe gallbladder attack not too long ago. It was unseen until the infection in the organ spread into his torso and almost into his blood stream. It was another part of the body that was affected that caused him to go to the ER and be placed in the ICU for four days. One of the most visible blessings of being a part of the body of Christ is that we take care of the other members, and we ourselves are cared for by them.

There is rarely a time when someone in the body of Christ, the church, is not in need of care, either physical, spiritual, or emotional. My own church body, my local assembly of believers, has experienced several deaths recently—two women have become widows in particular. There is an interesting verse that is applicable here. Look at James 1:27: "Pure and undefiled religion in the sight of *our* God and Father is this: to visit orphans and widows in their distress, *and* to keep oneself unstained by the world." There are many other advantages. But the point I want to make regarding women is that we are not created to live life in a vacuum.

Knowing what God's Word says and knowing we are to live in obedience to what He says, when combined, becomes one of our most powerful lines of defense. Getting wise, biblical counsel from

9: VICTORIOUS, CHRIST-HONORING LIVING

someone who knows God's Word and understands how it is to be applied accurately can be another invaluable benefit. Women are more inclined to sharing our problems. However, when you are in need of advice, help, or simply an ear to listen or a shoulder to cry on, be so very, very careful with whom you share marital problems. Only go to the most trusted and tested friend. As I mentioned before, everyone my sister went to told her to "divorce the bum." That advice was not biblical. How I praise the Lord she didn't listen. I am convinced the only reason she listened to and did the righteous thing was that she searched the scriptures, and the Holy Spirit guided her in what to do and what not to do.

In addition to the great advantages and blessings that come from being a regular attender and an active participant in a local assembly of believers is the fact that we are being obedient because we are instructed to. Look with me at Hebrews 10:23-25:

> [23]Let us hold fast the confession of our hope without wavering, for He who promised is faithful; [24]and let us consider how to <u>stimulate one another to love and good deeds</u>, [25]<u>not forsaking our own assembling together</u> as is the habit of some, but encouraging *one another*, and all the more as you see the day drawing near.

There are several very important reasons why we are to be active in a local church. But I believe one of the least thought-of is "stimulating each other to love and good deeds." The Greek word *paroxusmos* translated "stimulate" here is a word that means "to encourage someone to action or feeling."[35] Christ's body should extend God's love to each other (that which is unconditional and sacrificial and meets the needs of those whom God brings into our lives) and motivate other believers to actively work in or through the church to accomplish God's purposes for themselves and His kingdom. Be reminded of this by reading John 13:35:

> "By this all men will know that you are My disciples, if you have love for one another."

---
35 *The Complete Word Study Dictionary: New Testament*

GOD'S PORTRAIT OF A "RIGHTEOUS WOMAN"

THE LORD'S SUPPER (COMMUNION)

You are likely very familiar with what is commonly called "The Lord's Supper" or "Communion." There are a few things I would like for you to take note of in 1 Corinthians 11 that you may have never considered before. I understand I am giving you a long passage to observe. However I believe you will be blessed and encouraged by its insights. Carefully read 1 Corinthians 11:23-32, and I'll talk with you about it afterwards.

> ²³For I received from the Lord that which I also delivered to you, that the Lord Jesus in the night in which He was betrayed took bread; ²⁴and when He had given thanks, He broke it and said, "This is My body, which is for you; do this in remembrance of Me." ²⁵In the same way He *took* the cup also after supper, saying, "This cup is the new covenant in My blood; do this, as often as you drink *it*, in remembrance of Me." ²⁶For as often as you eat this bread and drink the cup, you proclaim the Lord's death until He comes. ²⁷Therefore whoever eats the bread or drinks the cup of the Lord in an unworthy manner, shall be guilty of the body and the blood of the Lord. ²⁸But <u>a man must examine himself</u>, and in so doing he is to eat of the bread and drink of the cup. ²⁹For he who eats and drinks, eats and drinks judgment to himself if he does not judge the body rightly. ³⁰For this reason many among you are weak and sick, and a number sleep. ³¹But if we judged ourselves rightly, we would not be judged. ³²But when we are judged, we are disciplined by the Lord so that we will not be condemned along with the world.

First of all, I believe that the Lord gave us, the church, the ordinance of the Lord's Supper for several reasons: (1) to make a conscious and deliberate celebration of the horrendous, unimaginable price Jesus paid for our salvation; (2) to celebrate the promise of His return—the soon coming of Christ Jesus for us, His bride, the church, which is often called the rapture; and (3) to assure the regular corporate gathering of individual churches for each member to confess their sins.

9: VICTORIOUS, CHRIST-HONORING LIVING

Look back with me at verse 27 which says, "Whoever eats the bread or drinks the cup of the Lord in an unworthy manner, shall be guilty of the body and the blood of the Lord." I must confess that I don't fully understand all that this statement means, because in our minds we know that no one has ever been worthy of anything that God supplies to us. However, this passage explains what it means to be unworthy and how a believer becomes worthy in this context. The person who physically consumes these two elements and has any unconfessed sin, that believer is in danger of receiving the consequences that are listed in verses 30–31. Why? Because by partaking of the Lord's Supper with unconfessed sin, that person "eats and drinks judgment to himself." God says that by that act, they are actually "guilty of the body and the blood of the Lord."

I am going to add a fourth reason why I believe God established this ordinance for the church. It is for corporate cleansing/purification. It is even given to us in verses 31–32 that "if we judged ourselves rightly, <u>we would not be judged</u>" (that is, judged by God). In other words, there are most always consequences for continuing to sin, but when our sins are confessed to God, there are times when He removes that discipline. Here in verse 32 God defines His judgment of believers to be discipline: "weak and sick, and a number sleep [pass away]."

GOD'S DISCIPLINE OF BELIEVERS

Hebrews 12:7-11 makes a clear statement on God's discipline. Look with me and be blessed by God's explanation of His discipline—its purpose and why it is necessary:

> [7]It is for discipline that you endure; God deals with you as with sons; for what son is there whom *his* father does not discipline? [8]But if you are without discipline, of which all have become partakers, then you are illegitimate children and not sons. [9]Furthermore, we had earthly fathers to discipline us, and we respected them; shall we not much rather be subject to the Father of spirits, and live? [10]For they disciplined us for a short time as seemed best to them, but He *disciplines us* for *our* good, so that we may share His holiness. [11]All discipline for the moment seems not to be

joyful, but sorrowful; yet to those who have been trained by it, afterwards it <u>yields the peaceful fruit of righteousness</u>. (Hebrews 12:7-11)

Just in case you might not have let verse 11 soak in deep into your soul, know that God's discipline of His children is never out of anger and never to harm us. Even though God fully understands His discipline may possibly bring you sorrow, He does it anyway because His discipline brings about peace and righteousness in the heart and mind of each and every believer who is trained by it.

While I am on the subject, I need to "chase a rabbit" again here. There is another reason for God allowing sorrow in our lives. Second Corinthians 7:9 says, "I now rejoice, not that you were made sorrowful, but that you were made sorrowful to *the point of* repentance; for you were made sorrowful according to *the will of* God, so that you might not suffer loss in anything through us." Sorrow is not pointless when it brings us to our knees in repentance and reliance on God.

OK, back to 1 Corinthians 11 we observed in previously. The warning given to us in 1 Corinthians 11:29-30 should propel every believer (and we know that this ordinance is only for believers) to make sure they are "fully confessed up," so to speak, before they partake of these elements. By the phrase, "if we judged ourselves rightly," God means that (1) if we agree with Him that any of our own specific actions are wrong, (2) if we are continuing to dwell on anything that God tells us not to, or (3) if there is anything that God has told us to do and we have refused to do it—these, among others, are sins against God. And if we confess these to be sin and determine never to participate in any of these in the future and will do what God has instructed us to do, we become worthy to partake of the Lord's Supper.

You noticed, I'm sure, that in verses 31-32 there is an incredible promise that when we confess any sin to God, He removes the discipline that He would have otherwise needed to extend. I truly believe that one of the greatest benefits of when an assembly of believers gathers to celebrate the Lord's Supper is "corporate cleansing" of the bride of Christ. I'm hoping that knowing these things will make you not want to miss and take every opportunity to participate in this God-established ordinance which we commonly call the Lord's Supper or Communion.

9: VICTORIOUS, CHRIST-HONORING LIVING

LOVE YOUR NEIGHBOR

Let me digress for a moment to explain something very significant that happened to me. At the time of my writing this book, I have within the recent past completed the incredible privilege of serving on our church's pastoral search committee. As is most often the practice of such committees, its members are charged with the assignment of listening to the sermons of prospective candidates to fill the position of senior pastor. There was one week during this process when I listened to three different pastors preach on the same passage—Luke 10:30-37. I'm not going to say much about Jesus' illustration here, because it is self-explanatory, but this passage is printed below for those who might want to refresh their memories regarding the story of the good Samaritan:

> [30]Jesus replied and said, "A man was going down from Jerusalem to Jericho, and fell among robbers, and they stripped him and beat him, and went away leaving him half dead. [31]And by chance a priest was going down on that road, and when he saw him, he passed by on the other side. [32]Likewise a Levite also, when he came to the place and saw him, passed by on the other side. [33]But a Samaritan, who was on a journey, came upon him; and when he saw him, he felt compassion, [34]and came to him and bandaged up his wounds, pouring oil and wine on *them;* and he put him on his own beast, and brought him to an inn and took care of him. [35]On the next day he took out two denarii and gave them to the innkeeper and said, 'Take care of him; and whatever more you spend, when I return, I will repay you.' [36]Which of these three do you think proved to be a neighbor to the man who fell into the robbers' *hands?*" [37]And he said, "The one who showed mercy toward him." Then Jesus said to him, "Go and do the same." (Luke 10:30-37)

The Lord used the repetition of my listening to this sermon topic three times in one week and combined it with Romans 5:8 to speak to me: "But God demonstrates His own love toward us, in that while we were yet sinners, Christ died for us." Through the combination of these two passages, God gave me an insight, a revelation into one of the most important assignments we have: "Love our neighbors as ourselves," according to Luke 10:27.

I can't explain how the simplicity of this truth had escaped me all my adult life. I now no longer have to worry about "who" is my neighbor—he or she is the person God has placed in my path who has a need that He wants me to fulfill. I now no longer have to wonder how it is that I love this person. God wants me to meet that particular person's need, which is the manifestation of God's kind of love.

Note that God doesn't tell us the specific details of *how*; He just tells us we are to love. God loved us by providing the answer to every person's greatest need. We were sinners in need of a Savior. The truth that is so simple, yet so profound, is that we love others whom God has brought to our attention or placed in our path—that is, the people who need something and God has given us the resources to meet that need. Their needs can be of such great variety, but we are to be the vessel through whom God manifests His love by meeting their immediate needs.

Your love might be manifested in something as simple as bringing a meal to a sick person. There may be a neighbor you casually greet in your yard, or maybe you have just seen a moving truck pull in nearby and you can welcome them with something tangible. It might be a visit to someone who is homebound and needs Christian fellowship. It could be as you sit with a grieving person and comfort them in ways that God will lead you. You may have the monetary resources that God wants you to give to someone in financial need. In other words, love is an action not an emotion. God's kind of love is an act of the will with the purpose of meeting specific needs of specific people to whom God sends us and has given the needed resources to meet that need. There are some of you who learned this life-transforming truth many years earlier than I did. But as I have shared this insight with others, they seemed to be as thrilled as I was to have it explained so simply. What had seemed to be a very ambiguous command has become clear and doable. I am so blessed by Franklin Graham's proclamation for every act of kindness he and his team deliver—it is delivered "in Jesus' name" and through gospel conversations whenever possible. Our question needs not be, *Who is my neighbor?*, but needs to be a response of meeting the need of any person with whom the Lord puts in our path that has an immediate need whereby we have been given by God the resources to meet that need. I used to define God's love only as an action that is unconditional and sacrificial. However, the foundational action is meeting that person's immediate need whom God has sent to you because He has given you the resources to do so.

I must admit that recently I saw a need while I was standing in a parking lot. I recognized there was a need for physical help, but for some reason, I didn't step forward to meet that need. I could give you some excuses, but they would be just that—excuses. The lady later was so distraught by her situation that she stopped, got out of her car, and with great distress explained her situation. It broke my heart that I didn't help, and the Lord chastised me to the point of godly sorrow and repentance. I didn't anticipate this illustration through my failure to manifest an act of God's love and with it explain to this precious elderly woman how much God loves her. I assure you that I got the point. Ouch! *Thank You, Lord, for teaching me through a circumstance that I pray I will never repeat.*

God's love is manifested in us through how we respond to others. As wives, we need to manage our home atmosphere so that it is a safe place where our husbands most want to be. Providing a safe place for your children to come home to is just as important. Use this principle of loving your neighbor in teaching your children how God's love is manifested. If you do not have children, "borrow" others. I have heard of families who have chosen not to give each other gifts but to spend that money on buying presents for the children in orphanages and taking their children with them to deliver the presents. Others don't have Thanksgiving dinner at their house but rather go to a Christian homeless shelter and help serve. I won't be presumptuous to tell you how best you might train your children to love others God's way. The Lord is the one with the greatest, most creative and beneficial ways. We just need to ask Him, then listen for the answer.

Always remember to use your acts of love to try to develop gospel conversations. I'm sure that you know as well as I do that children learn best by example. There is no one who has the time and opportunity that you do to "train up your child in the way he should go." I consider, and I think our Lord God does too, that the job of raising children (by your personal teaching and example) to love God and serve Him wholeheartedly is one of the most important jobs in all the universe.

ANGELS: GUARD AGAINST ERROR

Angels seem to be an extremely popular topic among many today, including among Christ followers. As such, there are a couple of things the Bible is explicit about that could be profitable for us to remember:

1. No human has ever or will ever become an angel when they die. Angels are created beings which are in a separate category of God's created beings. One of the jobs they have been created to do is found in Hebrews 1:13-14: "But to which of the angels has He ever said, 'Sit at My right hand, until I make Your enemies a footstool for Your feet'? Are they not all ministering spirits, sent out to render service for the sake of those who will inherit salvation?" (Hebrews 1:13-14).

2. We are never to ask an angel to do anything. As we have just read in Hebrews 1, angels are "ministering spirits" that God sends out to help believers or those who will later become believers.

It has been well documented in God's Word that angels do on occasion take on human appearance and deliver messages and even come to the aid of God's children. It has also been well documented in history where a Christ-follower was in desperate need of help and there was no human around to help. But none-the-less, physical help came to them through angels who had taken on human appearance. For example, many Christians have been praying for years for those who are called by God to proclaim the gospel in countries where the persecution of Christians is common, even to the point of martyrdom. At the time of the writing of this book, our country has left Afghanistan with hundreds of Christians abandoned. As we should, we have been praying for their safety: *Lord, there doesn't seem to be any humans there that are able to help, but I know You can send an angel in human appearance to guide and protect them to a safe place, and I ask You to do so.*

9: VICTORIOUS, CHRIST-HONORING LIVING

Even as we are encouraged by what our God has purposed for angels to do, please note the warnings we are given as well from Colossians 2:18-19:

> ¹⁸Let no one keep defrauding you of your prize by delighting in self-abasement and <u>the worship of the angels</u>, taking his stand on *visions* he has seen, inflated without cause by his fleshly mind, ¹⁹and not holding fast to the head, from whom the entire body, being supplied and held together by the joints and ligaments, grows with a growth which is from God.

It is important that we be warned about who angels are and who they are not. Never are they to be worshiped as stated in Colossians 2, but we are not to go to them directly for help either. In other words, we should not try to communicate with them, ask them to do anything for us, etc. They indeed are ministering spirits sent to render service to us. However, it is God who sends them, not us. Second Corinthians 11:14 explains why:

> No wonder, for even Satan disguises himself as <u>an angel of light</u>.

We also learn in 1 Corinthians 6:3, "Do you not know that we will judge angels? How much more matters of this life?" This verse conveys to Christ followers our true relationship with the unseen spiritual world of angels. Yes, they are used by God to minister to His children, but we are to keep in mind that they are not superior beings. Someday Christians will judge angels. Truly an eye-opening fact that is worth remembering.

GUARD YOUR RESPONSES

The following is simply a concern of mine through personal experience and observation. Those of us who minister in our spiritual giftedness and calling in the arena before people are frequently complimented by others. Obviously these times are precious to us and encourage us greatly, knowing all along and publicly proclaiming in various ways that we know it is our God who is empowering and anointing us for service.

Years ago, I read somewhere that at the end of each day we should (figuratively speaking) give our God a bouquet of flowers with a sweet aroma as a "sacrifice of praise" for His bountiful provision that day. Isn't that a beautiful word picture and worth remembering? All this to say, how is it that we should handle the praise given to us by people? First, let me say that it should never be a rebuke similar to, "Don't give me praise; it is God." As true as that statement is, such a response is almost a slap in the face to the one who was just trying to encourage you by saying how much you blessed them. So, what do you say then? An encouraging response to give is something like, "Thank you so much. Our God is so good, and I am grateful He blessed you today."

> Let your speech always be with grace, *as though* seasoned with salt, so that you will know how you should respond to each person. (Colossians 4:6)

The way I express this command in Colossians 4:6 is to always let your speech be seasoned/laced with grace. I have learned that with the Lord's power I can address most any circumstance in a kind and encouraging way, even when something needs to be corrected. Have you ever had someone come to you with good advice, especially times when the Lord has already shown you the way of that good advice? Even though it would be correct to say, "I already know that," how much more of a blessing would it be to that person to respond with something like, "Thank you so much for sharing that with me. That is confirmation of what I sensed the Lord wanted me to do." Of course, there are many more illustrations, but I believe you share with me the instructions in Proverbs 15:1: "A gentle answer turns away wrath, but a harsh word stirs up anger."

GUARD YOUR MIND

The world and culture in which we live is continually becoming more and more ungodly and evil in its beliefs and practices. When you are listening to any person speak (especially in all aspects of media), please don't allow yourself to be influenced by what they say. I personally advise all believers to make it a practice to *not* be guided by what you see, much less by what you hear. The enemy of

9: VICTORIOUS, CHRIST-HONORING LIVING

our souls, Satan himself, is manifesting his evil destructive ways not only through lies but also through manipulating what is seen visibly. The deceptions and lies of the devil and his minions that are accepted as truth by so many today make one shiver inside at the thought of their ramifications.

We must test the words of any spiritual leader we listen to. At least one person who will read this book will ask the questions, *What do you mean by "test" their words?* Or, *How do I test what someone says to be truth or not?* So glad you asked. I'm sure many of you have heard that when someone is trained to discover counterfeit bills, the method that is used is *not* to examine the counterfeits. They learn to recognize what is counterfeit by carefully studying and learning the feel and look of that which is genuine.

We as believers are trained to recognize what is false by studying God's Word, that which is true and without error. Knowing what is clearly and accurately given to us in God's Word prepares us to recognize false teachers. I plead with you to determine to make it your lifelong habit to deposit God's Word deep within your heart to the extent that you not only *know* but also *believe* what God says to be true and trustworthy to the point of obedience. Knowing and embracing God's truth will guide, protect, and change you more and more into the image of His Son, our Savior, Jesus Christ the Nazarene by the power of the Holy Spirit.

Second Timothy 2:15 commands us to "Be diligent to present yourself approved to God as a workman who does not need to be ashamed, <u>accurately handling the word of truth</u>." There are many today who hold high levels of spiritual influence that are preaching or teaching principles that are in direct opposition to what God's Word clearly states. One of the most well-known, popular preachers on television today has preached (I heard him say it myself) that there is more than one way to God. Jesus said in John 14:6, "Jesus said to him, 'I am the way, and the truth, and the life; <u>no one comes to the Father but through Me.</u>'"

Determine to make it your habit to choose not to listen to any person you know who has taught or is currently teaching actions, information, or doctrine that is contrary to the clear teachings in scripture. I promise such a habit will help guard anyone of us from being deceived by false teachers who seem to be everywhere in the days in which we live. I have made the decision not to listen again to one of my past favorite teachers because I know that something he has taught in the recent past is not biblically true and that I am not smart enough to catch all the errors he may teach in the future. Yes, in today's world, that really does lessen the listening pool.

GUARD YOUR CHILDREN

Perhaps in the history of our great country, there has never been a time when our children were in more danger. Again, I am speaking from personal experience when I say that our children and grandchildren are faced with time and opportunity to become involved in ever-increasing destructive, evil, sinful behavior. There is open opportunity for our youth to obtain drugs easily, to some of whom the taking of one pill can be so lethal it kills. As I mentioned earlier, sexual immorality today among many is considered a normal and acceptable social activity. I cannot claim enough wisdom to begin to advise you on how to raise your children, but scripture tells us in Ephesians 6:4b to raise them in the "discipline and instruction of the Lord."

There will be wonderful times in the future for you to become good friends with your children. However, while they are under your authority, they desperately need involved parents who will risk their children's anger in order to "train them up in the discipline and instruction of the Lord." As I mentioned earlier, Dr. James Dobson taught me years ago, and it has proven to be true, that most children balk and fuss, some even pushing over the boundaries, regarding the rules and restrictions you set. However, these rules and boundaries subconsciously give them security. Most often, in their subconscious brains these boundaries are the things that they internally receive as safety and love.

I realize I am repeating a warning that I have not only covered well but that you are perhaps well acquainted with yourself. There is unseen danger lurking in the shadows of much social media and even in our schools, as has been revealed. The kids in today's culture and time most often reject the warnings that much of the information they are receiving from many outside sources is brainwashing their minds toward evil and destructive ways. I do so pray that the Lord will give you new, creative, and effective ways to dismantle, to intercept,

9: VICTORIOUS, CHRIST-HONORING LIVING

and to guard your child(ren) from this evil they are bombarded with constantly.

GUARD YOUR CHILD'S EDUCATION

Beware, determining which university/college you will send your children off to can be one of the most difficult events you and your child will ever go through. In many cases, college is the place where a teen is forced to put their parents' teaching to the test—where their lifelong beliefs will be contradicted and mocked and where their behavior will be unseen by their parents. I believe most if not all of you who have gotten this far in this book are much more concerned about your individual child(ren)'s future welfare than anyone else could ever be. I just want to encourage you to continue to keep close to all their activities. Just as you should be included in your children choosing friends (maintaining proper "veto power"), I encourage the same when helping your child(ren) choose a college to attend. There are excellent academic institutions that continue to maintain a culture where Christian behavior and beliefs are not only acceptable but are encouraged and nurtured. I am confident that your careful research and God's guidance will lead you to the best place for your child's higher education.

Recently, many, many of our school districts are propagating what has been titled officially as "Critical Race Theory" (CRT)—or disguised under another name. Many, but thankfully not all, city or county school boards are making decisions regarding what they want to teach regardless of what the majority of parents want and believe. I have personally read what CRT is saying. Among the text, homosexuality is presented as a good and viable alternate lifestyle. However, I think one of the most damaging premises is that there is more than one race. God has created only one race, and there is still just one race—the human race which has been and continues to be created in God's image. Every person who has ever lived is a descendant of Adam and Eve. And even further down the family tree, everyone alive today is a descendant of Noah and his wife through their three sons. There are no other races, just the one, although there are different "nations and tribes and tongues and peoples," according to Revelation 14:6.

GOD'S PORTRAIT OF A "RIGHTEOUS WOMAN"

Also, there are only two genders—male and female. It has been revealed that both homosexuality and transgenderism is often being taught as good, and it is encouraged and also being included in many schools' teaching curriculum starting at very young ages. I don't think parents today can afford not to be very informed in their child's activities and what they are taught at their schools.

GUARD YOUR WORD CHOICES

We are instructed to use biblical words when biblical subjects are discussed. Second Timothy 1:13 commands us to "Retain the standard of sound words which you have heard from me, in the faith and love which are in Christ Jesus." Instead of the word *abortion*, I personally use the term *killing babies* because that is exactly what it is. Another common word people use is *gay*. God's standard of a "sound word" is *homosexuality*. To so many among us, *gay* is the word they use because they have determined it is the most common, acceptable, and non-offensive. There are more examples, but I think you get the idea of the 2 Timothy 1:13 command. Words mean something— God's words not only mean what He says they mean, but they also carry within them the divine power to accomplish what God has sent them forth to accomplish.

I caution each of us to be careful how we voice our differences of opinions—in our churches and everywhere else. First Corinthians 11:18-19 says, "For, in the first place, when you come together as a church, I hear that divisions exist among you; and in part I believe it. For there must also be factions among you, so that those who are approved may become evident among you." God forbids us to cause division or strife, according to Jude 18-19 and Proverbs 6:16-19:

> [18][T]hey were saying to you, "In the last time there will be mockers, following after their own ungodly lusts." [19]These are the ones who cause divisions, worldly-minded, devoid of the Spirit. (Jude 18-19)

> [16]There are six things which the Lord hates, yes, seven which are an abomination to Him: [17]Haughty eyes, a lying tongue, and <u>hands that shed innocent blood</u>,[36] [18]A heart

---

36 Note: this certainly covers killing unborn babies.

that devises wicked plans, feet that run rapidly to evil, ¹⁹a false witness who utters lies, and <u>one who spreads strife among brothers</u>. (Proverbs 6:16-19)

There are certainly doctrinal issues that we must "fall on our swords" over (figuratively speaking, of course). These are issues that revolve around foundational principles for salvation: that Jesus is the Son of God who took on human flesh; lived a perfect, sinless life; died on a cross as a substitutionary sacrifice for the sins of the world; was raised bodily from the dead on the third day for our justification (declared to be made the righteousness of God); and has ascended into heaven to sit at our Father God's right hand. When it comes to these essential beliefs of the Christian faith, it is vital that you hold fast to your convictions.

However, there are many other doctrinal beliefs that may not be agreed upon within even a single body of believers as well as among different denominations. We are certainly free to have our opinions, but we are not free to be so adamant about them that we demand people join us in our opinion or they will be slandered by us in our church and elsewhere. This is the essence of causing division and strife among brothers. I am sorry to say that I have been in churches where this very thing has caused the church to literally split in half. I believe that our God doesn't turn a blind eye to such behavior; there are and will be consequences. However, as I have mentioned several times, God does not let us choose when or how He will discipline such behavior. Ephesians 4:1-3 speaks clearly on this subject:

> ¹Therefore I, the prisoner of the Lord, implore you to walk in a manner worthy of the calling with which you have been called, ²with all humility and gentleness, with patience, showing tolerance for one another in love, ³being diligent to preserve the unity of the Spirit in the bond of peace.

GUARD AGAINST GOSSIP

There have been times in my past when I was put in the position where I had to answer someone with the following "principle." On rare occasions, someone would try to tell me something that was very negative and accusatory against a person in my church. The answer the Lord would normally put on my heart was, "I really don't believe that could be true," and then I change the subject. There were other times when this person would not stop speaking negatively about someone, and I would have to say, "Please stop. I just don't want to hear about this," or something similar. To my great joy, over the years, one woman in particular got the idea and rarely ever shared gossip (at least with me). I truly believe she finally understood that I was unwilling to listen to these things. The following passage in 1 Peter 3 is very sobering when we look at the consequences stated there. A popular children's song may come to mind as you read: "be careful little tongue what you say."

> [10] The one who desires life, to love and see good days, must keep his tongue from evil and his lips from speaking deceit.
> [11] He must turn away from evil and do good; He must seek peace and pursue it. (1 Peter 3:10-11)

GUARD YOUR CHILDREN FROM YOUR MARITAL ISSUES

There is another issue that I don't think some Christian parents are as cautious about as they need to be. The safety that children feel when surrounded by their parents' love and respect for one another is incalculable. The truth is that the genuineness of any person's true self is lived out and revealed in the privacy of their own home. If there are serious disagreements between you and your husband, of course, they need to be discussed, but only in private and away from your children's ears. According to God's Word, your husband has the final say in settling these decisions as the leader of the home. And indeed, it is your husband who is responsible for and accountable to God for these decisions, not you. I have heard it said and agree that the husband who either doesn't seek his wife's opinion or totally disregards her opinions is a fool and can be depriving himself of important and necessary information required to make good and informed decisions. Again, discussions about things you and your husband are in disagreement on are often necessary and beneficial but not in the presence or the hearing of your children. Because there

9: VICTORIOUS, CHRIST-HONORING LIVING

are so many divorces in today's culture, I have heard it stated that when a child hears their parents "discuss their differences harshly," it often leads to fearing that their parents will be divorcing soon.

GUARD YOUR FOCUS

You may have heard the saying, "A person can be so heavenly minded, they are of no earthly good." Did you know there is a scripture passage that states the exact opposite? It is found in Colossians 3:1-2:

> ¹Therefore if you have been raised up with Christ, keep seeking the things above, where Christ is, seated at the right hand of God. ²<u>Set your mind on the things above</u>, not on the things that are on earth.

GUARD FROM WHOM YOU SEEK ADVICE

Many people, including Christians, blame their past for their present difficulties. As I have mentioned previously, when my sister was young, she was molested by our father. She decided at some point in her marriage to reveal this fact to her husband, which caused genuine irreputable damage to their marriage. Later when she was dealing with marriage/separation struggles with her unbelieving husband, she was advised to divorce him. She decided to live life God's way and not by the advice many in her church gave her at the time of her separation from her husband. My sister was a counselor, teacher, and encourager of the gospel of Jesus Christ. She gave me permission to share her story, and through the years I have connected women with her who have also experienced sexual abuse. She was able to minister to these women of the victory she found in Jesus.

Let me clarify. We do not have to have experienced the same circumstance as another to be able to minister to them. It is God's Word that does the healing, not our experience. Because I know that God's Word is able to give each and every believer in Jesus Christ the answer and guidance to be more than a conqueror in living out every circumstance they ever encounter in total victory, I do not hesitate to give counsel according to God's Word, even though I have never walked in their shoes.

In my opinion, it is important when seeking out biblical counsel not to seek advice from someone who is still in the midst of a trial similar to yours. These situations often result in sharing miseries and consoling one another. However, it will not be until someone has gotten to the other side of their trial in victory that they are equipped to be able to counsel and encourage another according to God's wisdom and ways. Then they are able to tell you how God can and is able to meet your needs specifically through His Word of instructions and promises because He has faithfully met their needs to the place of victory! Second Corinthians 1:3-4 will be food for your soul:

> ³Blessed *be* the God and Father of our Lord Jesus Christ, the Father of mercies and God of all comfort, ⁴who comforts us in all our affliction so that we will be able to comfort those who are in any affliction with the comfort with which we ourselves are comforted by God.

From this passage in 2 Corinthians 1, I not only see that God does indeed comfort us in our afflictions, but I also see that the comfort we receive from the Lord during our afflictions and trials then becomes a vehicle through which God can use to help us comfort others. I heard someone say years ago, "Don't waste your cancer." I guess I can say through the testimony of this scripture passage that we should not waste our afflictions.

This last admonition regarding "from whom you take advice" will be more difficult than others for many of us, especially for those in leadership who are committed to listening to the opinions of those whom you are responsible to lead. It is so important that leaders know the areas of need that can be revealed through the counsel of others. However, the task of discerning which ear you are to pay attention can be daunting. There is a stark example given to us in the account of how Rehoboam would "reign over the southern kingdom of Judah" after the death of his father, King Solomon. I'm not going to go through with you the account given to us in 1 Kings 12 and 2 Chronicles 10, but Rehoboam rejected the council of wise experienced men and was persuaded by his self-serving, inexperienced friends to make a terrible decision. I guess what I am trying to convey here is that leadership requires close attention to whom you allow

9: VICTORIOUS, CHRIST-HONORING LIVING

yourself to be influenced, but it also requires much prayer and divine discernment in choosing to whom you will listen and to what is being advised. Again, God has promised to give each of us wisdom if we will ask according to James 1:5-6. Our part is not only to ask but to listen to and obey what the Lord reveals to you. I believe it is not only incumbent on us who are under Christian leadership to follow this leadership but also to pray diligently for them as they seek godly counsel.

CHAPTER 10

A Snapshot of God's Declared Future

Many say that neither the book of Daniel nor the book of Revelation can be understood. I am in total and absolute disagreement with that conclusion. In both of these books in God's Word, God gives us very important details regarding His declared future. First and 2 Thessalonians reveals other critical information about our Lord's return that we would be wise to diligently study as well. I have tried to relate these truths about "God's declared future" in a way that those who desire to come to at least an overview understanding will be able to. The Lord instructed me to add this subject to the book. The purpose primarily is to give you hope, peace, and anticipation of what He has planned before the foundation of the world was laid. Read and be amazed at the many details that our all-sovereign and good God has given us to know in advance of these events before they become reality and are fulfilled. Because these prophesies are recorded in God's Word, we will be able to recognize them as part of God's predetermined plans.

My encouragement is that you read this chapter slowly, asking the Lord to give you understanding. He always does if any of us ask Him. Forewarned is indeed forearmed. My prayer is also that you will be at peace as you learn from God's Word and be enabled to view our country's—even the world's—circumstances with confidence and hope because you now are able to recognize many events as God's revealed plans and purposes.

Jesus is coming back for His bride (the church). *Be ready to meet your Bridegroom!* Living righteously—that is, living out the life God has purposed for women—includes our being spiritually and emotionally prepared by God's revelation before it occurs. This is part of God's transformational process of His children so that when we see Him face to face, He will say, "Well done, good and faithful slave. You were faithful with a few things, I will put you in charge of many things; enter into the joy of your master," according to Matthew 25:23.

Have you ever had the opportunity to study the books of Daniel, Revelation, and/or 1 and 2 Thessalonians in depth? I am going to somewhat shift gears in this chapter. At the time of this writing, I have recently finished ten months of teaching the book of Daniel to my Sunday school class. I am also at this time leading a weekly Precept Bible study class on the book of Revelation (which is my third time to do so). Needless to say, eschatology (biblical study of future things) is very much on my mind these days. I will not attempt to teach you all I have learned from God's Word about the events of the last years humans will occupy this present earth nor even of the years that will precede those times. However, as God-fearing women, it is important to have a solid overview of what God has revealed in His Word regarding the prophesied future to the degree that we will be equipped spiritually and emotionally to persevere. To view these times as clear, foretold events that will usher in the second coming of the Lord Jesus Christ to earth to set up His earthly kingdom for one thousand years is of immense value to all followers of the Lord Jesus Christ.

One of the major tenets of the Christian faith is our confident assurance (my definition of *hope*) that Christ Jesus will return for His bride—that is, those who have been saved by faith and placed by His Spirit into the body of Christ, His church. Jesus came the first time to give His life as a ransom for many to pay our sin debt, according to Mark 10:45: "For even the Son of Man did not come to be served, but to serve, and to give His life a ransom for many." As He told His disciples that He would give His life (which He did

10: A SNAPSHOT OF GOD'S DECLARED FUTURE

on the cross and then was raised bodily from the dead), He also told them that He would return again for them. Look with me at John 14:1-3, what Jesus spoke, and Acts 1:9-11, what Luke recorded of a statement made by two angels on the day Jesus visibly ascended into heaven forty days after His bodily resurrection from the dead. There were two angels that appeared to Jesus' disciples immediately after He ascended into heaven and then sat down at the right hand of God the Father, and what they communicated is recorded in Acts 1:9-11.

> ¹"Do not let your heart be troubled; believe in God, believe also in Me. ²In My Father's house are many dwelling places; if it were not so, I would have told you; for I go to prepare a place for you. ³If I go and prepare a place for you, <u>I will come again and receive you to Myself</u> that where I am, *there* you may be also." (John 14:1-3)
>
> ⁹And after He [Jesus] had said these things, He was lifted up while they were looking on, and a cloud received Him out of their sight. ¹⁰And as they were gazing intently into the sky while He was going, behold, two men in white clothing stood beside them. ¹¹They also said, "Men of Galilee, why do you stand looking into the sky? This Jesus, who has been taken up from you into heaven, <u>will come in just the same way as you have watched Him go into heaven</u>." (Acts 1:9-11)

It has been a two-thousand-year-plus quest for man to try to determine exactly when Jesus will be returning in the clouds for His bride, the church, and then seven years later when He will return to the earth to set up His earthly kingdom to reign for a thousand years. God's Word clearly states that we will not know the day or the hour of Jesus' return, according to Matthew 24:36: "No one knows about that day or hour, not even the angels in heaven, nor the Son, but only the Father."

This passage carries with it some very fascinating nuances. During the time of Jesus' earthly ministry, there were specific traditions that the Jews followed in the engagement and the wedding ceremonies. In those days, there was an actual ceremony for the engagement (the Jewish word was *betrothal*) of a Jewish male to a Jewish female. In fact, this ceremony produced a legal binding covenant agreement of the couple, and it could only be broken by a legal divorce. This practice can clearly be seen by what Joseph planned to do when he learned that Mary (to whom he had already become legally betrothed) was pregnant. Matthew 1:18-19 (ESV) says, "Now the birth of Jesus Christ took place in this way. When his mother Mary had been betrothed to Joseph, before they came together, she was found to be with child from the Holy Spirit. And her husband Joseph, being a just man and unwilling to put her to shame, resolved to divorce her quietly." The common order was that after the betrothal occurred, the bridegroom would go back to his father's house and begin to prepare the place that would be his and his wife's future home. Many times, these quarters were an attachment to the father's house. When the father (only the father) decided the quarters were ready and the time was right, he would tell his son to go get his bride. When he returned with her, there was a wedding ceremony followed by a banquet with many guests.

When Jesus returns for his *bride*, the church, we see the following:

> ¹Now concerning the times and the seasons brothers, you have no need to have anything written to you. ²For you yourselves are fully aware that the day of the Lord will come like a thief in the night. ³While people are saying, "There is peace and security," then sudden destruction will come upon them as labor pains come upon a pregnant woman, and they will not escape. ⁴But you are not in darkness, brothers, for that day to surprise you like a thief. ⁵For you are all children of light, children of the day. We are not of the night or of the darkness. (1 Thessalonians 5:1-5 ESV)

It is evident that Paul had taught the members of the Thessalonian church much about the Lord's return. We call this event the rapture. Paul says to them, "You have no need to have anything written to you concerning the times and the seasons." The Greek word *chronos* used here that is translated "times" is defined as follows: "This word perceives time quantitatively as a period measured by the succession of objects and events and denotes the passing of moments." The Greek word *kairos* translated "seasons"

10: A SNAPSHOT OF GOD'S DECLARED FUTURE

(ESV) is partially described as follows: "When used as the plural are times at which certain foreordained events take place."[37]

Paul states that these Thessalonians believers "are fully aware that the day of the Lord will come like a thief in the night." Then he goes on to say that Jesus will not come as a thief in the night *to them* (Christians) because they were not in darkness—they were children of light. We don't know for sure just how much of the details Paul had taught them were written in letters to the other churches, but he also mentions in 1 Thessalonians 5:3 the sudden coming of Christ Jesus was compared to labor pains/birth pangs. So according to 1 Thessalonians 5:1, we are to know/recognize the "times and the seasons," but Matthew 24:36 makes it clear we will not know the day or the hour.

It is interesting to note that both Matthew 24:8 and Mark 13:8 record Jesus' statements regarding the signs of the coming "ends of the age," and both use the words *birth/labor pangs*. Paul also used the same description in 1 Thessalonians 5:3. In the Matthew and Mark passages, you will discover that many of the listed "birth pangs" are present-day, recognizable events. There are many Christians who believe that scripture warns us that we are to be alert and ready for Jesus to return at any time. Many believe that not only have the "birth pangs" begun but also that we are getting closer and closer to the actual "birth" itself—that is, that Jesus' return for His bride is getting very close. Hallelujah, what a Savior! So we know for sure that we won't know the day or the hour, but we can and should know "the times and the seasons." Paul adds to our knowledge about Jesus' return in 2 Thessalonians 2:1-9, which is an interesting response to the fact that there were those in the Thessalonian church who believed that they had missed Jesus' rapture of the church (verse 1: "our gathering together to Him"). Paul's response to them leaves present-day Christians some interesting and informative insights given to you in the scripture passage below.

> ¹Now we request you, brethren, with regard to the coming of our Lord Jesus Christ and <u>our gathering together to Him</u>, ²that you not be quickly shaken from your composure or be disturbed either by a spirit or a message or a letter as if from us, to the effect that the day of the Lord has come. ³Let

---

37 *The Complete Word Study Dictionary: New Testament*

GOD'S PORTRAIT OF A "RIGHTEOUS WOMAN"

no one in any way deceive you, for *it will not come* unless the apostasy comes first, and the man of lawlessness is revealed, the son of destruction, ⁴who opposes and exalts himself above every so-called god or object of worship, so that he takes his seat in the temple of God, displaying himself as being God. ⁵Do you not remember that while I was still with you, I was telling you these things? ⁶And you know what restrains him now, so that in his time he will be revealed. ⁷For the mystery of lawlessness is already at work; only <u>he who now restrains will do so</u> until he is taken out of the way. ⁸Then that lawless one will be revealed whom the Lord will slay with the breath of His mouth and bring to an end by the appearance of His coming; ⁹*that is*, the one whose coming is in accord with the activity of Satan, with all power and signs and false wonders. (2 Thessalonians 2:1-9)

The way these nine verses are written makes it kind of trickly to determine the sequential order of the events Paul mentions. The three phrases, "the coming of our Lord Jesus Christ," "our gathering together to Him," and "the day of the Lord," I believe, are speaking of the same event. The phrase "the day of the Lord" represents the "umbrella event," which consists of both the "coming of our Lord Jesus Christ" and "our gathering together to Him." Paul was reassuring these Christians in the Thessalonian church that they had not missed the rapture; there were certain events that must happen, which had not yet occurred, before they would meet Jesus in the clouds. The following shows the sequential order of events (as best as I can discern) mentioned in the above passage:

1. *The apostasy comes* (to depart, to forsake, to fall away;[38] v. 3). Be sure to apply 1 John 2:19 here: "They went out from us, but they were not *really* of us; for if they had been of us, they would have remained with us; but *they went out*, so that it would be shown that they all are not of us."

2. *The "restrainer" is taken out of the way.* Most believe "the restrainer" mentioned in verse 7 is the Holy Spirit. I am not one of them; however, we do agree that the "what" (this noun is neuter; is inanimate) of verse 6 is the church.

---

[38] *The Complete Word Study Dictionary: New Testament*

10: A SNAPSHOT OF GOD'S DECLARED FUTURE

3. *The "Lawless One" is revealed.* Most conservative Christians who believe the Bible is in its entirety without any error, agree the Lawless One mentioned in verse 3 is the antichrist. I am also one of them.

4. *The Day of the Lord comes* (vv. 2-3). In this context, I believe "the Day of the Lord" in verse 2 is described in verse 1, and it is "the coming of our Lord Jesus Christ and our gathering together to Him"—that is, the rapture.

The "Day of the Lord" in this context is not a single period of twenty-four hours but is a period of time that begins with a specific event and ends with a specific event. Many believe, and I am one, that the "Day of the Lord" has its beginning with the rapture of the church and culminates with the literal, physical return of Jesus Christ with the saints to this present earth to rule and reign for one thousand years as King of kings and Lord of lords.

The "restrainer" of 2 Thessalonians 2:1-9, I believe, is God's appointed guardian angel for the church (as opposed to the widely held belief that this "person" is the Holy Spirit). Let me start with some of the foundations for such a strong belief. We know that God created these heavenly beings to be messengers and guardians of His creation, including humans.

As we have already seen, Hebrews 1:14 says, "Are they [angels] not all <u>ministering spirits,</u> sent out to render service for the sake of those who will inherit salvation?" Daniel 10:13–12:4 records for us the conversations that an unnamed angel had with Daniel. We not only learn in these verses that angels are busy in the unseen heavenly realm but also that there is warfare going on in the heavenly realm between the angels on God's mission and demons (fallen angels who follow Satan's mission). These demonic angels were trying to keep God's angels from accomplishing their assigned duties. In Daniel 10:13 this unnamed angel spoke of Michael as one who came to help him and in Daniel 10:21 as the only one who "stands firmly with me against these *forces* except Michael your prince." This unnamed angel was assigned to be a guardian over Darius, the king of Media (the king whom Daniel served), according to Daniel 11:1: "In the first year of Darius the Mede, I [the angel] arose to be an encouragement and a protection for him."

Now let's observe Daniel 12:1, where we are told that Michael was and is today the guardian angel over the Jews, God's chosen people.

> Now at that time Michael, the great prince <u>who stands guard</u> <u>over the sons of your people</u>, will arise. (Daniel 12:1)

It is my strong opinion that, just as God has assigned Michael (who is among the angelic hierarchy established by God) to watch over and guard the Jews, God has also appointed a strong angel with the assignment to watch over and guard the church/the bride of His Son, our Lord Jesus Christ. I believe that God's guardian angel over the church is the "restrainer." Because of 2 Thessalonians 2:7, we know that the "restraining of lawlessness . . . is now at work" and would be a major part of this angel's assignment.

Another reason I believe the Holy Spirit is *not* the restrainer is that I do not believe the Holy Spirit will be "taken out of the way," as 2 Thessalonians 2:7 declares will happen to the restrainer. I'm convinced that those who are to be saved during the last seven years (that is commonly called the tribulation that precedes the Lord's physical return to earth) will be saved and permanently indwelt by the Holy Spirit the same way as we are today. Revelation 14:6, 12 states that the gospel of Jesus Christ will be preached to "every nation and tribe and tongue and people" on the earth:

> ⁶And I saw another angel flying in midheaven, having an <u>eternal gospel</u> to preach to those who live on the earth, and to every nation and tribe and tongue and people; . . . ¹²Here is the perseverance of the saints who keep the commandments of God and their <u>faith in Jesus</u>. (Revelation 14:6, 12)

The fact is, those who are saved during these last seven years will be saved by faith in the gospel of Jesus Christ, just as all have been since the new covenant was inaugurated through His blood. There has not been a "newer covenant" made by God for salvation. This new covenant of salvation through Jesus which was made for the Jews and the Gentiles has not been altered nor eliminated. This new covenant of grace through faith in Christ Jesus promises the permanent indwelling of the Holy Spirit, which has not been replaced

10: A SNAPSHOT OF GOD'S DECLARED FUTURE

or made void and will be the same until Jesus returns to earth to set up His earthly kingdom.

There are a few additional passages given to us in the book of Daniel that reveal what God plans for the future. The following is more of a commentary than a verse-by-verse exposition. As I have mentioned, it took me ten months to teach this book to my Sunday school class, so I will do my best to be concise and clear in just a few pages.

Daniel is one of my very favorite books of the Old Testament. I am so inspired by this young man who determined from the beginning of his captivity in Babylon in 605 BC (many believe he was probably around fourteen years old) that he would not defile himself by eating the provisions given to him in the king's court. Throughout the approximately sixty-five-plus years that he served in the courts of pagan kings, he never wavered from this worship of, trust in, and obedience to the only true God. Because of Daniel's unfailing love for and service to Jehovah God (and probably for more reasons), God chose him to be the recipient of His "blueprint" for all future worldwide kingdoms to rule on this earth, including that which Jesus will set up.

Daniel 2 records for us a dream of Nebuchadnezzar, the king of Babylon. Daniel and his three Jewish friends prayed that God would give Daniel the interpretation of this dream. And indeed, God not only gave Daniel the accurate interpretation of Nebuchadnezzar's dream but the actual content of his dream. The dream was of a large statue in which God revealed five future worldwide kingdoms and the future of the present kingdom. All but the "head of gold" would be future kingdoms unknown at that time, which was around 603 BC. These specific kingdoms represented by certain body parts of the statue are listed below. Note: A rendering of how this statue might have looked is following my explanation of the meanings of this statue.

1. *The first worldwide kingdom* was represented by the head of gold of the statue, which was Babylon and was at that time ruled by King Nebuchadnezzar from 605 BC until 539 BC. Keep in mind, these are kingdoms that would rule the entire known world at their time in history.

2. *The second worldwide kingdom* was represented by the breast and arms of the statue and was revealed by God to

be the combined kingdoms of the Medes and the Persians (which is named in Daniel 5:28; 6:8, 12, 15), which would begin their reign in 539 BC (about sixty-four years later). Remember the numbers go *down* in the years prior to the beginning of "AD," which was supposed to be the year of Jesus' birth. However, most experts today believe they were off by three or four years.

3. *The third worldwide kingdom* was represented by the belly and the thighs of the statue and represented the kingdom of Greece which began in 331 BC, some 272 years after Nebuchadnezzar's dream of this statue. The name of this worldwide kingdom would not be revealed until about fifty-three years later through one of Daniel's dreams. The name is recorded as Greece in Daniel 8:21; 10:20; and 11:2.

4. *The fourth worldwide kingdom* was represented by the two legs of iron of the statue, which was biblically unnamed; it has been named by humans as the Roman Empire. This kingdom is pictured in Daniel 7:7a (Daniel's first prophetic dream) as a "dreadful, terrifying and extremely strong beast which had ten horns." The Roman Empire's worldwide reign began in 146 BC and lasted until about 476 AD. The Roman Empire was the last worldwide kingdom which was prophesied and has already been fulfilled. There has been no worldwide kingdom that ruled over the whole earth since the Romans. However, there were two more prophesied worldwide kingdoms in Daniel 2 and Daniel 7 which are yet to be fulfilled.

5. *The fifth worldwide kingdom* was represented by two feet with ten toes in Nebuchadnezzar's statue. This part of the statue is also an unnamed worldwide kingdom, and it has not yet been formed nor has begun to reign. Daniel's first dream recorded in Daniel 7 pictures these same prophesied kingdoms, but his was illustrated through the figures of animals, not a statue. Daniel 7:24 records that out of the fourth kingdom (the Roman Empire) the fifth kingdom will arise, pictured as ten horns.

10: A SNAPSHOT OF GOD'S DECLARED FUTURE

Most who have studied prophecy for years agree that this fifth worldwide kingdom (yet to come) will be composed of ten kingdoms that will come out of the nations which were originally part of the old Roman Empire. Many have thought these ten kingdoms would be the European Union. I do not. The Roman Empire not only spread over most if not all of today's European countries but was also spread over several Middle-Eastern nations, including Turkey, Syria, Iraq, Egypt, and part of the Soviet Union. This fifth worldwide kingdom will come to pass in God's timing and will be the kingdom which will be, soon after it is established as a worldwide ruling authority, ruled solely by the antichrist.

6. *The sixth worldwide kingdom* was represented by a stone, cut without hands, that struck the statue on its feet and became a great mountain and filled the whole earth, according to Nebuchadnezzar's dream (Daniel 2:35, 44-45). This stone represents the Lord Jesus Christ when He comes physically to the earth to set up His kingdom to reign over the whole earth for one thousand years as the King of kings and the Lord of lords.

Let me remind us that these worldwide ruling kingdoms were prophesied in both Nebuchadnezzar's dream of the statue in Daniel 2 and partially in Daniel's dream of the animals in Daniel 7. These were foretold by God some six hundred years before the birth of our Lord Jesus Christ.

Daniel 9:23-27 is a passage that contains a wellspring of information that we need to examine and begins with an angel speaking to Daniel. This passage records the angel's explanation and interpretation of Daniel's third vision to him. Read through these verses, and I'll provide an interpretation based on my research, and various reputable biblical scholars agree:

> ²³At the beginning of your [Daniel's] supplications the command was issued, and I have come to tell *you*, for you are highly esteemed; so, give heed to the message and gain understanding of the vision. ²⁴"<u>Seventy weeks have been decreed for your people and your holy city</u>, to finish the

transgression, to make an end of sin, to make atonement for iniquity, to bring in everlasting righteousness, to seal up vision and prophecy and to anoint the most holy *place*. ²⁵So you are to know and discern *that* from the issuing of a decree to restore and rebuild Jerusalem until Messiah the Prince *there will be* seven weeks and sixty-two weeks; it will be built again, with plaza and moat, even in times of distress. ²⁶Then <u>after the sixty-two weeks the Messiah will be cut off</u> and have nothing, and the people of the prince who is to come will destroy the city and the sanctuary. And its end *will come* with a flood; even to the end there will be war; desolations are determined. ²⁷And he will make a firm covenant with the many for one week, but in the middle of the week he will put a stop to sacrifice and grain offering; and on the wing of abominations *will come* one who makes desolate, even until a complete destruction, one that is decreed, is poured out on the one who makes desolate." (Daniel 9:23-27)

10: A SNAPSHOT OF GOD'S DECLARED FUTURE

©1999 Precept Ministries International

Revelation Part 3
The Gentile Domination of Israel

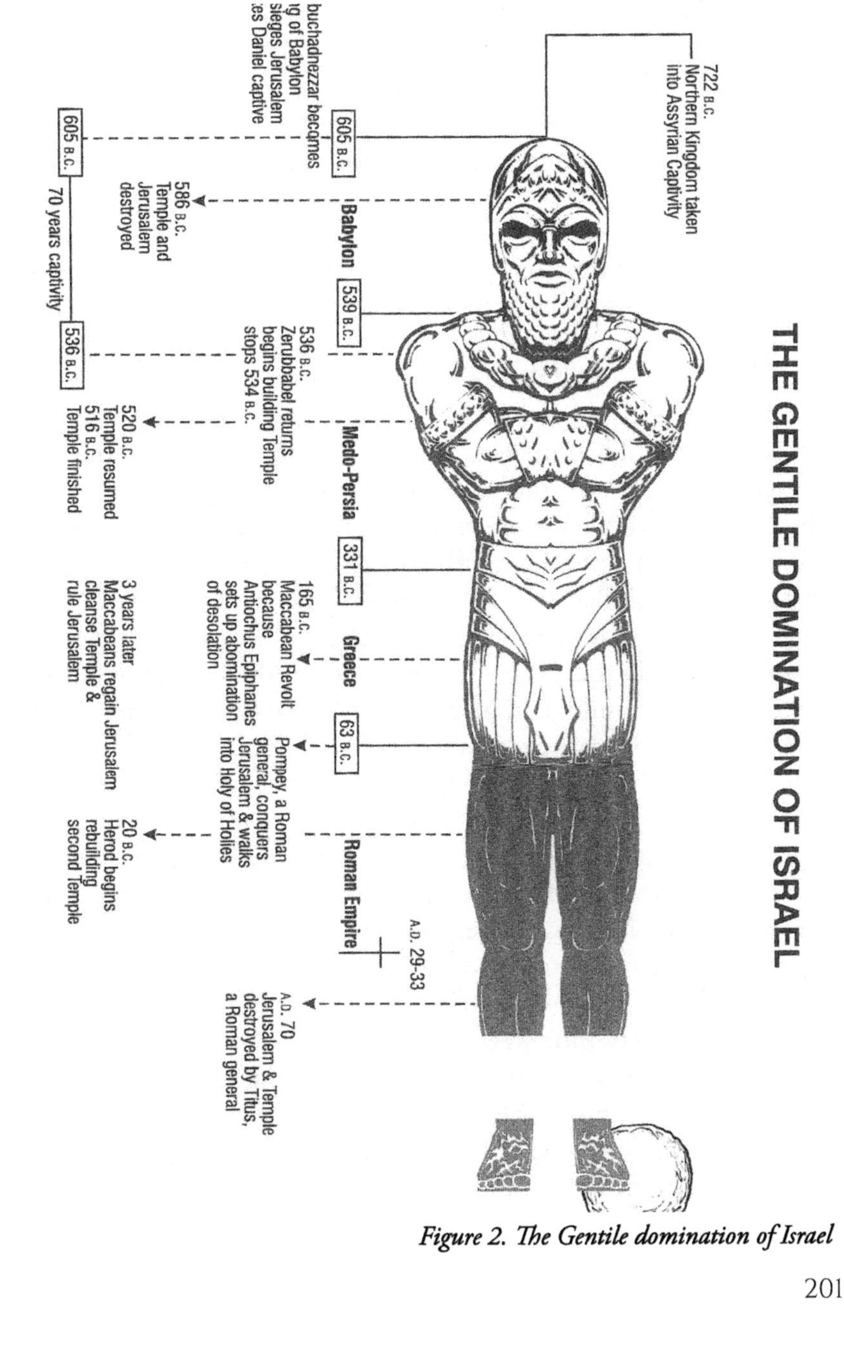

Figure 2. *The Gentile domination of Israel*

GOD'S PORTRAIT OF A "RIGHTEOUS WOMAN"

The "seventy weeks" mentioned in Daniel 9:23-27 have been decreed specifically for the Jews (Daniel's people). The Hebrew word *sabua* that is translated "weeks" in this passage is actually the Hebrew word for "sevens, a group of seven days or seven years, etc."[39] We are told in verse 24 that there have been decreed literally "seventy sevens"—that is, seventy groups of seven days or seventy groups of seven years. History proves that these events prophesied here did not occur in seventy groups of seven days. So a literal interpretation would have to be seventy groups of seven years equaling 490 years, which works out perfectly with what history reveals has already been fulfilled, plus one more period of seven years that is yet to be fulfilled. The first period addressed is seven weeks (forty-nine years) plus (and) sixty-two weeks (434 years), which equals sixty-nine weeks (483 years).

The beginning of these seventy weeks or 490 years decreed for the Jews were prophesied to begin with the issuing of a decree to restore and rebuild Jerusalem, according to Daniel 7:25. The book of Nehemiah records the event of God sending Nehemiah and other Jews to Jerusalem to rebuild the wall around Jerusalem, which enabled them to restore and rebuild Jerusalem itself. This Daniel 9 prophecy was fulfilled by a decree issued by Artaxerxes in 445 BC, which gives us the start date of the prophesied 490 years, namely the seventy weeks. So the times given were "from the issuing of a decree to restore and rebuild Jerusalem *until* Messiah the Prince" (Daniel 9:26). Recall my mention of the combination of two different periods of time (weeks) in verse 25. I have been told that the mention of seven weeks (forty-nine years) in verse 25 refers to something significant occurring regarding the Jews, perhaps the completion of the rebuilding of Jerusalem. The next time frame mentioned in verse 25 is sixty-two weeks, which equals 434 years. Verse 26 states "after 434 years" (sixty-two weeks) Messiah would be cut off. If you add the forty-nine years (seven weeks) to the 434 years (sixty-two weeks) you get 483 years (sixty-nine weeks).

In about 539 BC it was given to Daniel through a vision that from the issuing of the decree to restore and rebuild Jerusalem until the Messiah will be cut off would be 483 years. Scholars have calculated that from the time when the Persian King Artaxerxes'

---

39 *The Complete Word Study Dictionary: Old Testament*

10: A SNAPSHOT OF GOD'S DECLARED FUTURE

issued the decree to rebuild the wall of Jerusalem until Jesus rode the donkey into the city of Jerusalem on the week of His crucifixion was exactly 483 years (sixty-nine weeks).

Daniel 9:26 also prophesied that "the city [Jerusalem] and the sanctuary [the rebuilt temple in Jerusalem] would be destroyed," which was fulfilled in 70 AD by a Roman general. By the way, the Roman Emperor Vespasian had told his General Titus not to destroy the Jewish temple in Jerusalem. But God's prophetic plans must be fulfilled, and Jerusalem and the temple were totally destroyed. There was not one stone left on another, as Jesus prophesied in Luke 21:6.

History accounts for 483 years (sixty-nine weeks) of the 490 years (seventy weeks) spoken of in Daniel 9:25-26 that were decreed for the Jews. What is true about many prophecies in scripture is that there are events that are not mentioned. In this case, a very long interlude between week sixty-nine (483 years) and week seventy (seven years) isn't mentioned in Daniel 9:23-27. This interlude is spoken of in scripture as the "time of the Gentiles." This "time of the Gentiles" is mentioned by Jesus Himself in Luke 21:24: "And they will fall by the edge of the sword, and will be led captive into all the nations; and Jerusalem will be trampled underfoot by the Gentiles until the times of the Gentiles are fulfilled."

Let's read Daniel 9:26-27:

> ²⁶"Then after the sixty-two weeks the Messiah will be cut off and have nothing, and the people of the prince who is to come will destroy the city and the sanctuary. And its end *will come* with a flood; even to the end there will be war; desolations are determined. ²⁷And he will make a firm covenant with the many for one week [seven years], but in the middle of the week he will put a stop to sacrifice and grain offering; and on the wing of abominations *will come* one who makes desolate, even until a complete destruction, one that is decreed, is poured out on the one who makes desolate."

Note again that Daniel 9:27 addresses a singular "week" (seven years). This one week (seven years) is needed to complete the 490 years (seventy weeks) that have been decreed for the Jews. These last remaining seven years (one week) begins with, "He will make a firm covenant with the many for one week." The "he" of verse 27 has been connected with the people who would destroy Jerusalem and the temple in verse 26. These people were Gentiles of the then prophesied Roman Empire which occurred in 70 AD. Remember that the fifth kingdom will be composed of ten nations that would have originally been part of this fourth kingdom—that is, it would come out of the original Roman Empire (the fourth kingdom prophesied in Daniel 2 and Daniel 7).

Clearly, the prophesied future can be very tedious and complex to explain. Regardless, I hope you will be encouraged that our Sovereign God has revealed to us in His Word what the last seven years of man's rule on this earth will be like.

Let's go back and examine a specific passage that will help us better understand why Daniel 9:27 speaks of a *single person* when this kingdom is originally composed of ten nations. Look with me at Daniel 7:8, 20-26, describing the first of Daniel's personal dreams:

> ⁸"While I was contemplating the horns,⁴⁰ behold, another horn, a little one, came up among them, and three of the first horns were pulled out by the roots before it; and behold, this horn possessed eyes like the eyes of a man and a mouth uttering great *boasts*. . . . ²⁰and *the meaning* of the ten horns that *were* on its head and the other *horn* which came up, and before which three *of them* fell, namely, that horn which had eyes and a mouth uttering great *boasts* and which was larger in appearance than its associates. ²¹I kept looking, and that horn was waging war with the saints and overpowering them ²²until the Ancient of Days came and judgment was passed in favor of the saints of the Highest One, and the time arrived when the saints took possession of the kingdom. ²³Thus he said: 'The fourth beast will be a fourth kingdom on the earth, which will be different from all the *other* kingdoms and will devour the whole earth and tread it down and crush it.⁴¹ ²⁴As for the ten horns, <u>out of this kingdom ten kings will arise; and another will arise after them</u>, and he will be different from the previous ones

---

40 The context is "ten horns."
41 "[A] fourth kingdom" mentioned in verse 23 is referring to the Roman Empire.

10: A SNAPSHOT OF GOD'S DECLARED FUTURE

and will subdue three kings.⁴² ²⁵He will speak out against the Most High and wear down the saints of the Highest One, and he will intend to make alterations in times and in law; and they will be given into his hand for a time, times, and half a time.⁴³ ²⁶But the court will sit *for judgment*, and his dominion will be taken away, annihilated and destroyed forever."

In my years of studying prophecy, I, along with many others, have come to the conclusion that this fifth worldwide kingdom prophesied in Daniel 2 and 7 will be a kingdom which will begin as a ten-nation worldwide ruling confederacy. Each of these kingdoms/nations will be ones which were part of the original Roman Empire and will collectively rule over all the nations on earth at that time. This ten-nation confederacy will embrace an eleventh king/kingdom (who is the "little horn" of Daniel 7:8) and will come into rule—not by power but by shrewdness according to Daniel 8:25. This eleventh king will be the antichrist, and when he comes into the ten-nation confederacy, he will personally remove three kings of the original ten. The antichrist will become the leader of this worldwide kingdom, which will then become an eight-nation confederacy (Daniel 7:24).

Daniel 9:27a will then become a reality: "And he will make a firm covenant with the many for one week." The seventieth week of Daniel, in my opinion, will begin with the antichrist as the sole ruler of this worldwide kingdom when he makes a covenant with the Jews/Israel for seven years (one week)—that is, these seven years will be the last remaining years which "have been decreed for the Jews." When these seven years are completed, the full 490 years will have been fulfilled. I have heard it speculated that the Jews will make this covenant in order to rebuild their new temple in Jerusalem. We are not told what will cause the Jews to make a covenant with the antichrist, but this speculation sounds compelling to me. When a new temple is built in Jerusalem, and indeed there will be a new temple built in Jerusalem, I believe Jews will flock to Israel from all over the world.

We know there will be a temple completed and sacrifices will have begun by the middle of this prophesied last week (seven years).

---
42 "[T]his kingdom" mentioned in verse 24 is referring to the old Roman Empire.
43 The "time, times and half a time" = three and a half years.

GOD'S PORTRAIT OF A "RIGHTEOUS WOMAN"

Daniel 9:27b tells us the antichrist "will put a stop to sacrifice and grain offering; . . . on the wing of abominations." Daniel 12:11 speaks of the event: "From the time that the regular sacrifice is abolished and the abomination of desolation is set up, *there will be* 1,290 days." These 1,290 days represent the last half of the seven years spoken of as the seventieth week of Daniel.[44]

Daniel 9:27 and Daniel 12:11 both prophesy of "the abomination of desolation" occurring in the middle of the seventieth week of Daniel. Daniel 12:11 speaks of 1,290 days, which would also be "in the middle of the week," as Daniel 9:27 states. This event was also prophesied by Jesus Christ Himself. Look at Matthew 24:15-21. This exact event is also recorded in Mark 13:14-19.

> [15]Therefore, when you see the ABOMINATION OF DESOLATION which was spoken of through Daniel the prophet, standing in the holy place (let the reader understand), [16]then those who are in Judea must flee to the mountains. [17]Whoever is on the housetop must not go down to get the things out that are in his house. [18]Whoever is in the field must not turn back to get his cloak. [19]But woe to those who are pregnant and to those who are nursing babies in those days! [20]But pray that your flight will not be in the winter, or on a Sabbath. [21]For then <u>there will be a great tribulation</u>, such as has not occurred since the beginning of the world until now, nor ever will. (Matthew 24:15-21)

This event that is titled "the abomination of desolation" was prophesied both by Daniel and Jesus and is also mentioned and described in 2 Thessalonians 2:4: "Who opposes and exalts himself above every so-called god or object of worship, so that <u>he takes his seat in the temple of God, displaying himself as being God</u>." This event, which is somewhat veiled, is also mentioned in Revelation 13:1-3, 5-6. The "him" mentioned in verse 5 is referring to the antichrist, which is described as a "beast" in Revelation 13:1-3. The "forty-two months" in verse 5 is also three and a half years, according to the Jewish calendar.

---

44 In the Jewish calendar, 1,290 days equal three and a half years.

10: A SNAPSHOT OF GOD'S DECLARED FUTURE

> ¹And the dragon⁴⁵ stood on the sand of the seashore. Then I saw a beast coming up out of the sea, having ten horns and seven heads, and on his horns *were* ten diadems, and on his heads *were* blasphemous names. ²And the beast which I saw was like a leopard, and his feet were like *those* of a bear, and his mouth like the mouth of a lion. And the dragon [Satan, according to Revelation 12:9] gave him his power and his throne and great authority. ³*I saw* one of his heads as if it had been slain, and his fatal wound was healed. And the whole earth was amazed *and followed* after the beast; . . . ⁵There was <u>given to him</u> a mouth speaking arrogant words and blasphemies, and authority to act for <u>forty-two months</u> was given to him. ⁶And he opened his mouth in blasphemies against God, to blaspheme His name and His tabernacle, *that is*, those who dwell in heaven. (Revelation 13:1-3, 5-6)

I finish this detailed explanation of "God's declared future" knowing that it is very long and most probably very difficult to follow by just reading through it. I don't intend these explanations to cause you to believe what I believe about these prophesies, but I hope that it will whet your appetite to the point of your desiring to study these passages yourself.

Within the last year, I compiled all the reasons that I have learned from God's Word to explain why I believe in a pre-tribulation (pre-seventieth week of Daniel) rapture. Although I understand there are a couple of passages in the book of Revelation that do give some credence to those who believe in a mid-tribulation rapture, I do not interpret these passages the same way. I believe the preponderance of evidence in God's Word leads to the conclusion that the rapture will occur before the last seven years as detailed in Revelation 5–19. There are many godly biblical scholars who do not agree with my interpretations. This is not a salvation issue and certainly not an issue worth fighting over, however it is important and worth a personal study. The following are six reasons I embrace a pre-tribulation rapture of the church:⁴⁶

---

45 Satan, according to Revelation 12:9.
46 During my years of studying eschatology, the biblical study of end times/final things/last things, I concluded that when the New Testament mentions

GOD'S PORTRAIT OF A "RIGHTEOUS WOMAN"

1. Daniel's seventieth week is for the Jews and Jerusalem.

    ^{24}"Seventy weeks have been decreed for your people and your holy city, to finish the transgression, to make an end of sin, to make atonement for iniquity, to bring in everlasting righteousness, to seal up vision and prophecy and to anoint the most holy *place*. ^{25}So you are to know and discern *that* from the issuing of a decree to restore and rebuild Jerusalem until Messiah the Prince *there will be* seven weeks and sixty-two weeks; it will be built again, with plaza and moat, even in times of distress. ^{26}Then after the sixty-two weeks the Messiah will be cut off and have nothing, and the people of the prince who is to come will destroy the city and the sanctuary. And its end *will come* with a flood; even to the end there will be war; desolations are determined. ^{27}And he will make a firm covenant with the many for one week, but in the middle of the week he will put a stop to sacrifice and grain offering; and on the wing of abominations *will come* one who makes desolate, even until a complete destruction, one that is decreed, is poured out on the one who makes desolate." (Daniel 9:24-27)

2. The rapture will not come unless the "man of lawlessness" (the antichrist) is revealed, which I have dealt with previously.

    ^{1}Now we request you, brethren, with regard to the coming of our Lord Jesus Christ and our gathering together to Him, ^{2}that you not be quickly shaken from your composure or be disturbed either by a spirit or a message or a letter as if from us, to the effect that the day of the Lord has come. ^{3}Let no one in any way deceive you, for *it will not come* unless the apostasy

---

either "the Day of the Lord" or the "coming of the Lord," and when the context is speaking to believers, most always (I've found only one exception) each of these phrases is referring to the Lord's return for His bride/the rapture (in the air) and not to Jesus' physical return to earth to set up His kingdom, which is at the very end of the seven years of tribulation—that is, the seventieth week of Daniel.

10: A SNAPSHOT OF GOD'S DECLARED FUTURE

comes first, and the man of lawlessness is revealed, the son of destruction, ⁴who opposes and exalts himself above every so-called god or object of worship, so that he takes his seat in the temple of God, displaying himself as being God. ⁵Do you not remember that while I was still with you, I was telling you these things? ⁶And you know what restrains him now, so that in his time he will be revealed. ⁷For the mystery of lawlessness is already at work; only he who now restrains *will do so* until he is taken out of the way. ⁸Then that lawless one will be revealed whom the Lord will slay with the breath of His mouth and bring to an end by the appearance of His coming; ⁹*that is*, the one whose coming is in accord with the activity of Satan, with all power and signs and false wonders, ¹⁰and with all the deception of wickedness for those who perish, because they did not receive the love of the truth so as to be saved. (2 Thessalonians 2:1-10)

Order of Events in 2 Thessalonians 2:1-10:

- *First:* Apostasy comes (v. 3).
- *Second:* The "restrainer is taken out of the way" (v. 7), "*then* the lawless one will be revealed" (vv. 6–8).
- *Third:* The lawless one is revealed in his time (vv. 3, 6, 8).
- *Fourth:* The Day of the Lord comes (v. 3: the Day of the Lord will not come unless the man of lawlessness is revealed).

3. The rapture will not come as a "thief in the night" to believers; we are not in darkness.[47]

   ¹Now as to the times and the epochs, brethren, you have no need of anything to be written to you. ²For you yourselves know full well that the day of the Lord will come just like a thief in the night. ³While they are saying, "Peace and safety!" then destruction will come upon them suddenly like labor pains upon a woman with child, and they will not escape. ⁴But

---
47 The context is believers' relationship to the rapture.

you, brethren, are not in darkness, that the day would overtake you like a thief; ⁵for you are all sons of light and sons of day. We are not of night nor of darkness; ⁶so then let us not sleep as others do, but let us be alert and sober. ⁷For those who sleep do their sleeping at night, and those who get drunk get drunk at night. ⁸But since we are of *the* day, let us be sober, having put on the breastplate of faith and love, and as a helmet, the hope of salvation. (1 Thessalonians 5:1-8)

4. The rapture will keep believers from experiencing God's wrath when it is poured out on the earth. Revelation 6:15-17 records the responses of those who experienced the results of Jesus breaking the sixth seal of the seven seal judgments.

⁸But since we are of *the* day, let us be sober, having put on the breastplate of faith and love, and as a helmet, the hope of salvation. ⁹For <u>God has not destined us for wrath</u> but for obtaining salvation through our Lord Jesus Christ. (1 Thessalonians 5:8-9)

¹⁵Then the kings of the earth and the great men and the commanders and the rich and the strong and every slave and free man hid themselves in the caves and among the rocks of the mountains; ¹⁶and they said to the mountains and to the rocks, "Fall on us and hide us from the presence of Him who sits on the throne, and from the wrath of the Lamb; ¹⁷for the great day of their wrath has come, and who is able to stand?" (Revelation 6:15-17)

5. The timeframe of the tribulation described in Revelation consists of two, three-and-a-half-year segments. Together these two segments equal the same timeframe used in Daniel 9:27. Revelation 11:3 and 12:6 mentions 1,260 days, which equals three and a half years in the Hebrew calendar and occurs in the first three-and-a-half-year segment.

10: A SNAPSHOT OF GOD'S DECLARED FUTURE

> "And he will make a firm covenant with the many for one week [7 years], but in the middle of the week [at the end of the first three and a half years] he will put a stop to sacrifice and grain offering; and on the wing of abominations *will come* one who makes desolate, even until a complete destruction, one that is decreed, is poured out on the one who makes desolate." (Daniel 9:27)

> "And I will grant *authority* to my two witnesses, and they will prophesy for twelve hundred and sixty days, clothed in sackcloth." (Revelation 11:3)[48]

> Then the woman fled into the wilderness where she had a place prepared by God, so that there she would be nourished for one thousand two hundred and sixty days. (Revelation 12:6)[49]

6. The church is not mentioned in the book of Revelation after the seven letters to the churches in Revelation 2–3. Some believe (and I am among them) that John the apostle's vision in Revelation 4:1-2 could be a veiled reference to the rapture of the church before the seventieth week of Daniel begins. It is notable that the event John saw when he was taken up into heaven was Jesus' future breaking of the seven seals fixed on the scroll that begins the 70th week of Daniel—i.e., the seven years of tribulation that are described in Revelation 6–19.

> ¹After these things[50] I looked, and behold, a door *standing* open in heaven, and the first voice which I had heard, like *the sound* of a trumpet speaking with me, said, "Come up here, and I will show you what must take place after these things." ²Immediately I was in the Spirit; and behold, a throne was standing in heaven, and One sitting on the throne. (Revelation 4:1-2)

---

48 This time frame is the first portion of the total of seven years.
49 This time frame is during the second and last portion of the total of seven years.
50 "these things" in verse 1, I believe, refer to the "times of the Gentiles"—that is, the church age as mentioned in Luke 21:24.

> "[A]nd they will fall by the edge of the sword, and will be led captive into all the nations; and Jerusalem will be trampled underfoot by the Gentiles until the times of the Gentiles are fulfilled." (Luke 21:24)

What follows is my summary of future events (sequentially) revealed in the passages in God's Word that I covered in this chapter. I have also added several events with their corresponding scripture references that I did not cover. There is much that could be said about these additional events, but this is not the time nor the place. However, the scripture references given will get you to the right place for your own personal study.

The bottom line of my intention for giving you this list that I have compiled from my own personal study of God's Word over many years is to create in those who read this book a conscious and deliberate decision to make yourself spiritually and emotionally ready for Jesus' return for His bride, the church. Stay close to Him in prayer, in Bible study, and in obedience, and listen for the trumpet to sound. Know and recognize the signs of Jesus' return—the "birth pains"—so that you are able to establish a biblical worldview that will equip you to accurately assess both current and future circumstances and events.

Summary of future events:

1. Ten nations will come together, will form a ten-nation confederacy, and will take over worldwide rulership.

2. The antichrist is revealed.

3. The rapture of the church occurs when Christians will meet Jesus in the clouds and receive their glorified, eternal bodies just like Jesus' after His resurrection.

4. The antichrist makes a seven-year covenant with Israel.

5. The seventieth week of Daniel begins and is completed—that is, the so-called "seven years of tribulation"—and occurs as described in Revelation 5–19.

6. The "Bema Seat" judgment is held. This will be where the works of each believer will be judged, and we will receive our rewards or experience the loss of rewards. This event

10: A SNAPSHOT OF GOD'S DECLARED FUTURE

will be held in heaven sometime between the rapture and our return to earth with Christ Jesus for the thousand-year reign with Him (2 Corinthians 5:10).

7. The marriage and the marriage banquet for Christ and His bride, the church, will occur in heaven. Revelation 19:7-19 (especially verses 7 and 9) gives us reason to speculate that the "marriage of the Lamb" and the "marriage supper" will happen just prior to Jesus' return to earth with His bride (all genuine believers) in her wedding garments made of fine linen (Revelation 19:8).[51]

8. Jesus comes, along with His saints, to earth the second time to establish His sovereign rule over all the earth (Revelation 19:11-20:6).

9. The war of the great day of God, commonly known as the Battle of Armageddon, will occur. Jesus will smite the nations and rule over them with a rod of iron (Revelation 19:15).[52]

10. The beast (antichrist) and the false prophet along with all those who had taken the mark of the beast will be killed by a sword, which will come from the mouth of Jesus, and then will be thrown into the lake of fire (Revelation 19:20-21).

11. Satan will be bound and then thrown and locked into the abyss for a thousand years (Revelation 20:1-3).

12. Jesus and His saints (us) will rule and reign over all the earth for a thousand years (Revelation 20:4).

13. Satan will be released after a thousand years is completed in order to gather a multitude of nations for the final battled called the Battle of Gog and Magog. Fire from heaven will come down and devour them (Revelation 20:7-9).

14. Satan will be thrown into the lake of fire for all eternity at the end of the thousand-year reign of Christ (Revelation 20:10).

---

[51] The "fine linen" is the "righteous acts of the saints." Let's be about creating much "fine linen" for the most beautiful wedding garment possible.

[52] The kings of the whole world will have been gathered by three unclean spirits at Har-Magedon for this battle (Revelation 16:13-16).

15. All who rejected the person and work of God's Son, Jesus Christ, will be judged at the Great White Throne Judgment and then thrown into the lake of fire (Revelation 20:12-15).

16. God will create of a new heaven and a new earth, and the new Jerusalem "will come down out of heaven from God" (Revelation 21:1-2).

17. All believers in the Lord Jesus Christ will live throughout all eternity, ruling and reigning with Christ in the presence of Father God and our Lord Jesus Christ (Revelation 21:3-7; 22:5).

I want to repeat that I am not in any way meaning to disparage the beliefs and/or conclusions of anyone else regarding my stated beliefs and conclusions stated in this book—including my thoughts on the subject of "God's prophesied future events." I do so hope and pray that the writings in this chapter regarding our Savior's second coming will have whetted your appetite for your own future study in God's Word. I am hopeful that this study brings with it the elimination of any fear and the confident assurance that God has a plan and is always about working out His plan. That you will become assured that God will provide all you need for "life and godliness through the true knowledge of Himself and His Son, Christ Jesus." I believe our returning to 2 Peter 1 and observing verses 2-11 one more time will not only remind you again of God's promises to us but will also remind you of some extremely important instructions. Carefully observe these life-changing verses and examine your own life as you do. The rewards could prove to be invaluable and will be eternal.

> [2]Grace and peace be multiplied to you in the knowledge of God and of Jesus our Lord; [3]seeing that His divine power has granted to us everything pertaining to life and godliness, through the true knowledge of Him who called us by His own glory and excellence. [4]For by these He has granted to us His precious and magnificent promises, so that by them you may become partakers of *the* divine nature, having escaped the corruption that is in the world by lust. [5]Now for this very reason also, applying all diligence, in your faith supply moral excellence, and in *your*

10: A SNAPSHOT OF GOD'S DECLARED FUTURE

moral excellence, knowledge, ⁶and in *your* knowledge, self-control, and in *your* self-control, perseverance, and in *your* perseverance, godliness, ⁷and in *your* godliness, brotherly kindness, and in *your* brotherly kindness, love. ⁸For if these *qualities* are yours and are increasing, they render you neither useless nor unfruitful in the true knowledge of our Lord Jesus Christ. ⁹For he who lacks these *qualities* is blind *or* short-sighted, having forgotten *his* purification from his former sins. ¹⁰Therefore, brethren, be all the more diligent to make certain about His calling and choosing you; for as long as you practice these things, you will never stumble; ¹¹for in this way the entrance into the eternal kingdom of our Lord and Savior Jesus Christ will be abundantly supplied to you. (2 Peter 1:2-11)

May our Lord's peace and anticipation reign in your hearts from the revelations God has given to us about His Son, our Lord Jesus Christ's soon coming return to gather His bride (the church) to Himself for all eternity.

CHAPTER 11

Now What?

So, ladies, what does all this mean? *Now what?* I believe that the following parable Jesus taught His disciples will be very profitable for all of us to observe at this time. This event occurred on the Mount of Olives two days before the Passover when He would be "delivered up for crucifixion" according to Matthew 26:1-2. This parable is found in Matthew 25:13-31. The reason for and the subject of this teaching is that the disciples asked Jesus, "What will be the sign of Jesus' return and the end of the age?" (Matthew 24:1-3). Read Matthew 25:13-31 first, and then I'll share with you what is so very applicable from Jesus' words to one of the foundational reasons this book has been written—to be ready and on the alert for Jesus' second coming.

> [13]"Be on the alert then, for you do not know the day nor the hour. [14]For *it is* just like a man *about* to go on a journey, who called his own slaves and entrusted his possessions to them. [15]To one he gave five talents, to another, two, and to another, one, each according to his own ability; and he went on his journey. [16]Immediately the one who had received the five talents went and traded with them, and gained five more talents. [17]In the same manner the one who *had received* the two *talents* gained two more. [18]But he

GOD'S PORTRAIT OF A "RIGHTEOUS WOMAN"

who received the one *talent* went away, and dug *a hole* in the ground and hid his master's money. [19]Now after a long time the master of those slaves came and settled accounts with them. [20]The one who had received the five talents came up and brought five more talents, saying, 'Master, you entrusted five talents to me. See, I have gained five more talents.' [21]His master said to him, 'Well done, good and faithful slave. You were faithful with a few things, I will put you in charge of many things; enter into the joy of your master.' [22]Also the one who *had received* the two talents came up and said, 'Master, you entrusted two talents to me. See, I have gained two more talents.' [23]His master said to him, 'Well done, good and faithful slave. You were faithful with a few things, I will put you in charge of many things; enter into the joy of your master.' [24]And the one also who had received the one talent came up and said, 'Master, I knew you to be a hard man, reaping where you did not sow and gathering where you scattered no *seed*. [25]And I was afraid, and went away and hid your talent in the ground. See, you have what is yours.' [26]But his master answered and said to him, 'You wicked, lazy slave, you knew that I reap where I did not sow and gather where I scattered no *seed*. [27]Then you ought to have put my money in the bank, and on my arrival I would have received my *money* back with interest. [28]Therefore take away the talent from him, and give it to the one who has the ten talents.' [29]For to everyone who has, *more* shall be given, and he will have an abundance; but from the one who does not have, even what he does have shall be taken away. [30]Throw out the worthless slave into the outer darkness; in that place there will be weeping and gnashing of teeth. [31]But when the Son of Man comes in His glory, and all the angels with Him, then He will sit on His glorious throne." (Matthew 25:13-31)

First of all, what we do with what God has entrusted to us in this life on earth has everything to do with how we will spend eternity in heaven in the presence of our Lord and our God. *Everything!* This message to His disciples covered those who are saved and those who

11: NOW WHAT?

were proven by their actions not to be saved. The subject is told us in Matthew 25:1, which starts with "the kingdom of heaven will be comparable to ten virgins" (verses 1-12), and then Jesus transitions to an illustration of "a master and his slaves." Even though I'm not including the details of the first part regarding the ten virgins, it is helpful to connect Jesus' response to the "foolish virgins" who were not prepared for the "bridegroom's coming to get his bride." This is how Jesus responded to these unprepared, foolish virgins in Matthew 25:12: "But he answered, 'Truly I say to you, I do not know you.'" Then Jesus' narrative about the "kingdom of heaven" continues with Matthew 25:13-31, which you have just read.

Another very important fact we want to notice in this passage is that the "master" was going on a journey and "entrusted" his possessions to his slaves. Speaking of this "slave" issue, it is written that all believers are "bondslaves" of Jesus Christ, according to Colossians 4:12: "Epaphras, who is one of your number, a bondslave of Jesus Christ, sends you his greetings, always laboring earnestly for you in his prayers, that you may stand perfect and fully assured in all the will of God." It is important that the master in this parable did not tell his slaves how long he would be gone, but it was understood they would be accountable to him when he did return. It is written in 1 Corinthians 4:2, "In this case, moreover, it is required of stewards that one be found trustworthy." Each slave was entrusted with the amount of money that was "according to his own ability." Their master returned, and an accountability of what had been entrusted to each of them occurred. The first two slaves had immediately put to work what each had been given, and each had increased his master's money twofold. Both received the same response from their master: "His master said to him, 'Well done, good and faithful slave. You were faithful with a few things, I will put you in charge of many things; enter into the joy of your master.'" We can't miss the fact that their reward was "entering *the joy of their master.*" The slave who had done nothing to increase what his master had entrusted to him had literally "hid his money in the ground." It was placed in the ground out of his sight with no intent to make any increase in his master's possessions. This slave received the following response: "Throw out the worthless slave into the outer darkness; in that place there will be weeping and gnashing of teeth. But when the Son of Man comes in His glory, and all the angels with Him, then He will sit on His glorious throne." There is much to be learned from this parable, but we will cover only a few things.

We learn from this parable that not only are Christians given specific *abilities* and with the abilities specific *works* through which we are to produce an increase in the "Kingdom of Heaven" and also to bring glory to His great name with what He has entrusted with us. The most significant ability we are given is found in Acts 1:8: "But you will receive power when the Holy Spirit has come upon you; and you shall be My witnesses both in Jerusalem, and in all Judea and Samaria, and even to the remotest part of the earth." And Ephesians 2:8-10 promises, "For by grace you have been saved through faith; and that not of yourselves, *it is* the gift of God; not as a result of works, so that no one may boast. For we are His workmanship, created in Christ Jesus for good works, which God prepared beforehand so that we would walk in them."

Jesus used parables to illustrate a specific spiritual lesson using a story whose language, setting, and cultural context was understandable to those He was speaking. Through the parable, they were able to gain deep insight into the core message Jesus needed them to understand. This chapter is intended to bring into focus the core messages that I have attempted to communicate through these chapters. While I pray that the details in each chapter have helped you gain deeper understanding of what God's Word says to us, I also want to make sure that you don't focus so intently on the minutiae of the biblical discussion that you miss the overall purpose for which the book was written. My heart, as evidenced through a lifetime of teaching women, is to disciple women. Success in discipleship demands that the biblical teaching and spiritual insights find faithful expression in real life. As Jesus offered parables to help supply spiritual truths in real life, my aim for this final chapter is to highlight the core truths that I hope and trust the Holy Spirit will give faithful expression to in all our lives.

God has promised to each of those who has put their faith in the Person and work of Christ Jesus that we will be provided all we need to accomplish all the "good works, which God prepared beforehand so that we would walk in them." The following promises given to us in God's Word are essential for us to know, remember, and believe.

11: NOW WHAT?

And my God will supply all your needs according to His riches in glory in Christ Jesus. (Philippians 4:19)

³⁶"Just as it is written, 'FOR YOUR SAKE WE ARE BEING PUT TO DEATH ALL DAY LONG; WE WERE CONSIDERED AS SHEEP TO BE SLAUGHTERED.' ³⁷But in all these things we overwhelmingly conquer through Him who loved us.'" (Romans 8:36-37)

No temptation has overtaken you but such as is common to man; and God is faithful, who will not allow you to be tempted beyond what you are able, but with the temptation will provide the way of escape also, so that you will be able to endure it. (1 Corinthians 10:13)

⁷He said to them, "It is not for you to know times or seasons that the Father has fixed by his own authority. ⁸But you will receive power when the Holy Spirit has come upon you, and you will be my witnesses in Jerusalem and in all Judea and Samaria, and to the end of the earth." (Acts 1: 7-8 ESV)

My prayer and goals for all that is written in this book is the following:

1. That it will help guide you into God's Word, through which He will either draw you to Christ Jesus for salvation or transform you more and more into the image of Jesus Christ, the Son of the living God.

2. That each of you will know the *truth*, which will set you free either (1) from the slavery of sin, to be saved by the inherent power contained in every single word of the gospel of Jesus Christ or (2) from the lies that may have unknowingly held you captive.

3. That you would be enlightened about the "times and seasons" of Jesus' return and be able to prepare for His return and to evaluate the current events through the lens of biblical prophecy.

4. That you would be encouraged to seek to increase your true knowledge of our God and Savior, to live life in obedience

to God's Word, and to eagerly anticipate Jesus' return, all of which will aid in empowering you to become God's living *Portrait of a Righteous Woman*.

5. That you may not fear the actions being taken by government leaders or any others but will be comforted that our God is sovereignly orchestrating events for the purpose of setting all things in right order for His sending His Son, Christ Jesus, back to get His bride, the church of Jesus Christ.

6. That you come to know and become consciously aware that God's Spirit has been given to each believer at salvation not only to guide us but to give each one of us "resurrection power" to effectively accomplish all that He has ordained that we accomplish in and for His kingdom.

And…

7. That your intimacy in your relationship to our Lord and Savior would grow exponentially as you learn more about His character, His ways, and His deep love for you. God's incalculable love for you is so deep that He gave His life to have you be with Him for all eternity.

Be ready, at peace, and content no matter the circumstances. In a phrase of the vernacular of today, "God's got this." Be about the creation of your own wedding garment (Revelation 19:8). Our sovereign, living God will never leave His throne. No person or thing can thwart God's plan.[53] And through this book, I pray you have learned much about God's plan and instructions for you personally. May you continue to meditate on God's Word and focus your eyes on the end goal: to persevere and be content until the day you see Christ face to face, knowing you have put forth a fight to become a righteous woman of God.

I acknowledge that this book contains some difficult passages from God's Word to understand and walk in obedience to. The major purpose for this book is to bring to your attention what God has said in His Word, that you will carefully read what God says and let Him teach you personally what He means by what He says and how

---

53 "I know that You can do all things, and that no purpose of Yours can be thwarted" (Job 42:2).

you are to apply His instructions, along with His promises, to your life. Then, as you know and obey your God, He will bring to you the joys, contentment, and rewards of living in His presence. As I have mentioned several times, God rewards obedience and at times He must discipline our disobedience. It cost God and Jesus way too much, and He loves us way too much to leave us in our sin that is destructive to our own lives and ministries. Look at 2 Corinthians 3:2-5 and be encouraged and inspired.

> ²You are our letter, written in our hearts, known and read by all men; ³being manifested that you are a letter of Christ, cared for by us, written not with ink but with the Spirit of the living God, not on tablets of stone but on tablets of human hearts. ⁴Such confidence we have through Christ toward God. ⁵Not that we are adequate in ourselves to consider anything as *coming* from ourselves, but our adequacy is from God. (2 Corinthians 3:2-5)

Our God tells us that He prefers obedience to sacrifice. Listen to God's voice through the prophet Samuel in 1 Samuel 15:22-23:

> ²²Samuel said, "Has the LORD as much delight in burnt offerings and sacrifices as in obeying the voice of the LORD? Behold, to obey is better than sacrifice, *and* to heed than the fat of rams. ²³For rebellion is as the sin of divination, and insubordination is as iniquity and idolatry. Because you have rejected the word of the LORD, He has also rejected you from *being* king."

Please do not think that I believe that it is easy to obey God's Word in very difficult and greatly challenging circumstances. I know, and hope you know also, that our flesh is in constant warfare with the Holy Spirit Who dwells within us, according to Galatians 5:17: "For the flesh sets its desire against the Spirit, and the Spirit against the flesh; for these are in opposition to one another, so that you may not do the things that you please."

There is another war we are fighting every day and sometimes every minute of some days. Very recently I had a conversation with a lady from my Precept Bible study about what to do when you experience a lack of peace (having very unsettling emotions). She was in spiritual warfare, holding her "shield of faith" (a part of God's full armor spoken of in Ephesians 6:16-17) in perfect position to "extinguish the fiery darts" with which the enemy of our souls was bombarding her very being. Satan himself is relentless in his schemes to cause some to doubt God's goodness and His promised power by His Spirit to overcome the devil's temptations. But we have spiritual weapons to fight the devil in his warfare against us, and the Holy Spirit gives us guidance and divine power to fight through each and every instance of either evil schemes or downright full-blown warfare. *Thank You, Lord. It is proven in the lives of those who are totally devoted to You and to following Your "instruction manual: God's Word," that victory is not only possible, but You promise that victory can be experienced in our daily lives. We are always empowered to bear up under any and all circumstances as more that conquerors in Christ Jesus our Lord.* Philippians 4:19 promises, "And my God will supply all your needs according to His riches in glory in Christ Jesus."

I am not immune to Satan's attacks. I have during this past season of my life and ministry encountered many attacks from the enemy of our souls. Praise the Lord, He continues to remind me that spiritual warfare requires spiritual weapons—that they are powerful enough to defeat anything the enemy throws at me. These spiritual weapons are so powerful that every instance of their use "in faith" brings victory to overcome to the point that "fullness of joy and contentment" returns. More importantly, this is the result with many of those the Lord has brought to me to disciple according to His Word. One whose husband passed away suddenly with no known past physical problems. One whose husband fought cancer for a long period of time and then passed away. One whose daughter is continuing to live a homosexual lifestyle. One who is encountering persecution in her workplace. Each is living by the power of the Holy Spirit as *God's Portrait of a Righteous Woman* because they not only know our Jehovah God of the Bible intimately, but they know and totally believe and trust that He will provide them with what He has promised in His Word.

There is a particular person the Lord brought into my life who has exemplified how the Lord continues to work in the midst of very difficult circumstances. She joined my Sunday school class as a person who thought they were saved, but after hearing the gospel over several years, God truly saved her. She was addicted to alcohol,

11: NOW WHAT?

but not too long after she was saved, she was convicted that the alcohol had to go. It took a while, but she finally was victorious over this addiction by our God's great grace and the power of the Holy Spirit. She was married to an unsaved husband, which always brings great challenges when one spouse gets saved and the other doesn't. The Lord taught her how to live as more than a conqueror in Christ as she lived "as a new creation" in her home. For several years she shared with her support group her faith and "God's way" to genuinely overcome an alcohol addiction and not be tethered to a twelve-step program for the rest of her life. From the beginning of her salvation, she was committed to knowing God's Word and to continually being transformed by the renewing of her mind, according to Romans 12:1-2: "Therefore, I urge you, brethren, by the mercies of God, to present your bodies a living and holy sacrifice, acceptable to God, *which is* your spiritual service of worship. And do not be conformed to this world, but be transformed by the renewing of your mind, so that you may prove what the will of God is, that which is good and acceptable and perfect." It was her belief in and the practice of God's ways in His Word that God released His inherent power to overcome and be a useful and fruitful vessel in the Potter's hands. She continues to be a 2 Timothy 2:21 vessel, which says, "Therefore, if anyone cleanses himself from these *things*, he will be a vessel for honor, sanctified, useful to the Master, prepared for every good work." To Him be all glory.

As I mentioned in the chapters dealing with (1) wives voluntarily subjecting themselves to the leadership of their own husband and (2) divorce and remarriage, these are very challenging circumstances to handle in the way God describes. I am consciously aware that some of you have deep wounds that are yet to be healed from horrific experiences you have endured in the past. I have no wish nor intent to ignore nor diminish these deep hurts in your lives. God knows who and how someone has sinned against you. Those sins were not just against you but also against our all loving, all-sovereign God whom you worship and serve. He does not ever let those who are guilty go unpunished, according to Romans 12:19: "Never take your own revenge, beloved, but leave room for the wrath *of God,* for it is written, 'Vengeance is Mine, I will repay,' says the Lord." However, be consciously aware that there is a great Physician/

Healer of all hurts and wounds—His name is Jesus. He is able and desires to heal your hurts from within your soul.

Jesus Himself promised us in Acts 1:8 that we will receive power by the Holy Spirit. The Apostle Paul was in prison suffering persecution for preaching the gospel when he wrote the following letter to the church in Philippi. Hear him speak about experiencing suffering and hardship in Philippians 1:19-20:

> [19]For I know that this will turn out for my deliverance through your prayers and the provision of the Spirit of Jesus Christ, [20]according to my earnest expectation and hope, that I will not be put to shame in anything, but *that* with all boldness, Christ will even now, as always, be exalted in my body, whether by life or by death.

The power and provision of the Holy Spirit, "the Spirit of Jesus Christ," Whom Jesus sent to permanently indwell every believer, is available and willing to guide and provide whatever is needed to live victoriously through any and all circumstances we may encounter. The Holy Spirit's guidance and power can hardly be explained every time, but His work can most often be easily identified.

Lest anyone of us ever feel or even say at times, *These circumstances are just too hard for me*, we must be reminded of what our always faithful and good God has promised to His children in the following passages in His Word, the Holy Bible.

> "But you will receive power when the Holy Spirit has come upon you; and you shall be My witnesses both in Jerusalem, and in all Judea and Samaria, and even to the remotest part of the earth." (Acts 1:8)

> No temptation has overtaken you but such as is common to man; and God is faithful, who will not allow you to be tempted beyond what you are able, but with the temptation will provide the way of escape also, so that you will be able to endure it. (1 Corinthians 10:13)

> [1]Now, brethren, we *wish* to make known to you the grace of God which has been given in the churches of Macedonia, [2]that in a great ordeal of affliction their abundance of joy

and their deep poverty overflowed in the wealth of their liberality. (2 Corinthians 8:1-2)

^{37}But in all these things we overwhelmingly conquer through Him who loved us. ^{38}For I am convinced that neither death, nor life, nor angels, nor principalities, nor things present, nor things to come, nor powers, ^{39}nor height, nor depth, nor any other created thing, will be able to separate us from the love of God, which is in Christ Jesus our Lord. (Romans 8:37-39)

"The thief comes only to steal and kill and destroy; I [Jesus] came that they may have life, and have *it* abundantly." (John 10:10)

Now to Him who is able to keep you from stumbling, and to make you stand in the presence of His glory blameless with great joy. (Jude 24)

^{12}Beloved, do not be surprised at the fiery ordeal among you, which comes upon you for your testing, as though some strange thing were happening to you; ^{13}but to the degree that you share the sufferings of Christ, keep on rejoicing, so that also at the revelation of His glory you may rejoice with exultation. If you are reviled for the name of Christ, you are blessed, because the Spirit of glory and of God rests on you. (1 Peter 4:12-13)

You will make known to me the path of life; in Your presence is fullness of joy; in Your right hand there are pleasures forever. (Psalm 16:11)

Do not be grieved, for the joy of the LORD is your strength. (Nehemiah 8:10b)

^{9}And He has said to me, "My grace is sufficient for you, for power is perfected in weakness." Most gladly, therefore, I will rather boast about my weaknesses, so that the power of Christ may dwell in me. ^{10}Therefore, I am well content with weaknesses, with insults, with distresses, with persecutions, with difficulties, for Christ's sake; for when I am weak, then I am strong. (2 Corinthians 12:9-10)

GOD'S PORTRAIT OF A "RIGHTEOUS WOMAN"

The Lord has led me to deal with many different subjects in this book. Some will have simply affirmed your doctrinal beliefs. Some subjects will be new to you, that you have never come across or thought about before. However, I am confident that for some subjects that are dealt with in this book, you have also dealt with them, and your conclusions are the opposite of what I believe to be true. I am *not* asking you to simply believe what I believe, but I am asking that you revisit and study these issues in God's Word in the context they appear. As you do, ask God to give you revelation not only regarding what He is saying and what He means by what He has said, but exactly how you are to apply these truths to your life—that is, how to live out the life God has purposed for *you*.

There is a treasure trove of information within this book. This wealth I am referring to is not my words, which have no inherent power to change anyone's heart or behavior. *Influence*, hopefully . . . *permanently change*, NO. It is God's Word alone, sprinkled throughout these pages, that sanctifies according to John 17:17: "Sanctify them in the truth; Your word is truth." The Greek verb *hagiazo* that is translated "sanctify" in this passage is defined as, "to make clear, render pure" and also "spoken of persons, to consecrate as being set apart of God and sent by Him for the performance of His will."[54]

One thought to leave you with is from a passage that we observed earlier—Titus 2:3-5:

> ³Older women likewise are to be reverent in their behavior, not malicious gossips nor enslaved to much wine, teaching what is good, ⁴so that they may encourage the young women to love their husbands, to love their children, ⁵*to be* sensible, pure, workers at home, kind, being subject to their own husbands, so that the word of God will not be dishonored.

"Older women" is the Greek noun *presbutis* and is defined as "an aged woman."[55] However, I would propose that this particular "older woman" must include *spiritually older* women as well. The older women are instructed to teach younger women in several specifically

---

54 *Complete Word Study Dictionary: New Testament*
55 *Complete Word Study Dictionary: New Testament*

11: NOW WHAT?

named arenas of behavior that I covered in a previous chapter of this book. I urge each of you to locate a biblically qualified "older woman" to mentor and disciple you in what God's Word says about these behaviors that produce a "righteous woman." If you qualify as an "older woman," I urge you, if you are not already doing so, to get busy about pouring your life into the "younger women"—discipling them in God's Word that declares His ways in order that they may become *God's portrait of a righteous woman*. You will be forever grateful to God for His leading and empowering you to participate in the advancement of His kingdom in both quality and quantity, whether you are the discipler or the one who is being discipled. Always keep uppermost in your conscious mind that it is God Who is at work in you, both to will and to work for *His* good pleasure, according to Philippians 2:13.

To those who have finished this book, I want to tell you how privileged and blessed I am that you did. If there is anything I said, anything that has aided in your spiritual growth, or any issue that I have dealt with that you have heard our God speak to you about, I acknowledge that this has come from the inspiration and revelation of our merciful and gracious God. I give Him all the honor, glory, praise, and thanksgiving. May God and God alone be exalted.

Amen and Amen.

If you would like to continue studying God's Word with me, please use the link or QR code below to review my unedited digital audio and video recordings of my weekly Bible studies and Sunday school classes: **bit.ly/marie-strain**

ABOUT PRECEPT & KAY ARTHUR

⸜⸝ Precept®

For the last half-century, Precept has been training leaders, creating resources, and developing a Bible study method to help people grow in their relationship with God. Through television, radio, writing, and speaking, God has used Precept to reach millions of households with His truth. Precept was founded by Jack and Kay Arthur and they served as co-CEOs of Precept until 2012 when their son David assumed the position.

- Since 1970, Precept has been equipping small group Bible study leaders to discover the truth of Scripture for themselves, but not by themselves.
- Precept authors and publishes Bible study resources that help individuals know God through His Word and be changed by the truth they discover.
- Precept recruits, equips, and resources Bible study leaders who take God's life-changing Word to their communities.
- Through partnerships, translation efforts, and cross-cultural ministry, Precept provides international believers with the tools they need to study the Bible.

To learn more about Precept, visit their website at **www.precept.org**.

KAY ARTHUR

Through television, radio, writing, and speaking, God has used Kay Arthur to reach millions of households with His truth. Kay is the author of over 100 books and Bible studies, with over ten million in print. Four of her books have received the prestigious Gold Medallion Award. Kay taught and hosted Precepts for Life™, reaching more than 75 million households each day through radio and television in more than 30 countries for more than 20 years. Precepts for Life is available online today at **PreceptsforLife.com**. Kay continues to collaborate with the Precept team on Bible study resources.

MORE FROM INNOVO PUBLISHING

Suffering, Endurance, Character, and Hope - by Abigail Walker

Blinders Triilogy - by Kristy Shelton

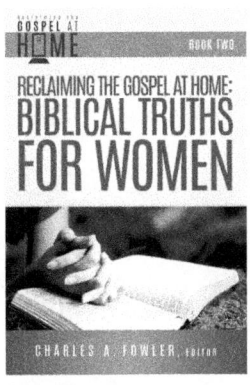

Therefore I Hope in Him
- by Joyce Rogers

Biblical Truths for Women
- by Charles A. Fowler

Totally Grace-FULL
- by Cynthia Hopson

MORE FROM INNOVO PUBLISHING

Sober - by Jessica Whalen

The Souls I Gave Away - by Deborah Kirk

The Girl with the Zebra Leg - by Lynette Johnson

Paisley Little - by Deb Grizzle

Goodnight, Sweet - by Leah Stanley

Caring for a Loved-One with Alzheimer's - by Leah Stanley

Mr. How Do You Do Learns to Pray - by Kelly Johnson

A Minute with Molly - by Judy Bollweg

www.ingramcontent.com/pod-product-compliance
Lightning Source LLC
Chambersburg PA
CBHW061256110426
42742CB00012BA/1933